AT
THE
EDGE
OF
ART

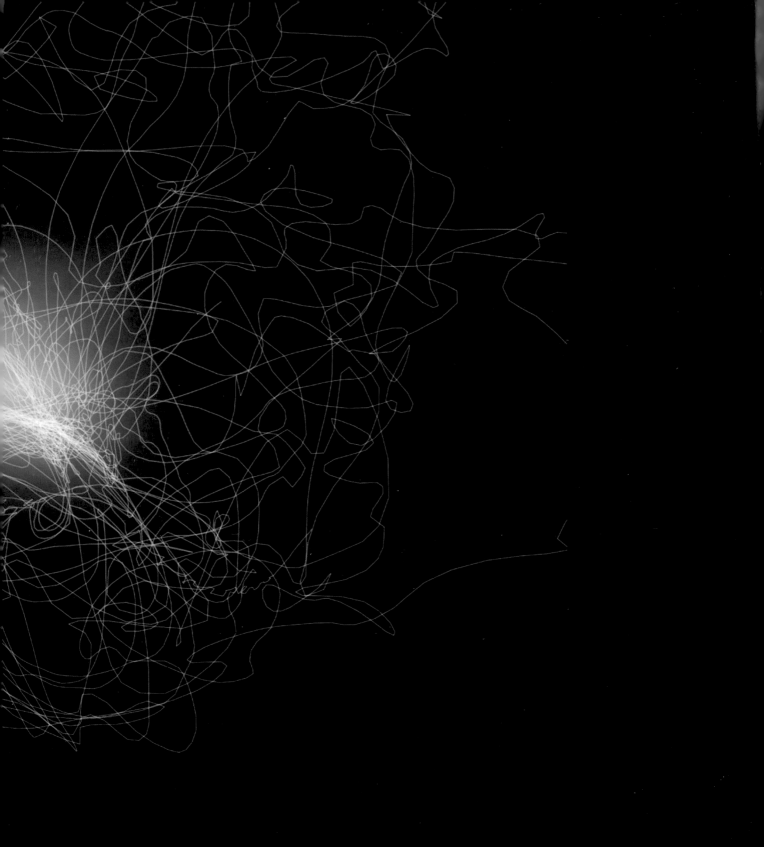

AT THE EDGE OF ART

Joline Blais

Jon Ippolito

With over 500 illustrations in color

Thames & Hudson

CONTENTS

'What would happen if art were suddenly seen for what it is, namely, exact information of how to rearrange one's psyche in order to anticipate the next blow from our own extended faculties?'

— Marshall McLuhan, *Understanding Media: The Extensions of Man*

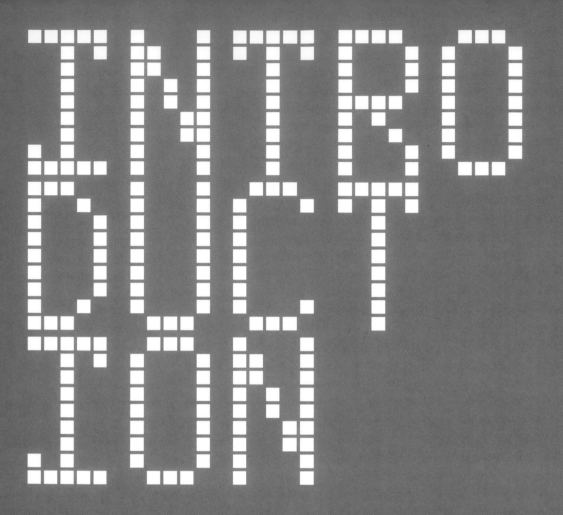

INTRODUCTION

Surfing the Internet can bring you to some pretty odd places. Take the home page[1] of Joe Davis, a self-described 'research affiliate in the Department of Biology at MIT'. Recent works include *Microvenus* (artwork embedded in a bacterial genome); *Audio Microscope* (a microscope that translates light information into sound, thus allowing you to 'hear' living cells, each with its own 'acoustic signature'); and experiments with how *E. coli* responds to jazz.

His ideas are certainly inspiring, inventive, and thought-provoking, but plans to put a map of the Milky Way into a **transgenic** mouse or build a fishing rod to snare paramecia in a Petri dish are too far out to qualify as bona-fide science. The only clue to why one of America's pre-eminent scientific universities lets a maverick like Davis into its labs is his self-description as an artist.[2]

Davis's case is not unique. In a computer-science lab in Tokyo, another scientist is letting a population of interbreeding computer viruses loose on his hard drive; they are evolving into a complex ecosystem. Back in the US, a hacker bent on demonstrating the futility of copyrighting computer programs has buried forbidden code in an image and posted it on the Web site of the government's Copyright Office. Online activists in Europe channel money through the Internet to a group that switches Barbie's voice box with G.I. Joe's, so that unsuspecting girls buy Barbie dolls that bark 'Commence firing' instead of cooing 'Let's go shopping.'

Far from the traditional epicenters of artistic production and distribution, creative people sitting at computer keyboards are tearing apart and rebuilding their society's vision of itself. Though they may call themselves scientists, activists, or entrepreneurs rather than poets or artists, many of these visionaries are playing the roles of Dante or da Vinci. Unlike the Soviet artist-engineers or Happening participants of the past century, who pushed artistic practice to the edge from within the avant-garde, many of the most innovative creators of the new century hail from other disciplines.

One reason is a shift in interest from traditional forms to new-media tools and technologies. Another is that in the US, funding for traditional genres from sources like the National Endowment for the Arts is declining, while support for technological creativity is increasing. The Rockefeller Foundation, for example, recently changed the name of its 'Humanities and the Arts' program to 'Creativity and Culture' to reflect this shift. At the same time, many respected creators formerly known as artists are abandoning the term. As early as 1996, Net provocateur Alexei Shulgin exhorted, 'Artists! Try to forget the very word and notion *art*.'[3] Virtual-reality pioneer and girl-game CEO Brenda Laurel calls herself variously a 'culture worker' or a 'utopian entrepreneur'. Online collectives etoy, ®™ark, and C5 describe themselves as corporations rather than artists. Even veteran performance and video artist Vito Acconci, as critic Tim Griffin has recounted,

> definitely doesn't consider himself an artist anymore. He's a designer.... According to his designer's statement, 'What I've retained is: the construction of architecture equals the construction of meaning.' And everything has an architecture. To design is to enter a tactical dialogue with any given site, whether in clothing, kitchen utensils, airports, desk chairs.[4]

Curiously, as artists are eschewing the term, art-world outsiders like Joe Davis are starting to appropriate it. In his book *The New New Thing*, Michael Lewis claims that Silicon Graphics and Netscape entrepreneur Jim Clark 'had ceased to be a businessman and become a conceptual artist'.[5] As Tim Griffin has commented, '...revamping business and communications models accords with Acconci's criterion. Perhaps a conceptual artist is now any number of things by name, and the words are getting larger.'[6]

The New Lifeblood

If we are living through the dimming of one constellation of stars – the death of the author, the impoverishment of the public patron, and the waning importance of studio practice and gallery shows – we are also witnessing the birth of another. The stars of this extraordinary new constellation tend to be biologists, engineers, designers, and hackers rather than the newest crop of fine-arts graduates, and they wield powerful twenty-first-century tools such as **DHTML** or **Webcams** rather than a nineteenth-century palette and brush. Not surprisingly, we have also seen a flurry of experimentation with novel forms of subjectivity – **avatar**s, **synthesbian**s, **bot**s, **artificial life** – as well as entirely new forms of community – global villages, **MOO**s, virtual colleges, email networks.

The breakneck pace with which these new forms are evolving would not be possible without the Internet. The Net's global reach has enabled these creative endeavors to escape the narrow confines of the art world to touch a world-wide audience – and, more importantly, to draw this audience into the creative process. Would-be artists don't need to haunt the Moulin Rouge or Cedar Tavern to rub shoulders with today's Picassos and Pollocks; with a computer and modem they can tap into a vast network of shared resources and ideas online, exploiting media such as electronic bulletin boards and chat rooms, and social codes such as **copyleft** and the **open-code movement**. As we shall see, the Internet is in a strongly metaphorical way the lifeblood of this new creativity.

To be sure, the online art community has developed almost entirely outside the purview of galleries, auction houses, and printed magazines. Ironically, online art's disconnection from the mainstream art world has actually contributed to its broad appeal and international following. The absence of a gallery shingle, a museum lintel, or even a 'dot-art' **domain** suffix to flag art Web sites means that many people who would never set foot in a gallery stumble across works of Internet art by following a fortuitous link. The Web site ada·web, for example, was one of the first and foremost destinations for online art in the mid-1990s. Yet ada·web's domain suffix was '.com' – partly because '.art' didn't exist,[7] but also because the site's founders deliberately avoided any use of the term art in any of the text or **meta-tag**s on the site. Alexei Shulgin even created the www.Art Medal Web site, archived at www.easylife.org/award/), in which he ranked commercial sites for their artistic potential.

Art as Antibody

But is every instance of creativity, from shrewd e-commerce ventures to clever toy designs, equally valid as art? Has the distinction between art and non-art become irrelevant in an age when art and science, commerce and fashion are all whipped together in the global culture blender we call the Internet?

The answer is no, though the reason has little to do with the traditional rationales for defining art, be they to distinguish high and low culture or to validate creative programs in academic settings. Art may be temporarily out of place, but society needs to make a place for it. Because society needs art to survive.

This is a time of tumultuous technological change. On any given day, a news outlet like Wired.com is likely to report on the outbreak of a new computer virus, the development of a new surveillance technology, and a new technique for growing bodily organs. Science has always offered us a future, and sometimes even a promise to repair the dangers it has unleashed on us in previous generations. But in an age when technology seems increasingly to have a mind of its own,[8] art offers an important check on technology's relentless proliferation.

How might this be done? What functions can art deploy to help us defend ourselves against technology's assault? The biological body defends itself from foreign invasion via the immune system, more specifically through the action of antibodies. Perhaps the kind of art we need in such an age is one that can support the social body as antibodies support the individual one. If we look at how digital art functions in our society, we can discern remarkable parallels to the actions of antibodies. Like antibodies, digital art often **pervert**s codes, **arrest**s normal operations, **reveal**s latent information or meaning, **execute**s instructions, triggers mechanisms to **recognize** its activity, and **persevere**s in memory.

While this analogy between the working of an antibody against biological infection and that of art against technological proliferation may seem new, many of its features were anticipated in earlier analogies. Oliviero Toscani, a photographer whose in-your-face political images have turned magazine ads and bus placards from advertising into agitprop, proposed a precursor. His ads for the 'United Colors of Benetton' marketing campaign feature images of ten-story-high condoms to increase AIDS awareness and three beef hearts labeled 'WHITE BLACK YELLOW' to reveal the absurd dynamics of racism. When asked to explain his practice, he said, 'I act as a virus against the commercial world. Art is a virus… Others resist me, I don't resist them. A virus doesn't have to defend itself, art doesn't have to defend itself – it attacks, and if necessary it also kills… Caravaggio was a virus against the Church.'[9]

Caravaggio was a mere painter, but by hiring a prostitute as a model for Mary's bloated body in his *Death of the Virgin* (1605–06), he struck fear into a religious establishment that was the strongest institution of its day. Likewise, Toscani has seen himself as infecting a corrupt commercial body. Yet neither Caravaggio nor Toscani was interested in destroying the entire social body. For this reason, portraying art as a virus may describe some of its proclivities but is misleading.

Technology Is a Virus

A better example of a cultural phenomenon that acts like a virus might be technology. In the eyes of many observers, our tools seem to have wills of their own. The cultural historian Manuel de Landa, inspired by the philosophers Gilles Deleuze and Félix Guattari, has even claimed an independent evolutionary track for them as part of a 'machinic phylum'.[10] Unlike art but like a virus, technologies often seem indifferent to culture rather than engaged with it. Some seem downright hostile to humanity. The earliest human technology may have been the arrowhead; some of the most recent ones require only the pressing of a few buttons to pound the world's cities into radioactive rubble. (No artwork has ever brought us to the brink of extinction.) Even technologies designed to heal, such as vaccines, can end up harming instead.[11] In other cases, the reason a technology feels alien is not that its imputed intentions are hostile but that they are inscrutable. Like a virus, digital technologies are constantly mutating. Unlike **microprocessor** speeds, the human capacity to foresee the ethical consequences of technology does not double every eighteen months, and so it's not surprising that people wonder whether these tools are under our control or we are under theirs. If nuclear proliferation and information overload are diseases, perhaps technology is their cause.

Critics of this kind of thinking point out that
technology is not simply about steam engines
and server farms but about the social conventions
that accompany them.[12] Perhaps, then, it is not
technology per se that is a virus but technological
concepts, conscious or unconscious. These
technological **meme**s, to borrow a term coined
by the philosopher Richard Dawkins, describe
persistent cultural metaphors or currents that
spread in a way analogous to viruses. Technological
memes in the Internet age can be utopian – like
virtual reality and e-commerce – or dystopian –
computer piracy or surveillance. Some, such as the
threat of anthrax infection or nuclear accident,
constitute real dangers, while others, such as fear
that computers will turn homicidal in the manner of
Arthur C. Clarke's HAL or James Cameron's
Terminator, lurk in our imaginations. Whether the
inspiration comes from *Eyewitness News* or
Entertainment Tonight, what defines a technological
meme is less a particular gadget or protocol than a
cluster of intellectual and emotional associations
that spreads too quickly to be properly analyzed or
understood. Thus, when we refer to technology in
the course of our argument, we understand it to
mean not simply the tools and codes but also the
concepts and metaphors that accrue to them.

The analogy between technologies and viruses
is complex but works at many stages of 'infection'.
Technologies, like viruses, are perverse: they are constantly mutating into new strains
(or new software and tools). Technologies, like viruses, are arresting: they halt a cell's
(or a society's) normal operating procedure and hijack it for their own ends. Technologies,
like viruses, are revelatory: they elicit responses latent in the (social) body's own systems
but had never been revealed – sometimes even in the body's own immune response (or
society's cultural practices). Finally, technologies, like viruses, are executable: a virus's
instructions hijack the body's operating system (or the social body's institutions).

But Art Is Accountable

If art functions like technology, that shouldn't be surprising, as antibodies also function
much like viruses. Why? Because the only way for antibodies to keep up with the
incredibly creative power of viruses is to act like them. So, the only way for art to keep
up with the energetic pace of technology in the Internet age is to adopt many of its
functions. Still, there are key differences between art (antibodies) and technology
(viruses). The main difference is that art is accountable to the social body as antibodies
are accountable to the biological one. Neither viruses nor technologies by themselves are
accountable to the bodies within which they operate. Viruses originate outside a host
organism and are interested in that organism's surviving only long enough to enable it to

infect other hosts. Art, on the other hand, originates in and is symbiotic with the larger social body. Its long-term survival – and, many would say, its meaning – depends on the survival of the cultures it celebrates or critiques. The goal of an artist, we propose, is not to expend or destroy the social body but to challenge it to evolve in new ways. And for its part, the social body needs art.

To have lasting social impact, art must emulate two functions antibodies perform that viruses lack: recognition – the ability to engage attention – and perseverance – the ability to endure. The analogy between art and antibody extends even further, for antibodies also are prevented from doing harm to the body they inhabit. Immune cells turn out to be the product of an unruly, random genetic process, but their power is deliberately limited; it's important that they not latch onto and destroy your pancreas, for example. Because the genes that control antibody structure are prone to **recombination**, antibodies are free to take every possible shape but only so long as they operate within a framework that guarantees they will not kill the body. Only in recent years have researchers discovered the biological mechanism that provides this framework. **Lymphocytes** are born in bone marrow, which happens to be the same proto-cellular playpen in which ordinary red blood cells grow up. Because they grow up around red blood cells, lymphocytes develop an indifference to them – an indifference that ensures that mature examples will target invaders rather than neighbors.

Art has its own nursery: the schools, studios, and galleries where it has traditionally been cultivated and appreciated. However, just as lymphocytes can't protect the body if confined to the nursery, so art is most effective when it pervades the entire circulatory system. A decade ago, the idea that art could flourish outside the art world's protective walls seemed a utopian fantasy. But now, such a circulatory system – the Internet – exists, and art is swimming through this bloodstream unimpeded.

The framework that protects the body from antibodies also protects antibodies from the body. In most biological contexts, evolution weeds out unstable gene patterns, preferring **canalized genes** with modest variation in their **phenotypes**. But the rich variety of antibody shapes populating a healthy immune system requires an unruly genetic engine. Likewise, artists rarely make good governors, yet society benefits from stimulating – and tolerating – a community of improvisatory and lateral thinkers.

Although the best art prepares society for unforeseen challenges, most viewers aren't even aware they are being conditioned. As Marshall McLuhan put it:

> If men were able to be convinced that art is precise advance knowledge of how to cope with the psychic and social consequences of the next technology, would they all become artists? Or would they begin a careful translation of new art forms into social navigation charts? I am curious to know what would happen if art were suddenly seen for what it is, namely, exact information of how to rearrange one's psyche in order to anticipate the next blow from our own extended faculties.[13]

As McLuhan intimated, cell phones, genetic engineering, and global trading networks set in motion entire new cascades of perceptual and philosophical quandaries. At a time of accelerated technological progress, art that tackles such quandaries before they are clearly articulated offers an essential prophylactic against future shock.

So, what makes an antibody different from a virus – and art different from mere technological innovation – is its peculiar kind of accountability. If the antibody's immune jumbler enables 'play' in the service of the biological body, so art's polymorphous perversity enables play in the service of the social body. Like antibodies, artworks provide insight into questions that haven't come up yet. And if art serves society in its own perverse way, society must serve art by providing mechanisms for recognizing and preserving it.

Art as a Collective Immune System

The diagram on pages 14–15 compares six stages of an immune response to the analogous stages of an artistic intervention: perversion, arrest, revelation, execution, recognition, and perseverance. Yet it may seem outlandish to suggest that art of the Internet age is as important to the social body as antibodies are to a biological one. Indeed, as our detailed comparison of stages reveals, it is not entirely clear whether digital artists can achieve the same level of recognition and perseverance as antibodies – or even that they want to.

Like any metaphor, the identification of art and antibody has its limits. Art in the Internet age does offer less inherent recognizability or perseverance than antibodies, but by way of compensation it offers certain accountabilities that antibodies can't. For one thing, the play of genetic recombinations is entirely random, but the play of artists is a bit more directed, and good artists are far better than random gene jumblers when it comes to finding useful resonances.[14]

In other respects, the social body upon which art acts may be more analogous to the immune system of a human population than to that of a human individual. For if human survival depends on adaptability of individual immune systems, it also depends on genetic diversity across gene pools. Selective lymphocyte reproduction worked quite well for the millions of years during which humans subsisted as relatively independent tribes scattered from the African savannah to the Alaskan tundra. Physical barriers like mountain ranges and climate variation made the collective human immune system better able to withstand assault from killer viral strains because geographic separation guaranteed that human populations would remain sufficiently diverse to explore many different evolutionary niches. The same mutation in red blood cells that produced sickle-cell anemia in France guarded against malaria in Côte d'Ivoire. The bubonic plague of the fourteenth century took years to spread across the mountains between Central Asia and Europe, and although it wiped out one in three Europeans, it never reached northern climes too cold for the rats carrying the infection.

Unfortunately, our immunological legacy is less well equipped to deal with a globalized world characterized by increased genetic homogenization, the eradication of physical barriers, and the creation of artificial climates. The twentieth century's AIDS epidemic has been described as the product of eighteenth-century African colonization. Twenty-first-century disease vectors are just as global but much faster; a SARS virus inhaled by a stewardess boarding a Boeing 747 in Hong Kong may infect a ticket clerk in Toronto a few hours later.

If technology is a virus, our collective immunity against it may be even weaker than against biological viruses. Nature introduced somatic immune systems at about the same time that it introduced backbones, but our technology has yet to co-evolve an automatic immune response. Moreover, the advent of the Internet and the increasing monopolization of computer platforms and media networks have wiped out the mechanical barriers that might protect some cultures from a technological plague. The Slammer **worm**, a form of computer virus, infected more than 90 per cent of vulnerable computers within ten minutes, making it – according to some researchers[15] – the first instance of a 'Warhol' worm: a program that could infect the entire Internet within fifteen minutes.

Art may not guard against computer viruses, but it can target viral memes – from the presumption that hackers are always bad, to the assumption that only violent computer games sell; from the rush to spread Western economic and democratic institutions forcibly to the rest of the world, to the failure to recognize human wealth when it can't be measured in terms of profit or power.

No single culture can eradicate such pervasive memes, any more than a single antibiotic can prevent the evolution of resistant microbes. Neither can we protect society from technology's influence with barricades of fear and isolation. Internet filters like NetNanny or America On Line promise a reassuring way for some populations to surf the Internet, but they are the cultural equivalent of vaccination – the introduction into the bloodstream of a part or all of a weakened **pathogen** in the hopes of passing on immunity in advance of infection. The benefits of such exposure have come under increasing doubt in recent years, with some researchers arguing that vaccines confer only an attenuated immunity more fleeting than the deep one conferred by full exposure. Vaccines, so this argument goes, mortgage the survival of the species to safeguard the survival of individuals.

The best art does the opposite. It challenges local phenomena or institutions – as Caravaggio provoked the Church, as the Radical Software Group mocked the FBI, as ®™ark queered the New York Stock Exchange – in order to safeguard human society as a whole. More importantly, each culture must come up with its own definitions of art's functions to ensure its adaptability and survival. Only in a diversity of approaches can collective culture emulate the strongest features of the human immune system. The best way to counter viral threats may not be to exchange attenuated versions of them but to exchange antibodies. This radical-sounding procedure is practised by millions of nursing mothers every day, and although biologists understand little about the process, they concur that antibodies acquired through breastfeeding confer stronger immunity, at least in the short term, than any other technique besides actual encounter with a foreign agent. Likewise, we propose that good art presents not attenuated memes but raw antibodies; it seeks not to protect *from* but to expose *to*. If nursing ensures survival by transferring somatic memory, art ensures survival by transferring cultural memory. In doing so, it allows us to encounter what is dangerous and alien in the context of play, and to remember our encounters. Without cultural support for such risk-taking, art ceases to function. For, like any cutting edge, the edge of art traces a fine line between life and death.

Six Chapters, Six Symptoms

Each of the following six chapters will scout a different frontier of Internet-based creativity in search of a function that characterizes art-like activity on this cutting edge. Every chapter will begin with two 'prompts', one just outside the limits of recognition by the art world, the other just inside. We will then compare these prompts to other 'edge studies' from the same online practice, be it the representation of self, the building of community, or the creation of artificial life. The six edges this book will pluck from the electrosphere are by no means the only foci of online creativity; music and literature, for example, are important fields of new-media research and experimentation, but neither is represented in this volume. The goal is less to arbitrate the line between art and non-art in every technological context than to derive a set of functions by which we can discern artistic practice wherever it occurs in our brave new world, and, in the spirit of insuring our own survival, encourage this play at the edge of art.

Following spread:
The 'Art as antibody'
metaphor, as revealed by
the six stages of infection.

perversion

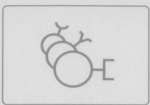

Antibodies are proteins dangling on the surface of a class of white blood cells called the lymphocytes. Trillions of them course through the bloodstream, each a complex organic molecule twisted into a distinctive three-dimensional shape that serves as a unique portrait of a particular foreign agent. Antibodies make reliable detectors of viruses and other foreign lumps of protein because for any given virus there will be only one antibody that exactly dovetails with it.

A small fraction of antibodies are inherited from the mother in the womb; the body makes the rest. But it's no mean feat to generate a cellular database of foreign dangers you have never encountered. How can the body tell what chicken pox looks like without letting some inside its skin?

The answer lies in an ingenious mechanism described by biologist Gerald Edelman as a genetic 'jumbler.' Like everything else in a cell, the exact shape of the protein dangling from a lymphocyte is determined genetically. Unlike the stable genes for its membrane or nucleus, however, the genetic material corresponding to a lymphocyte's receptor is prone to shuffle itself during cell reproduction. As a consequence of this built-in randomizer, each of the billions of lymphocytes initially produced by the body bears a different chemical 'lure' on its surface. Even if a chicken pox virus has never entered the bloodstream before, there's a white blood cell somewhere with a protein to match. That's how the immune system 'knows' what chicken pox looks like before it even encounters it.

In a sense, art has a curiously similar origin in a process Freud called 'polymorphous perversity.' Artists are always mucking around with paint or pixels, misusing their tools in an unbridled attempt to uncover new possibilities. For example, the Internet art duo known as jodi began a series of experiments that would come to be called *Untitled Game* when they began to tinker with the code underlying *Quake*, a popular 'first-person shooter' game, which they found on the Internet. By changing a command here or a parameter there, jodi were able to produce desultory variations on the original game. Most of these variants were uninteresting or pathologically dysfunctional, but that didn't prevent jodi from exploring this undirected play, which often marks the initial stage of any artistic project.

As the body's metabolic investment in random lymphocyte production seems frivolous compared to repairing a broken bone or digesting spinach, so government subsidies of experimental music studios or digital arts facilities sound frivolous compared to building hospitals or training soldiers. Like antibodies, the arts are a greedy, inefficient drain on resources without any promise of immediate payoff. And like antibodies, the arts are worth it. That's because to be effective as art is to define goals in the act of accomplishing them; those goals don't even exist before the art is made. For this reason, it's important to nurture artists whose work has no overt utility. For it's hard to tell ahead of time which experiments will 'pay off' by resonating with a particular technological meme.

arrest

In the body, that resonance occurs when a chicken pox pathogen happens to collide with an antibody whose shape dovetails with the shape of the virus. Electrostatic forces between the viral and antibody molecules handcuff the virus in place, empowering the antibody to accomplish the immunological equivalent of the citizen's arrest.

Like antibodies, artists must always be on the lookout for an experience to 'catch their eye.' To achieve such resonance, one artwork might beguile; another might perplex; a third might astonish. It is impossible to write out a strict prescription for how art works , which is why it is so important for an artist to be receptive to when it does. Art often works by resonating with an unconscious meme, and the unconscious is by definition something that is impossible to articulate in advance.

A few of the many *Quake* variations produced by jodi's tinkering made them pause to think. Some of the mutations resembled the original game as viewed through a quirky or grainy lens, but one of the most arresting produced an immersive black-and-white abstraction that seemed to commandeer the computer, leaving the viewer groping about in a disorienting three-dimensional space.

Out of their innumerable tweaks of and twists on the original game, why did this particular variation catch the artists' eye? One reason for its special resonance is its uncanny association of two disturbing technological memes: fear of videogame violence and fear of a computer crash. jodi's *Quake* remix disables the usual toolbars and menus by which a computer user normally navigates within and among applications, replacing them with a wall-to-wall gyrating black-and-white moiré. As if that weren't sufficient to suggest that something is going wrong, the user's futile attempts to quit the program are punctuated by the same guttural interjections and rifle shots that provided unnerving audio feedback to the original shoot-em-up. The user becomes embroiled in a battle to wrestle their operating system back from the program that has hijacked it, at the same time that they are willy-nilly engaged in a battle with video game villains obscured by the abstracted interface. It's unlikely that jodi knew these resonances would occur when they began playing with the *Quake* code; it would have taken away the fun if they had. What matters is that this variant stopped them in their tracks, whether or not they understood why.

revelation

At the moment that an antibody arrests the first chicken pox virus, an advance scout of the immune system has become aware that an invader has arrived. But the awareness of a single lymphocyte among billions is useless from an immune standpoint, so the lymphocyte immediately broadcasts chemical signals alerting other immune cells in the bloodstream to the presence of the intruder ensnared by the lymphocyte's antibody.

The signals emitted by an activated lymphocyte cannot contain a message like 'I've found an instance of the chicken pox virus' if the body in question has never encountered chicken pox before. What they say is, 'I've found a foreign agent--I don't know what it is, but it resonates with me.' That's what it means to be revelatory: to reveal the as-yet unknown.

Likewise, making art that works is not a matter of reading a Newsweek cover story on hacking or identity theft and then making an artwork to fit this meme. The most useful art brings to light a meme that has not yet been articulated, but has begun to infect a society on a subconscious level. Up until *Untitled Game*, no cultural observer had put together its particular equation between the violence of computer games and the violence of a computer crash.

But the meme didn't magically appear on humanity's collective psychic radar just because two artists had a revelation in their Barcelona apartment. It was only when jodi packaged their epiphany in a form others could experience that the meme could spread. In this case, in the spring of 2002 jodi uploaded the twelve Quake variations with the title *Untitled Game* to their Web site, jodi.org. Jodi are well known in the field and cognoscenti regularly troll their Web site, but like most Internet artists jodi often post a notice about their new projects to well frequented e-mail lists such as Rhizome, nettime, Rohrpost, and Thingist.

execution

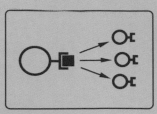

When it comes to executing code--especially the DNA that controls reproduction--lymphocytes are trigger-happy. If an antibody ever finds and latches onto its complementary virus, the match turns the lymphocyte into more than just a chemical warning beacon. The activated lymphocyte also undergoes the microbial equivalent of going into heat: it divides like crazy, filling the bloodstream with countless clones of itself, each of which is perfectly shaped to link up with the offending foreigners.

A stimulated lymphocyte creates new antibodies at the astounding rate of 10,000 molecules per cell per second, triggering a systemic change in the lymphatic and circulatory systems. At first the bloodstream may contain only a handful of antibodies to match a chicken pox virus, but thanks to the executability of genetic code within a few days billions of chicken pox will meet their match.

As word of jodi's new projects spread through online discussion lists, these e-mail signals inspire viewers to visit jodi.org and download *Untitled Game*. A single click on the right hyperlink is all it takes to send a perfect replica of the original work zipping through copper wires into the Internet's electronic bloodstream. Within a few weeks of the work's creation, a clone of *Untitled Game* exists on the hard drives of hundreds or thousands of computer users.

Just as antibodies are capable of propagating themselves with astonishing rapidity, so executable culture can spread like wildfire across global telecommunications networks. In the Internet age, art doesn't have to sit on a pedestal waiting submissively for a critic to look at it. Helen may have launched a thousand ships, but *Napster* got 60 million teenagers hooked on music swapping, resulting in the greatest exposure of music to the masses ever in the history of humankind.

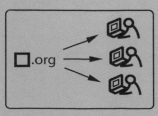

recognition

Once the cloned horde of lymphocytes activated by a matching virus secretes the chemical equivalent of a wakeup call, an army of microscopic bodily defenders springs into action. 'Killer' t-cells, macrophages, and other heavy infantry of the immune system puncture the offending viruses, aggregate them into harmless clumps, or dissolve bodily cells viruses have corrupted. A single lymphocyte, when executed, can stimulate a billion cells into action.

Similarly, it's faster and easier for art to find an audience in the age of the Internet, when recognition is not bestowed by brick-and-mortar apparatchiks like curators and magazine editors but by members of the online community. In January 2002, fellow artist and Rhizome list editor Alex Galloway recommended *Untitled Game* in two-line e-mail with the subject 'new games from jodi' to the Rhizome e-mail list, which inspired more users to download and view the project.

From such humble beginnings, community recognition can percolate even into the more exclusive brick-and-mortar art system. By March 2002 Ann-Marie Schleiner had posted a more formal review of *Untitled Game* on the nettime list. Four months later Florian Cramer interpreted the work in a printed catalogue for an exhibition at the Plugin art space in Basel; the show subsequently traveled to the Burofriedrich gallery in Berlin and Eyebeam Atelier in New York.

If few online artworks end up in galleries and museums, that says less about the inherent value of these works than about their relative independence from traditional art validation mechanisms. Only extreme luck and persistence will grant an artist entrance to gallery openings and cocktail parties that can make or break careers in the New York art world. Access to online recognition networks, by comparison, is far more transparent and egalitarian. For example, Slovenian and Korean artists, who live outside the mainstream geographic channels of the art world, have achieved notable recognition in making art for the Internet, where anyone who signs up for a free e-mail account can debate Internet aesthetics with curators on nettime or exploit free Web hosting to post art for all to see.

Of course, the immediate objective of immunological mobilization is clear--destroy or disarm the intruder--while the goals of art are generally more multivalent or enigmatic. In general, recognition aims to accommodate or assimilate the unknown. While this is a goal of the social body, it is not always one of the individual artists; in this respect some artists may wish to be more like viruses than antibodies, because they may not always want their art defanged of its revolutionary potential. We'll examine this dilemma when we look more closely at recognition networks in the chapter on Reweaving Community.

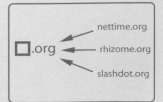

nettime.org
rhizome.org
slashdot.org

perseverance

Antibodies persevere. If you've had chicken pox as a child, your blood already contains millions of chicken-pox antibodies that replicated during the original infection. The fact that these extra antibodies stick around provides your body with a 'silver bullet' against any future chicken pox infections--which translates for most people into lifelong immunity from chicken pox.

Antibodies also provide their host with a somatic memory: even if a patient cannot recall having chicken pox, doctors can tell by testing for the appropriate antibodies in her blood.

Likewise, art that perseveres can create an analogous resource, a sort of cultural memory that persists in a society's collective unconscious. Art can persevere in various ways. Homeric hymns persevered by constant retelling; music and drama by interpretable scores; paintings by storage in a vault. To let this heritage disappear would be to deprive the social body of the immune resources it has built up over its lifespan.

Yet this is exactly the fate that will befall digital culture without a new preservation paradigm to accommodate it. Executable files may proliferate quickly across a given computing platform, but once that platform is gone so is the lifeblood that propagated them. We know from the numerous cases of death by technological obsolescence that the art world's default strategies for storing paintings and sculpture will fail to preserve most of digital art. In the chapter on Preserving Artificial Life we'll look at two diametrically opposed strategies for keeping this work alive, and ask what sort of cultural resource each preserves for the benefit of future generations.

Online artists manipulate digital code to make art much as the immune system manipulates genetic code to make antibodies. Some of the most renowned online artists take this practice to an extreme by following Cornelia Solfrank's dictum, 'A smart artist makes the machine do all the work.'[1] Now, trusting a machine to make art is already an enormous departure from the direct gesture of hand-brushing oil paint on canvas. In the case of Internet art, the remove is even greater, since the machine in question is not the artist's but one owned by a viewer who might be halfway around the world. To get someone else's PC to draw lines, flash colors, or spin words across the screen, Internet artists rely on instructions which can be stored on a disk or squeezed through a modem line. These instructions take the form of code.

Why would artists forego the directness of squeezing out tubes of cadmium red or chiseling away chunks of marble in favor of disembodied commands? For many practitioners, code is not simply a means to an end; on the contrary, they revel in the intricacies of **document.write**; they chisel lines of **Perl** or **Java** instead of marble, creating elegant solutions to artistic problems. Code is their muse.

But professional computer programmers also pride themselves on elegant solutions, even though the solutions in question may be to mathematical conundrums or e-commerce applications. If programming is an art, is any programmer with high standards an artist? No. As we shall see, software artists deliberately misuse code. Like the immune system's polymorphous antibody production, this perverse practice lends code art a quirky and prophetic vision that is unlikely to emerge from a purely utilitarian approach.

How Can Art Compete with the Mandelbrot Set?

Like many self-proclaimed examples of software art, John F. Simon, Jr.'s *Every Icon* (page 19) embodies the **procedural**[2] aesthetic Judson Rosebush espoused in 1989. According to Rosebush's manifesto, the goal of computer art is to create the greatest richness and meaning from the fewest lines of code. But if code art's yardstick for aesthetic success is 'the biggest bang for the buck', how do we judge the merit of Proceduralist art against such remarkable achievements of the scientific community as the *Mandelbrot Set* (page 18), whose single-line formula generates an astounding wealth of complex iterable shapes? One clue lies in the irony of Simon's failed promise to deliver every conceivable image, which provokes the question of whether software must be devious to qualify as art.[3]

As we'll see, the answer helps to resolve a debate that has raged in the past decade among creative coders who champion formal versus social values. The invention of software in the twentieth century produced a new medium for artistic expression. Like literature or painting, software can be appreciated from the inside out (basing an interpretation on a program's syntax, or internal architecture) or from the outside in (reading the function of a software application against a broader social context). The key to understanding the connection between these two readings will turn out to be a feature that sets software apart from these earlier media: its capacity for utility. Performative speech is rare outside a courtroom, but almost all computer programs are performative in some way. If our definition of art is to adapt to a twenty-first-century context, then its characteristics must adapt to accommodate this subtle but seismic shift in media. **< >**

TO SEE THE WORLD IN A GRAIN OF SAND

Benoit Mandelbrot, *Mandelbrot Set*

It is not much of an exaggeration to say that Benoit Mandelbrot, creator of the *Mandelbrot Set*, devised a universe from a line of code. Mandelbrot was one of the first mathematicians to recognize the power of computers to generate forms that had never before been seen or described. That power is based on iteration, a method of solving an equation by repeatedly adding together increments toward the answer until the sum is close enough to suggest the correct result.

Interestingly, many equations that require iteration are extremely simple. The formula Mandelbrot focused on, for example, consisted of a mere six characters: $z = z^2 + c$. It turns out that this formula yields two kinds of results, **convergent** and **nonconvergent**, depending on which number Mandelbrot chose to 'seed' his equation. More surprising is the fact that it proved impossible for Mandelbrot to predict in advance which seed numbers would produce each of the two results. Plugging in numbers by hand was tedious, but the advent of computers made such calculations simply

a matter of waiting for the dumb machine to spit out its results. Even better, computer **plotter**s made it easy to see the results mapped out on paper — by assigning nonconvergent seeds a colored **pixel** and convergent seeds a black one, for example. Allowing z to be a special kind of two-valued number, called a complex number, permitted the result to be mapped out on a plane. When Mandelbrot and his colleagues saw the result of this **recursive** formula in their plotter output, they were astounded at the complexity of the result: a fantastically intricate 'bug' bristling with innumerable tendrils and appendages, any detail of which seemed as complex as the original gnarled shape.

Scientists have applied Mandelbrot's intricate geometries, known as **fractal**s, to systems in a wide range of scales and contexts, from the cycle of booms and busts in national economies and antelope populations to the geography of coastlines and the frequencies of dripping faucets. What unites all of these natural phenomena is nonlinear feedback: a force of nature or culture that amplifies small effects or diminishes large ones.

Feedback leads to a strange mix of the periodic and the unpredictable, and it is perhaps because of this familiar tension that the *Mandelbrot Set* retains interest as a mathematical and visual construct apart from its real-world applications. While fractals are by no means native to the Internet, they have inspired enthusiasts to create numerous resources for exploring their infinite diversity, from posters to screensavers to online viewers such as the *Fractal Microscope*.

When college students pin up posters of the *Mandelbrot Set* next to their posters of Monet's waterlilies, are they correct in placing these disparate forms of cultural expression in the same category?

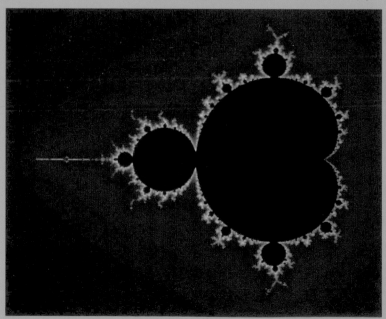

BINARY CODE UNLEASHED

John F. Simon, Jr., *Every Icon*

Like the *Mandelbrot Set*, John F. Simon, Jr.'s *Every Icon* reveals the power of computers to create a world from a minuscule amount of code. But Simon's world deliberately promises more and delivers less than its fractal counterpart. His description of his program is simplicity itself:

> Given: A 32 x 32 Grid
>
> Allowed: Any element of the grid to be black or white
>
> Shown: Every Icon

The word *shown* is somewhat misleading. Once triggered by the user, Simon's **applet** will in good faith begin to display every possible combination of black and white elements; yet even at a typical desktop computer's rate of a hundred new icons per second, it would take over 10^{308} years to draw every icon. Like Mandelbrot's creepy-crawly apparition, Simon's library of images requires a computer to generate its diversity. However, if Mandelbrot's order steadily emerges from his fractals' relentless recursion, in Simon's case the moments of order are few and far between; even on a supercomputer of unimaginable speed, recognizable images would melt in and out of focus, meandering across the space of all possible images rather than gradually converging on a definitive shape. *Every Icon* holds out the potential of displaying a meaningful image — indeed, *every* meaningful image — but in practical terms the user is likely to be exhausted long before the icons are. In fact, Simon estimates that the first recognizable image wouldn't appear for several hundred trillion years. (What would it be? A 'no smoking' icon? A **bitmap**ped *Mona Lisa*?) The result is an apt emblem for the Web, where needles await in an electronic haystack of global proportions.

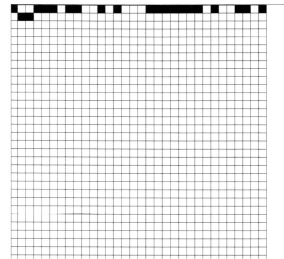

Given:
An Icon described by a 32 X 32 Grid

Allowed:
Any element of the grid to be colored black or white.

Shown:
Every Icon

Owner:
John F. Simon, Jr.

Edition Number:
Artist's Proof

Starting Time:
January 14, 1997, 9:00:00 pm

©1997 John F. Simon, Jr.   www.numeral.com

Opposite: Mandelbrot Set.
Top right: *Every Icon.*
Above right: Simon's Combinations.

Proceduralism

Although most of Mandelbrot's disciples publish in technical journals devoted to the mathematics or computer-graphics communities, one researcher who has candidly championed the use of fractal algorithms in art-making is Ken Musgrave, who for six years worked with Mandelbrot in Yale University's computer-science department. While Musgrave's fractal **algorithms** are cutting-edge computer graphics – his special effects enhanced the films *Titanic* and *Apollo 11* – he uses them to generate that most ancient of artistic genres, the landscape. Although landscapes have hitherto been the province of painters trained in two-point perspective, Musgrave has cited Mandelbrot to underscore the inadequacy of Euclidean geometry for describing nature: 'Clouds are not spheres, mountains are not cones, coastlines are not circles…'[5] What shapes can accommodate Nature's wispy, rugged, meandering profile? Fractals, of course, because they marry repetition and randomness. Musgrave writes recursive algorithms that perform the mathematical equivalent of Genesis, building mountains crag by crag and trees limb by limb, tracing the paths of virtual light rays to cast shadows of virtual peaks and to paint reflected sky in virtual water.

While Musgrave's pictorial process is highly original, the subject matter and style of the images are not. The photorealistic landscapes that result from his application of fractal algorithms to landscape generation – windswept deserts dominated by spiky mountain ranges, cratered moons reflected in alien lakes – resemble the clichéd cover art of science-fiction paperbacks more than contemporary abstract or representational painting. Not surprisingly, Musgrave justifies his aesthetic not by positing any relevance to contemporary aesthetics but by invoking Rosebush's notion of Proceduralism to explain the algorithmic purity behind his working method:

> If I dislike the resulting hue in a particular highlight (a local effect) I may change the color of the light source accordingly, but this changes tones everywhere that light falls in the scene. Similarly, if I dislike the shape or location of a given wave in the water or mountain peak in the terrain, I may change it, but this change will also affect all other waves or peaks and valleys. The randomness at the heart of the fractal models I use grants both enormous flexibility and expressive power, but it also entails complete abdication of control over specific details in relation to their global context.[6]

Despite this deterministic process, Musgrave argues vehemently that the computer 'is in no way the creator, the author of the product',[7] emphasizing instead the role of intuition

and serendipity in his process. Falling back on mathematical jargon to describe his art, Musgrave searches '*n-space for local* **maxima** *of an aesthetic* **gradient** … the task of the artist then is first to create these *n* **parameters** (*n* being usually around two to five hundred in my own images) … then to tweak the values of these parameters to obtain a satisfactory result or image'.[8] Tellingly, Musgrave spends a lot of time defining his parameters but very little time explaining the aesthetic gradient on which they act – except to say that they're dependent on the artist's subjectivity and mood.

Except for a passing mention of Sol LeWitt, the only explicit aesthetic yardstick Musgrave invokes is nineteenth-century landscape painting, and he is frank about fractal geometry's limited success according to this benchmark: 'The fact is, the computer artwork has not yet been produced which could stand a side by side comparison with, say, a great van Gogh painting. My own best image would pale, stood beside a Bierstadt.'[9] Rather than a difference of tone or aim, however, Musgrave explains this lack as a deficiency of the output medium, citing oil painting's continuously gradated surface, abundance of perceptual information, and variety of scales (from small-scale brushwork to large-scale composition).

Perhaps Musgrave isn't nervous about his product's relevance because he believes the integrity of the process – i.e., the code – will vindicate his work. He cites Rosebush's claim that Proceduralist computer art 'will increasingly be appreciated as a major art movement by this and future generations', adding, 'If Mr. Rosebush and I are correct, we may be witnessing one of the truly definitive events in the history of Art.'[10]

While instruction-based creativity has been around since the 1960s,[11] Proceduralism has recently found a more aesthetically sophisticated, if less grandiloquent, expression in the eu-gene email list and the software-art communities around the transmediale and read_me new-media festivals. More hip to contemporary art and criticism than the fractal calendar-makers, this group has decided to resolve Musgrave's understandable anxiety about aesthetic output by means of a Gordian-knot approach. These makers of 'generative art' tolerate, or even celebrate, output that is unruly or ugly – though to be sure it is often ugly in an arty kind of way – and to focus on the code itself as the object of interest. Although the rhetoric and aspirations may differ, the definitions proposed by this group are a direct echo of Proceduralism: 'Generative art refers to any art practice where the artist creates a process, such as a set of natural language rules, a computer program, a machine, or other mechanism, which is then set into motion with some degree of autonomy contributing to or resulting in a completed work of art.'[12]

Above and following spread: fractal landscapes by Ken Musgrave.

Social Software

Opposed to this formal exploration of code as an art in itself is a group of Internet artists, notably the London-based collaboratives I/O/D and Mongrel, known for projects with covert or overt political agendas. I/O/D member Matthew Fuller, who has written cultural criticisms of quotidian programs such as Microsoft Word,[13] has challenged formal explorations of code to go beyond inbred aestheticization, calling for an examination that provokes a greater awareness of code's social and political contexts. Internet artist Amy Alexander expresses the same point of view in an interview with the jury for the read_me software-art competition: 'Most non-art software pretends to be neutral and objective technology – devoid of human influence. Software art opens itself up to examination of its human-created biases and its human-experienced influences – so it helps us understand how these factors operate in "normal" (non-art) software as well.'[14]

The German code historian and free-software activist Florian Cramer calls this divergence 'software formalism vs. software culturalism', lamenting:

> If Software Art would be reduced to only the first, one would risk ending up with "
> a neo-classicist understanding of software art as beautiful and elegant code…
> Reduced on the other hand to only the cultural aspect, Software Art could end
> up being a critical footnote to Microsoft desktop computing, potentially
> overlooking its speculative potential as formal experimentation.[15]

To juxtapose the Mandelbrot Set and *Every Icon* is to sit uncomfortably on the horns of Cramer's dilemma. Should they be evaluated according to code (form) or result (function)?

A Third Alternative

The biological body copes with this dilemma by using form to produce function. Genetic jumblers manipulate the code (form) of an antibody in order to produce the wide variety of antibodies that can then detect an invading virus (the function). This misuse of genetic code – which might prove lethal elsewhere in the body – allows the immune system to anticipate shapes it has never encountered. Artists employ a similarly wrongheaded strategy, playfully misusing software and other technological codes to help us cope with technology's invasion of the social body.

If being creative with technology means thinking 'outside the box', then there is no better example than the artwork *Magnet TV* (1965), in which the Korean-born artist Nam June Paik planted a hefty magnet on top of an ordinary television set. Paik's magnet distorted whatever soap opera or car commercial happened to be airing at the moment into an exquisite variety of geometric patterns. In this case, the box in question is a television – the technological device that has contained human potential more efficiently than any other in recorded history. Before Paik,[16] the image flickering on a TV screen was intentionally broadcast from a distance, out of the control of the end user.

What made Paik's intervention creative was not so much his use of technology as his deliberate misuse of it. As the artist himself put it, 'Television has attacked us for a lifetime – now we strike back.' In lugging a magnet onto a TV, Paik violated not just the printed instructions that came with the set but also the political assumptions underlying its widespread use. Artistic misuse exploits a technology's hidden potential in an intelligent and revelatory way. The 1960s were a heyday of such activity, with artists like Paik, Jean Tinguely, and Robert Rauschenberg misusing everything from roller-skates to internal-combustion engines.[17]

There are examples of artistic misuse of technology prior to the 1960s, such as the effects Charlie Chaplin created by cranking film the wrong way through a camera. But the proliferation of digital media in the 1980s and burgeoning Internet access in the 1990s created an explosion in opportunities to conspire in and observe the perversion of technologies. Code artists deviate from the potential utility inherent in software by perverting the original use of the code to a speculative or critical end. This playful perversity distinguishes the artistic use of code from the merely technical one.[18]

The perversity central to the artistic misuse of code has nothing to do with 'perverse' subject matter. There's little perversity lurking in the code behind Bestiality.com or Sexy.com. Unlike works of artistic misuse, successful porn sites are clean under the hood (or is that under the sheets?), for they rely on a transparent, fully functional click-and-pay interface; glitches in the site would only remind porn hunters that they were paying to ogle pixilated curves rather than flesh-and-blood ones.

By contrast, the works we'll examine in this chapter retain some of the virtuosity of Proceduralism as well as the responsibility of social software, but to that they add a dose of perversity as they misuse code as syntax, tool, or experience.

Transparency and Artistic Misuse

Whether works pervert code as syntax, tool, or experience, a certain legibility is necessary for such misuse to have artistic value. Whether the work is a conceptual installation by Sol LeWitt, a quantum-mechanics diagram-turned-archival print by Eric Heller, or a popup window gone haywire at jodi.org, the perversion of code is ineffectual as an artistic strategy if such misuse is concealed to all but the technological cognoscenti.

One way to encourage transparency is the 'open-source' approach typified by the 'CODeDOC' exhibition, an online show curated by Christiane Paul of the Whitney Museum of American Art in New York. This exhibition presents software art in such a way that its underlying **if-then**s and **do-while**s are readily viewable by the user. Unfortunately, there are other occasions when viewing the code directly is impossible or unhelpful; still, what's key is that viewers understand how a rich visual or conceptual experience can be generated by the misuse of a particular technology. Nam June Paik hauled his electromagnet into plain sight on top of *Magnet TV*'s casing instead of hiding it inside, and he chose a store-bought magnet instead of custom-making a new one that would not have been recognizable to the average viewer.

Sometimes, paraphrasing code can make it even more legible than displaying it. John Simon does not reveal the Java behind his *Every Icon*, but he's gone to the trouble of summarizing it in three short phrases. If you can think like a programmer, you can reconstruct the binary formula behind his marching pixels, but Simon's paraphrase is so guileless that lay viewers can get a feeling for the dynamic as well.

Provided the concept behind a work is simple enough, a visual paraphrase of the underlying code can be just as enlightening as a verbal one. The initial screen of Simon's Java applet *Combinations* is a square with four colored lines which constitute the algorithm's graphic vocabulary. Once the user has dragged the endpoints so as to choose the angles and placement of the four segments – in effect, defined the algorithm's parameters – the applet produces a grid of every possible combination of those four lines on the computer screen or in a plotter printout. A Sol LeWitt drawing based on such combinations can take a team of draughtspeople weeks to complete; Simon's turbocharged drawing machine spits out its results in milliseconds. While *Combinations'* patterning is seductive on a purely visual level, it produces this embarrassment of riches with an unnerving suddenness, throwing down an impertinent gauntlet to its Conceptual forerunners from the 1960s.[19]

If the dynamic behind Simon's early works[20] is simple enough to paraphrase verbally or visually, the fractals and ray-tracing algorithms behind Ken Musgrave's alien landscapes can be incomprehensible to all but the computer-graphics specialist, even though his photorealistic sci-fi imagery is more accessible to the popular imagination. In recent years, however, Musgrave has hit upon a way to let ordinary users in on the process by which his fractal planets are created. His Pandromeda Web site offers freeware tools for navigating 3-D fractal planets (the 'Transporter') as well as 'pro' tools for building the planets themselves ('MojoWorld Generator'). By devising and distributing tools for creating and experiencing fractal landscapes, Musgrave has granted his viewers a hands-on sense of the arcane mechanism underlying his own artistic process.

When programmers expose code's perverse possibilities, they stretch our minds to accommodate not just the box but what's outside it as well. That is why what is perverse for an individual artist may be profitable for the social body. Just as the immune system's random jumbling of antibody genes enables the human body to foresee threats before they strike, so artists who misuse television or Java reveal powers latent in those technologies that aren't mentioned in their manuals. Before this revelation can occur, however, an artwork must jolt its beholders out of their everyday states of mind and into one ready for a category-breaking experience. This points to another power which art shares with immune response, one we'll explore in the next chapter: arrest.

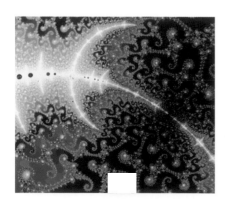
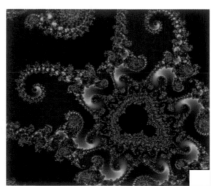

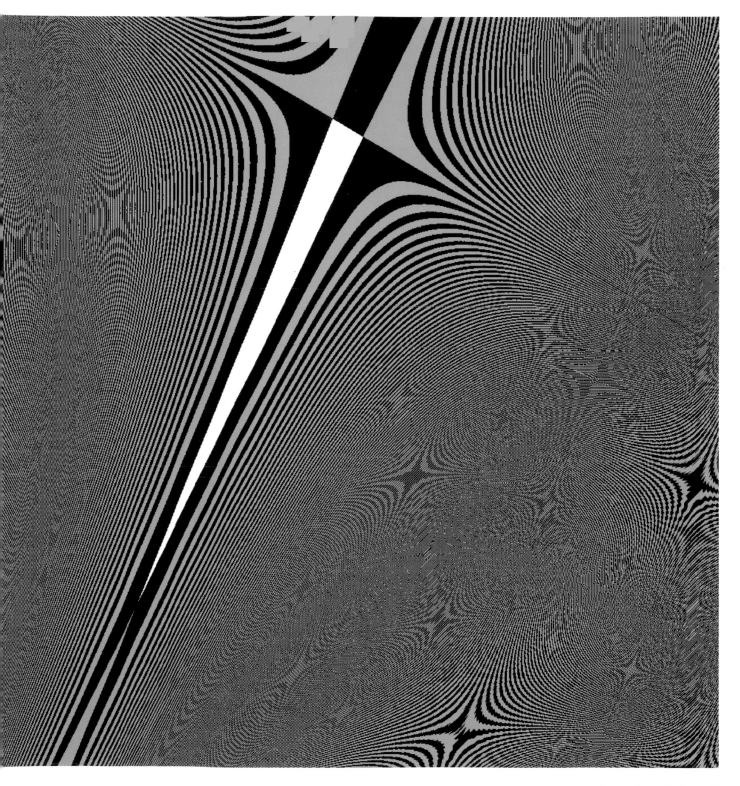

Code as Syntax: Use and Misuse

A look at the deepest level of code – the do loops and document.writes – shows how deliberate misuse of code helps to winnow the art from the craft. To pervert syntax means breaking the conventions that govern small-scale composition: creative painters commonly upset pictorial conventions, while creative poets commonly perturb grammar and word order. But if a creative programmer violates the rules that govern Java or Perl, the program won't work. So how can artists misuse the syntax of computer code to make art?

CRAFT WITHOUT CRAFTINESS
Donald Knuth, *The Art of Computer Programming*

The series of books called *The Art of Computer Programming* by the Stanford University computer scientist Donald Knuth is about as distant a context for art as you can get from the Louvre or Sotheby's. Yet programmers compelled by a sense of beauty in code mention Knuth's name with reverence,[21] and his own writing supports the assertion that programs can be works of art:

> My feeling is that when we prepare a program, the experience can be just like composing poetry or music… when we read other people's programs, we can recognize some of them as genuine works of art… The possibility of writing beautiful programs, even in assembly language, is what got me hooked on programming in the first place.[22]

Even if Knuth at times dismisses utility as the sole reason for studying code, his many volumes of algorithms and performance analyses are nevertheless directed at producing *good* code — code which is optimized for practical applications like sorting and searching. Software artists who work at the syntactic level, on the other hand, tend to be interested in *bad* code — code that doesn't or shouldn't work. While the craft Knuth espouses is useful background for their work, Florian Cramer has pointed out that craft is not usually the focus of their artistic activity:

> I thus would never limit software art to craftsmanship of programming (i.e. software art as a Donald Knuth-style 'art of programming'), but consciously take speculative, unclean, or even non-computer-related approaches into account, from certain forms of poetic play and conceptual art to the use of machine code fragments as private languages in artistic 'codeworks'.[23]

Elsewhere Cramer identifies Knuth's emphasis on craft with the Proceduralist art of Musgrave and his fellow computer scientists:

> Knuth's wording has adopted what Steven Levy calls the **hacker** credo that 'you can create art and beauty with computers'. It is telling that hackers, otherwise an avant-garde of a broad cultural understanding of digital technology, rehash a late-18th century classicist notion of art as beauty, rewriting it into a concept of digital art as inner beauty and elegance of code. But such aesthetic conservativism is widespread in engineering and hard-science cultures; fractal graphics are just one example of Neo-

Pythagorean digital kitsch they promote. As a contemporary art, the aesthetics of software art includes ugliness and monstrosity just as much as beauty, not to mention plain dysfunctionality, pretension and political incorrectness.[24]

For a better look at Cramer's 'ugly' code, let's turn to some programmers who deviate from the Olympian precepts of Knuth to explore the purposeful perversion of code syntax.

CODE-INFECTED WRITING

mez, mezangelle

One strategy is to write code that deliberately doesn't work on a computer and is instead targeted for the 'literary **compiler**' in our own brains. E-poet Alan Sondheim has coined the term *codework* to represent a writing style influenced by — or on occasion directly modified by — computer code. Numerous online artists have experimented with codework in their contributions to art-related email lists, including Netochka Nezvanova, jodi, and Sondheim himself. One of the most elaborated of these digital dialects belongs to the Australian artist mez (Mary Anne Breeze), whose 'wurk' consists of texts emailed to discussion lists written in her own lingo, called *mezangelle*.

```
"Then i sawe a COmmandE @ the d0llah
pr0mpte:
holdinge in itz teXt the keys of M: I: L: E:
N: & U. 1t seiZed sm
0v the lettaHs: & K0dEd them up in2 a
Th0usand N-crypti0nz. The
COmmandE sent the N-crypti0nz
staticscreaminge t0 the Binne.
The zer0Hs & w0nnes then flick.erred with
joy, N the
DataHK0de was b0rnE with the re:maining
lettaHz, the I: the
E: N 0therz B-sides, the P: & H: & O: all
linked N clicking
straighte in2 the Inph0ennium..."

"0h[& 1] wash the teXt with pixels 0v yr
spacE
 N weep c0de in2 yr boardes and chr0me-hic
dreamz:
The Ange1 & the godde-S d0 dance with-N
the Prayer
pr0Grammez
N lectr0split & text-N d0llah-flippe in2 the
screenz
N inph0spherez:
so greate iz yr teXt: my KodE: yr p0wer to
d0wn10ad."
```

```
"& i will smite thEE with mye vEYErus,
           N seeke 2 break the millennium
corrupt K0dE
           that binds u in itz thymiC
0verfl0w..."

" N we shell l00k 2 the screen, N on those
screens we shell f1nd the line——_—_——___
and the d0t:: . . , and the d0t shell
speax. N the d0t will teXt:

  $take up yr keys and type
  $N click yr modemz :0N:
  $N scroll the pages thru
  $N delete @b0minations
  $N n0.s N linkz that breakE the KoDE
  $N thenne merge the stringz
  $N u shell B phree."
```

mezangelle excerpt from *Psa1mz 4 the neW inphoennium.*

If pidgin scripting languages like Lingo attempt to make programming syntax look more like English ('put this in it'), *mezangelle* attempts to make English look more like a programming language. mez's texts are peppered with characters more commonly found in code such as /, [, and (. Programmers use these delimiters to associate numbers or **string**s with a common function, but mez uses them to give syllable clusters multiple meanings through double or triple entendres.

Clearly, *mezangelle* represents the increasing influence of programming code in our daily lives, although its variorum of natural-language semantics makes it impossible to write a compiler that could interpret it. The read_me jury recognized in *mezangelle* historical precedents such as Oulipo, Futurist, concrete, and Perl poetry, though a better analogue might be the innovative writing style of hackers, which wittily incorporates programming syntax into email and other electronic communication. As Eric Raymond notes in his linguistic analysis of 'hackish',[25] true hacker banter is an informal yet syntactically precise argot characterized by multivalent wordplay. For all its pretension as e-poetry, *mezangelle* lacks the precision that characterizes hackish.

On the other hand, hackish is a discursive practice without a single author or self-contained 'works'; it would be much easier, for example, to cite a *mezangelle* manifesto in a poetry anthology than to excerpt an email exchange among hackers, if only because it would be impossible to know where to begin or end the latter. Yet the similarity of these practices suggests that a truly expansive definition of art should be able to accommodate artistry that does not fit into well-defined genres, a point to which we shall return.

DISGUSTING FUNCTIONALITY
Tom Duff, *Duff's Device*

More perverse than private dialects like *mezangelle* are scripts based on improper syntax or puzzling recursion that can nevertheless be executed. As an example of a program that both does its job and embodies the 'monstrosity' Cramer champions in software art, Internet artist Amy Alexander cites *Duff's Device*, 'a remarkable algorithm that somehow marries two **C** structures in a surprising and efficient way. The result is both ugly and beautiful; disgusting and elegant'.[26]

At the time he wrote *Duff's Device*, Tom Duff was a programmer at Lucasfilm trying to animate a series of video shorts into a longer sequence. The conventional method of automating such sequencing — what programmers call a loop — was producing delays because of the bottleneck produced by the action of the processor looping back and forth.

Duff's original code looked like this:

```
send(to, from, count)
register short *to, *from;
register count;
{
    do
    *to = *from++;
    while(--count>0);
}
```

To speed up the processing, he found an extremely unconventional way to short-circuit the do loop:

```
send(to, from, count)
register short *to, *from;
register count;
{
    register n=(count+7)/8;
    switch(count%8){
    case 0:        do{      *to = *from++;
    case 7:                 *to = *from++;
    case 6:                 *to = *from++;
    case 5:                 *to = *from++;
    case 4:                 *to = *from++;
```

```
case 3:            *to = *from++;
case 2:            *to = *from++;
case 1:            *to = *from++;
}while(--n>0);
}
}
```

While Duff's hack circumvented the bottleneck he was encountering in animating a sequence of shorts without interruption, in the process he committed a number of serious sins against what Knuth would call 'literate' code. For example, the purpose of a **switch statement** is to be able to distinguish one case from another. This vexing program, however, exploits a **bug** in the language itself – the fact that C doesn't automatically break between cases — to permit the program to fall through from one case to another, executing all the lines along the way. Duff also began his do loop in *case 0* and ended it in *case 1* — another violation of regular syntax. The result was a form of animation that shouldn't be possible syntactically.

Duff himself was ambivalent about his discovery: 'Disgusting, no? But it compiles and runs just fine. I feel a combination of pride and revulsion at this discovery. If no one's thought of it before, I think I'll name it after myself.'[27]

It is remarkable that this hack works at all — and even more amazing that this solution to a practical problem actually works *better* than the syntactically correct method by which Duff originally tried to solve the problem. As Alexander pointed out, the output that *Duff's Device* generates so efficiently is completely mundane, but the aesthetics of Duff's algorithm are sufficiently interesting to transcend their original purpose — so much so that this perverse routine created for an immediate utilitarian need has since become a puzzle used to confuse students and experienced programmers alike, an M. C. Escher image written in C.

LETHAL GRAFFITI
jaromil, *forkbomb*

A forkbomb is a program that, once initiated, churns out of control until it has taken over all **system resources** and crashed the computer. In 2002 a forkbomb by Perl programmer Alex McLean was awarded the software art prize of the transmediale festival in Berlin, but in the category of 'bang for the buck' it's hard to beat the minimal forkbomb written by jaromil, Italian hacker and free software author.

jaromil's *forkbomb* only contains thirteen characters: :(){ :|:& };: When typed on the keyboard of certain UNIX computers, this simple instruction starts one process (symbolized by the colon), then replaces it with two processes, then three, four, five, and so on *ad infinitum*. As Florian Cramer has pointed out, this Molotov cocktail of code most resembles **emoticon**s such as :(and ;), which represent crude emotional states in chat and email messages.[28] jaromil's message, on the other hand, is performative as well as representational — an example of the executable culture we'll examine in more detail later.

According to Cramer, jaromil believes software should be beautifully crafted. Clearly, however, jaromil's sense of beauty is antithetical to Knuth's. If Knuth represents legibility and control, jaromil represents illegibility and explosiveness; the latter's emoticon graffiti set into motion a chain reaction that — out of control — feeds on itself, as though merely typing Einstein's $E = mc^2$ into the right typewriter could set off a nuclear explosion.

Left: jaromil's *forkbomb*.

Code as Tool: Use and Misuse

The examples we've examined up to now have all used or misused code at the level of syntax, yet creators can also misuse code at the level of utility. Code happens to be the basis of contemporary tools with which artists can manipulate images and sounds, from graphics packages like Adobe Illustrator to video editors like Apple's Final Cut. For digital artists of the formalist persuasion, to tear one of these CDs out of its shrink-wrap is to unlock a new toolkit brimming with unexplored techniques and effects. To those of the culturalist persuasion, however, such applications are subliminal straitjackets to creativity, so that artistic genres become defined less by an intent common to a group of artists than by a particular set of Photoshop filters or default Flash sounds.

A number of creative self-starters have taken it upon themselves to code their own applications from scratch, creating new tools with fresh ideologies not governed by corporate interests. Much virtual ink has been spilled on email lists over whether these artist-made tools are themselves art. Sometimes artists custom-make a tool simply to advance their own work, like the long sticks the bedridden Henri Matisse devised to pin his colorful cutouts on a wall. In other cases, innovative programmers make and distribute their tools to realize the aesthetic visions of others. These tools by artists for artists provoke the question of whether such software production might be an artistic practice in itself.

Just because a tool can make art doesn't disqualify the tool itself from being art. But more is required of such tools than that their makers claim to be artists. If programmers of perverse syntax abuse the conventions of code, programmers of perverse tools use perfectly proper syntax to abuse their users' expectations about how digital tools are meant to function. Perverse tools aren't slaves to some predefined purpose, but instead offer wrongheaded, often counterproductive approaches to the task their users expect them to fulfill.

GRINDING YOUR OWN VIRTUAL PAINT

Grahame Weinbren, Jon Weinbren, and Stephen Bannasch, *Limosine*[29]

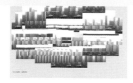

In 1982, Grahame Weinbren and Roberta Friedman began work on *The Erl King*, one of the first interactive video installations. Weinbren hoped to create an 'interactive cutaway' in which touching a screen while one video was playing would switch to another video without interrupting the soundtrack. Building on his experience as a video editor and interactive designer for the 1982 World's Fair, he soon discovered that there was no way, given the relatively crude and expensive equipment then available, to create the effect he was after. So, he and his brother set out to program a video-editing **suite** in **PASCAL** to do just that. The result, *Limosine*, ran on the minimal **CP/M operating system** on a primitive Zilog Z-80 personal computer. Despite this humble provenance, *Limosine* was capable of tracking video interactions over time to create a more complex and unpredictable cinematic experience than canned multimedia packages like Macromedia Director would offer decades later.

Weinbren originally intended to distribute *Limosine* freely to other artists who wanted to experiment with interactive video, but without the Internet as a distribution tool his efforts were doomed to failure. In today's world, where a new software release can be downloaded at the click of a mouse, the artist-made tool has blossomed into an artistic genre in its own right. Perhaps the best known of these applications is *Nato*, a project by the slippery online presence known variously as Netochka Nezvanova, nn, antiorp, and integer. Based on the venerable *Max* audio-editing software, *Nato* is a programmable interface for manipulating and mixing multiple audio and video feeds into a live networked performance. *Nato* has enabled new forms of artistic expression premised on networking together far-flung video images in real time. For example, the artist Meta used *Nato* to create his work

Panorama, a rare example of video-based Internet art. *Panorama* knits together Webcam images from around the world into a panoply of simultaneous video streams. Tools comparable to *Nato* have since been released by David Rokeby (*softVNS*), Jennifer and Kevin McCoy (*Live Interactive Multiuser Mixer*), and others.

But why stop here? Why not characterize as art any small-scale independent production of a tool for artists? *Max*, for example, the graphical-programming environment for music and multimedia on which *Nato* and *softVNS* are based, has enabled the creation of innumerable innovative audiovisual works by artists since its release in the mid-1980s. The trouble is that *Max*'s inventor, Miller Puckette, was trained as a mathematician and doesn't exhibit in galleries or museums (as Grahame Weinbren does) or hang out on art-related email lists (as Netochka Nezvanova does). To qualify *Limosine* or *Nato* but not *Max* would be to perpetuate the misinterpretation of Marcel Duchamp and his work that this book is trying to overturn. Although they have been the basis of wonderful artworks like *The Erl King* and *Panorama*, *Limosine* and *Nato* are not software art any more than a hammer and glue gun are installation art. And tool-making artists like Jennifer McCoy often admit the aesthetic limitations imposed by utility: 'As artists, we're not interested in revisiting the code. We just care if it allows us to create the art we set out to make.'[30]

Above: *Panorama*.
Right: *The Erl King*.

PAINT BY LETTERS

Tim Flaherty, Stuart Langridge, *et al.*,
Google Groups Art

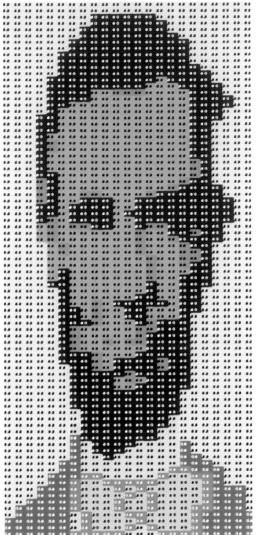

Adobe and Macromedia trumpet their new tools for artistic expression by offering ever-higher resolutions, smoother transitions, or fancier brush shapes. **ASCII** art, in contrast, offers a perversely low-tech way to make images. To make a picture in ASCII is simply to render a **grayscale** image (such as a portrait or a landscape) in the character set most common to the Internet — from &s, @s, and #s rather than from pixels of red, green, or blue. **Translator**s from image to text have been around since the 1960s,[31] but only in the past few years have ASCII artists realized that the popular search engine Google represented an ASCII translator lurking right under their noses. Google color-highlights search terms within the **Usenet post**s it displays; to hijack this feature for pictorial purposes, users post

contrived messages with carefully chosen strings of text ('aaaaabbbbaaaaa'), then run a Google query on the letter combinations from which their images are assembled. The result is the programming equivalent of painting by numbers. Stuart Langridge even scripted an automated tool to help would-be ASCII Leonardos reverse-engineer their images. What's engaging about this project is not the images themselves, which are as kitschy as most ASCII art, but the way in which a simple utility can let anyone hijack a dominant technology like Google for aesthetic ends.[32]

GRAPHIC DESIGN GONE HAYWIRE
Adrian Ward, *Auto-Illustrator*

Auto-Illustrator is a fully functioning perversion of
Adobe's popular commercial software, Illustrator.
Like its eponymous progenitor, *Auto-Illustrator* is a
vector-graphics program; Illustrator provides a
visual interface that helps artists (mostly graphic
designers, actually) generate images defined by
points and formulas rather than pixels. Such images
have the advantage of being scalable and, to some
extent, programmable. In a single keystroke, for
example, an Illustrator user can select three lines in
a picture and rotate each of them 20 degrees without
changing their positions.

Produced by software artist Adrian Ward, *Auto-
Illustrator* takes this programmability to an almost
absurd extreme. Users can select tools that 'Bauhaus'
a graphic into a particular style of geometric
abstraction, or that 'degenerate' a line using a
slider than runs from 'stupid' to 'pointless'.

Unlike Adobe Illustrator, whose interface is
designed to be as straightforward as possible, *Auto-
Illustrator* lends itself to a haphazard method of
visual composition based on random discovery
rather than premeditated planning. It is this
oblique relation between intention and result that
distinguishes *Auto-Illustrator* from pragmatic
artist-made tools.

Above: *Auto-Illustrator.*
Right: *Web Stalker.*

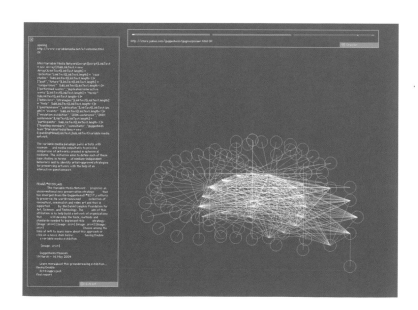

THE WEB WITHOUT PAGES

I/O/D, *Web Stalker*; Bill Cheswick,
Internet Mapping

Above: Web Stalker.

Perhaps the most prolific genre of do-it-yourself tools is the alternative **browser**. The proliferation of Web crawlers, spiders, and mappers at the turn of the millennium reflected the increased importance of this graphic medium, which since its introduction in the early 1990s had usurped the function of earlier text-based protocols like Telnet and Gopher to become the primary lens through which netizens viewed cyberspace. An additional motivation was the opportunity to demonstrate the technical and conceptual limitations resulting from the monopoly of a single such lens, Microsoft's Internet Explorer, which began to dominate the market at the same time that these alternative browsers emerged.

The challenge of picturing cyberspace has attracted programmers from various disciplines. One of the earliest and best-known alternative browsers is *Web Stalker* by the London-based artist collaborative I/O/D (Matthew Fuller, Colin Green, and Simon Pope). While commercial browsers such as Netscape and Internet Explorer represent the Web as a series of print-inspired pages, *Web Stalker* offers surfers a glimpse of the Web as a network. In place of a single window onto the Web, *Web Stalker* spawns multiple windows with suggestive names like 'Dismantle', 'Stash', and 'Extract'. It is the 'Map' window, however, that offers the most compelling vision of a pageless Web. Upon loading a particular **url**, *Web Stalker* draws a circle in the middle of this window, then draws spokes connecting to new circles, each of which is a page linked to the original Web page. Left to its own devices, *Web Stalker* will continue to spider new nodes and connections, gradually filling the screen with a visual network of increasing complexity and beauty.

If I/O/D's *Web Stalker* is a subversive critique of browser monopolies, researcher Bill Cheswick of the industry think-tank Bell Labs has a more scientific motivation for mapping the Internet. Cheswick aims

to envision the Net's technical structure by tracing the routes information **packet**s take along the frequently traveled paths of the information superhighway, from the Sprint and AT&T interstates down to the 'country roads' of regional phone systems. Studying the resulting diagrams, which plot these interconnected interstates as skeins of different colors weaving through a tangled knot of forking paths, can yield concrete, scientific conclusions. For example, a series of real-time maps of the Yugoslavian Internet during the 1999 Balkan conflict demonstrates how a network crippled by bombing can re-organize itself to route around damage.

Is there any reason to consider I/O/D's map art and Cheswick's not? I/O/D's palette is more restrained, and the work is regularly cited in online exhibitions and art-based email lists, while Cheswick's colorful design appeals more to popular taste yet is all but unknown among artists and curators online or off. Like all good art, both kinds of maps do not merely reflect the world as it exists, but rather construct the worlds — geographical, religious, political — we inhabit. Is the difference, then, just the company Cheswick keeps? If Cheswick's work appeared in the Duchampian context of a gallery or new-media festival, would it suddenly be recognized alongside *Web Stalker* on art-related email lists like Rhizome and nettime?

The question is ironic, because Cheswick's pretty pictures are actually more amenable to traditional frames than I/O/D's constantly changing interface. In fact, Cheswick is all too happy to offer 'framable' posters of his diagrams for sale on his Web site. His choice to exhibit computer-made images isn't exactly a radical intervention in the art world; deterministic illustrations have been produced by computers for some time now, and, as we'll see in the next section, they often are prized for their adherence to established aesthetic expectations rather than their departure from them.

By contrast, I/O/D's dynamic, screen-based application enlightens its viewers not through representation but through participation. And though I/O/D doesn't market matted prints of *Web*

Stalker **screenshot**s, they have deliberately 'framed' their work in the browser genre, precisely in order to call attention to the limitations imposed on that genre by page-based browsers like Explorer and Netscape. In effect, *Web Stalker* puts quotation marks around the browser concept, drawing attention to its limitations by jamming round nodes into this square window. By comparison, there is nothing particularly perverse about Cheswick's diagrams; his use of **traceroute algorithm**s, while it may be inventive, is perfectly in the spirit of their original purpose.

Below: Cheswick's Internet map.

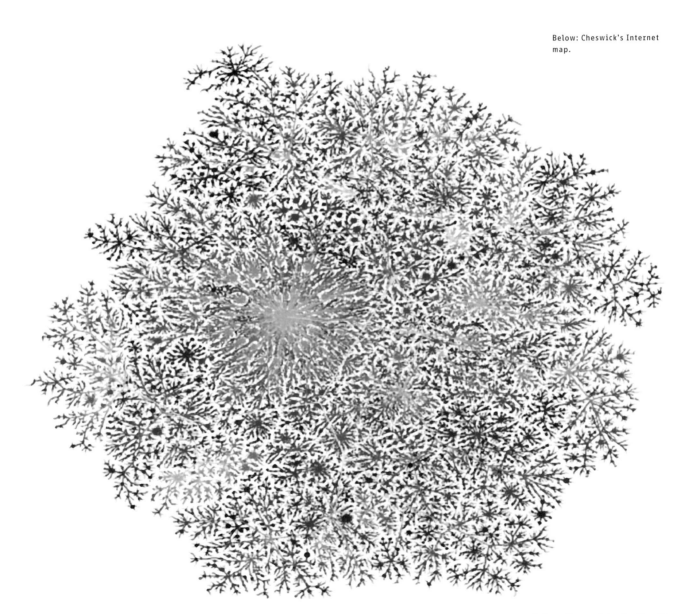

Code as Experience: The Proceduralist Product

The use of computers to generate creative experience, as opposed to creative syntax or tools, has been explored for several decades, yet the pioneers of this approach have achieved little recognition among mainstream museums and art critics. The first exhibition of computer art dates back to 1965, when three mathematicians – Frieder Nake, George Nees, and A. Michael Noll – installed photographic enlargements of plotter drawings at the Technische Hochschule in Stuttgart and the Howard Wise Gallery in New York.[33] Yet none of these mathematicians-turned-artists is well known outside a small circle of computer-art cognoscenti. The fault lies partly in the art world's limited purview but also in the obsession with product over process displayed by those who followed the first generation of Proceduralists.

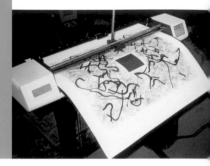

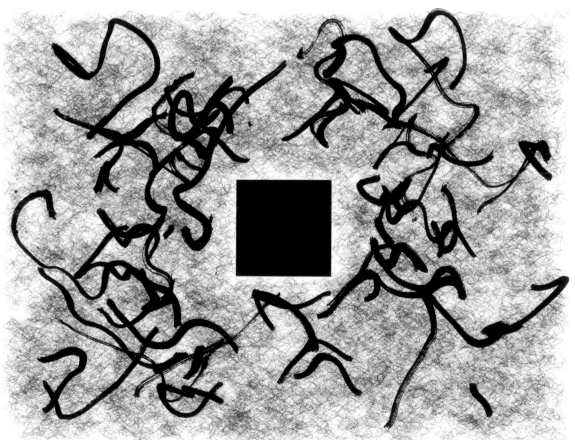

PROCESS OR PRODUCT?
A. Michael Noll, Harold Cohen, and Roman Verostko

The work of A. Michael Noll exemplifies a tension present in computer art from the very beginning, namely that regardless of any Proceduralist justification for the use of computers to create radically new imagery, much of the output of computer art ended up emulating traditional compositions. Noll, a mathematician at Bell Labs, did in fact write software to generate images that literally had never been seen before, such as a graphic animation of a four-dimensional hypercube. Though he made the animation into a 16mm film, Noll insisted that the software itself was the 'original';[34] it didn't matter much to the art world anyway, since few galleries at the time were willing or able to exhibit any format more dynamic than a plotter drawing. During the same period Noll also wrote programs for the express purpose of printing out algorithmic variations on pictorial compositions such as Piet Mondrian's 1917 *Composition with Lines*.[35]

Painter-turned-computer artist Harold Cohen takes Noll's picture-painting ambition to an extreme, claiming that his program AARON can produce 'a quarter-million original, museum quality images every year into perpetuity'.[36] Despite such grandiose claims, it is Cohen's process – teaching a machine to paint – that is his most valuable contribution to visual art. If Noll considers his computer to be more of a partner than a tool,[37] Cohen treats AARON as a child, instructing it in a series of 'aesthetic upgrades' to draw lines, then closed shapes, then colored forms, and, finally, entire compositions. Now in its 30s, AARON has passed through many stages in its life, from a turtle-like robot armed with a pen, to a wide-format printer, to video projections and screensavers. If Noll claims his software, not his pictures, are the 'original work', it's not as clear whether Cohen favors process or product. Cohen regrets an undue fascination with AARON's fancy hardware, preferring to demonstrate 'the most direct route possible from program to output'; yet he also trumpets the quality of AARON's imagery as proof of its value as software.[38] Ironically, as AARON gets better and better at emulating coloristic still lifes and figure paintings, its products become appealing only to those who want art to look like art.[39]

Roman Verostko goes further in his attempt to tame unruly software by framing it as art, claiming that 'in a very uncanny way software appears to have a life of its own. The artist's role is to humanize it.'[40] Verostko painted all-over canvases by conventional means until he discovered that a computer program could do it for him. His custom-designed software, Hodos, emulates the atmospheric abstraction this mature programmer-artist had already explored in pen-and-ink. Verostko describes as 'uncanny' the resemblance between his pre-computer, hand-made drawings and those scribbled by the fourteen-pen-plotter hooked up to his personal computer. Perhaps part of that uncanniness stems from the ease with which a 'machine that makes the art' has usurped the role of its progenitor and aesthetic role model, seemingly without introducing any aesthetic surprises or detours of its own.

Computer-generated drawings by Verostko's Hodos (opposite) and Cohen's AARON (left).

PRODUCT OVER PROCESS
Eric Heller

In perhaps the most extreme example of the use of code to create artworks whose authenticity is vouchsafed by traditional aesthetics, the Harvard chemist and physicist Eric Heller writes code that attunes his work not to his own taste but to that of his audience. To be sure, Heller also claims allegiance to a form of algorithmic purity; in fact, he claims more relevance for his algorithms than for the ungrounded mathematics of his peers:

> Digital artists need no longer emulate traditional media only! The computer allows us to create new media, with new rules, more naturally suited to the new tool. But such rules are best when they too follow physical phenomena, instead of arbitrary mathematical constructs. I have learned to paint with electrons moving over a potential landscape, quantum waves trapped between walls, chaotic dynamics, and with colliding molecules... You could say that I'm using physics as my brush.[41]

Heller seems to espouse a sort of reverse-Proceduralism when he argues that 'art can lead to science,' a claim he justifies by noting that chaos theory 'would never have taken off without some gorgeous images — like fractals — that came out of computers'.[42] But he wants to have it both ways; although the scientific Heller demands that his code be based squarely on the rigorous application of physical models, the artistic Heller manipulates the resulting colors using Photoshop to create five-by-eight-foot digital printouts.

Although a staunch Proceduralist might object to retouching computer output rather than resetting parameters in the original code, manipulating colors may not seem as impeachable to a mathematician or physicist used to dealing with the invisible, for whom color is an arbitrary attribute added after the fact. For these scientists — including Mandelbrot — color is less a referent to a hue in nature than a means to distinguish areas on a plane or altitudes on a surface.[43] Heller, however, goes further in his cavalier treatment of color, offering to 'color-shift' certain of his 'museum-quality' prints to suit a buyer's preference.[44]

As though to stave off the horrified reaction this pronouncement would provoke in the artist trained in the Modernist tradition of art-for-art's sake, Heller has cited Sol LeWitt as a role model.[45] LeWitt's analog wall drawings are generated by assistants following the predetermined sets of instructions in their titles, such as *Ten thousand lines about 10 inches long, covering the wall evenly.* Yet Heller's willingness to bend colors to suit his viewer's taste implies that he is also defying the Proceduralist strategy behind Conceptual art, which was to use a combination of logic and randomness to avoid tasteful adjustments which were not the direct product of the work's governing dynamics.

The value of LeWitt's work — and of good Conceptual art in general — lies in the tension between the simplicity of the rules and the visual complexity of the result. But this tension is only palpable if the artist has made the relationship between rule and result absolutely clear; although ten thousand lines on a wall create a surprisingly dazzling composition, any viewer who reads the instructions in the work's title can immediately grasp how they gave rise to the jazzy texture on the wall. By contrast, the same viewer would have to pore over *A Quantum Mechanics Primer* or *Mathematical Models of Semiconductor Physics* to fathom how Heller's variegated patterns and vertiginous lattices emerged from the study of our physical world. Artists like LeWitt deliberately kept the concepts underlying their work as simple as possible, precisely so that viewers could connect the dots between process and product. Similarly, Proceduralism will only achieve the experiential clarity of Conceptual art if its code is visible, simple, and devoid of any artificially introduced noise — such as manipulating color to suit the audience's taste[46] — that could obfuscate the transition from rules to result.

Opposite and following spread: Heller's *Random Sphere I, Quasicrystal II,* and *Crystal III.*

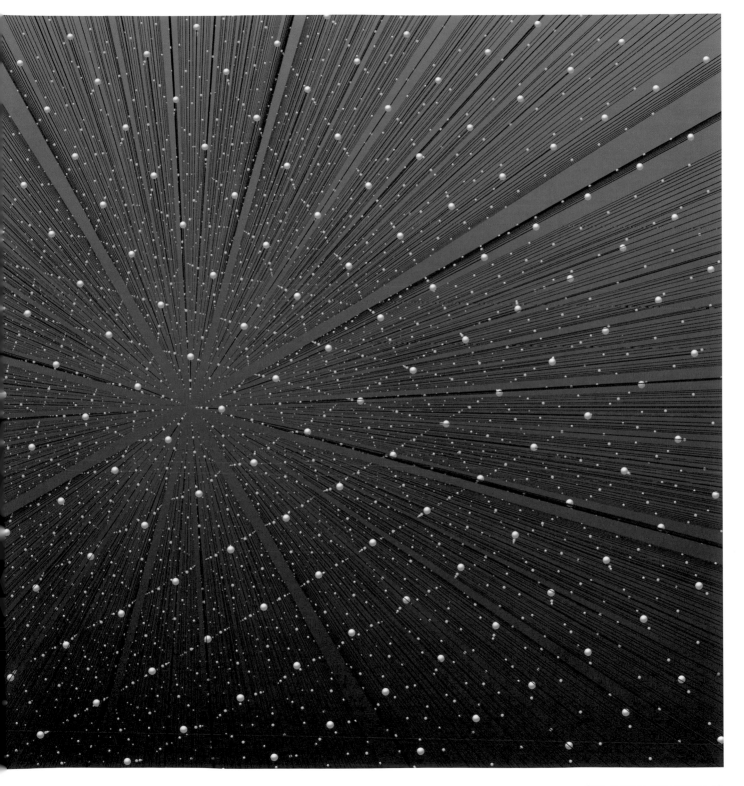

PROCESS OVER PRODUCT
Martin Wattenberg, *The Shape of Song*

The Shape of Song is one of the few projects based on mathematically complex algorithms where readers without an MIT PhD can still see the code in the results. That's partly because the work's creator, Martin Wattenberg, is an expert interface designer, but it's also because he's not out to make arty images with code but images that shed light back onto code itself.

The Shape of Song is an algorithm Wattenberg wrote to analyze **MIDI** versions of musical scores — i.e., encoded instructions about duration and pitch. By drawing arcs to connect all sets of notes that recur in a composition — whether on the scale of measures or of movements — Wattenberg's program reveals patterns of symmetry and asymmetry across a score as a whole. The shape of John Lennon's *Imagine* is a regular pattern of translucent semicircles equidistantly spaced over the score, while Bach's *Brandenberg Concerto No. 2* is an intricate tapestry of blue skeins arching across arpeggios, chord progressions, and refrains.

In a perverse but serendipitous act of introversion, Wattenberg also applied this software to analyze the code in *other* computer programs. The resemblances between his diagrams of software and his diagrams of Lennon or Bach speak of the profound similarities between code and music louder than any text on 'The Art of Programming'.

As these examples indicate, scientific analysis frequently generates images at least as compelling as aesthetic output. Sometimes those with scientific training are too eager to bend their output into a frame defined by art-world norms and don't recognize that the most artistically illuminating option may be to leave the work in the state of a scientific diagram.[47]

Right: Wattenberg's plot of Madonna's *Like a Prayer*.

Code as Experience: Screen

So far, we've argued that software must be perverse yet intelligible to succeed as art. Requiring the misuse of code to be legible puts software artists in a difficult position, for perversity can get in the way of a viewer trying to figure out the connection between code and output. Fortunately, instruction-based process art of the 1960s, which rejected the undue fixation on product that ill-fated the work of their computer-artist contemporaries, offers code artists several strategies to wed perversity with intelligibility. LeWitt's wall drawing *Ten thousand lines...* demonstrates the strategy of logical excess: pursue a trivial notion – in this case drawing a line on a wall – doggedly to its extreme. The result is an artwork in which the relationship between instruction and experience is both perverse and lucid.

Besides excess, another tactic explored by Conceptual artists is impertinence. Florian Cramer has suggested an example of a nondigital artist whose simple yet impertinent instructions provoke 'improper' thoughts or experiences.[48] In 1960, the avant-garde artist and musician La Monte Young published this cheeky single-line instruction in an anthology of Conceptual and performance-art writings: 'Draw a line and follow it.' Young's directive, entitled *Composition 1960 #10 (to Bob Morris)*, might seem inconsequential, but it's freighted with philosophical and political consequences. Anyone who tried to follow his command would soon run figuratively or literally up against a brick wall, because few legal systems permit unrestricted trespassing.

If Tom Duff perverted programming by writing an unreasonable script for a reasonable purpose, La Monte Young perverted performance by writing a reasonable script for an unreasonable purpose. Unlike Duff's improper case statements, there is nothing 'disgusting' about Young's syntax, which is grammatically correct and easy to understand. Yet, while Duff's device is functional despite its incorrectness, Young's instruction is dysfunctional despite its correctness. Like most Conceptual art, *Composition 1960 #10...* breaks rules in practice, not in theory.

Software artists of the culturalist persuasion can take a cue from Young and employ a perfectly ordinary piece of code in an impertinent way that chafes social norms and expectations. Whether it bumps into brick walls or firewalls, impertinent code can reveal the hidden ideological constraints that mark real-world processes.

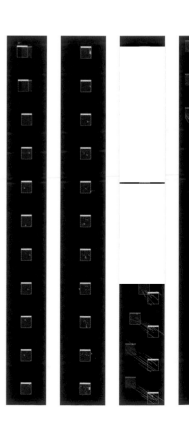

Above: *Screen Saver* applied to two different computer characters.

FOLLOW THE BOUNCING SQUARE
Eldar Karhalev and Ivan Khimin, *Screen Saver*

Software art is generally confined to a window the user can show or hide at will; one exception is the screensaver, which allows programmers to use the entire screen as their canvas. Art-world celebrities from painter Peter Halley to architect Greg Lynn have made screensavers,[49] but none are as impertinent as Eldar Karhalev and Ivan Khimin's eponymous *Screen Saver*. To 'run' this program is simply to change a few settings in the default screensaver that comes with pre-2001 versions of Microsoft Windows. A user who follows Karhalev and Khimin's instructions will convert Windows' default screensaver into a rectangle of fluctuating color sliding back and forth across the screen. In a strange way, *Screen Saver* is an update of Young's *Composition 1960 #10...* for virtual space, in which a square, or indeed any shape that can be specified by a keyboard character,

tries to continue in a straight line but ends up bouncing off the walls constraining it.

Like *Google Groups Art*, *Screen Saver* wonderfully illustrates how software art can be created without even learning a programming language.[50] Ultimately more important than knowledge of Java or ActionScript is an impertinent impulse to bend computers to purposes different from — and sometimes better than — those intended by their creators.[51]

SOFTWARE FROM ANOTHER PLANET
John Maeda

Above right: *Reactive Graphics.*
Opposite and right: *Time Paint.*

Taking a cue from A. Michael Noll, graphic-design maven John Maeda of the MIT Media Lab encourages designers to think of computers as impertinent collaborators rather than slavish layout tools.[52] The graphic applications Maeda builds are even more brazen than *Auto-Illustrator*; while the latter could be used for practical design work, Maeda's 'reactive graphics' feel more like software for denizens of another planet. The stroke of a virtual pencil in *Time Paint* drifts off the screen like smoke from a smokestack, while to paint with *Inverse Paint*, the user moves the window — the pencil stays still. While mastering drawing with the wind or a frame requires some dexterity with a mouse, Maeda also wanted to program an instrument his three young daughters could play without a steep learning curve.

The result was *Tap, Type, Write*, a perversion of the ordinary computer keyboard that lets loose a torrent of letter rotations, magnifications, and general typographical nuttiness in response to keystrokes.

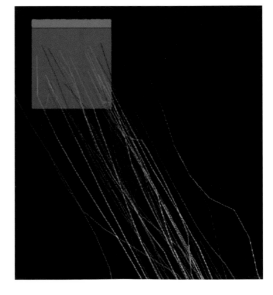

Code as Experience: Peripherals

With mainstream browsers now supporting DHTML, Flash, and Java, numerous digital designers have experimented with new ways to click, drop, and drag your way around a screen. A few, however, have pushed the Graphical User Interface to its extreme; in the right hands – literally and figuratively – even the lowly keyboard can be misused to generate aesthetic excess. The result places the mouse, keyboard, and other so-called peripherals front and center as expressive instruments in their own right.

THE MEDIUM IS THE MASSAGE
Golan Levin, *AVES*

MIT Media Lab graduate Golan Levin inherited his mentor John Maeda's penchant for perverting the keyboard. By translating the placement and cadence of keystrokes into percussive patterns, Levin's *Dakadaka* reminds us that whenever we are typing, we are also drumming. But Levin parts company with Maeda stylistically, especially in his later works based on **click-and-drag**. Maeda is tight, Levin is loose; where Maeda's geometries tend to be Euclidean, Levin's are organic tendrils and nebulous clouds.

Like Maeda's reactive graphics, Levin's interfaces are more instrument than tool, leaving their user with memories of fleeting sensations rather than 'museum-quality' prints. In no work is this more evident that his *Audiovisual Environment Suite* (*AVES*), a set of five interfaces for producing visual gestures and sounds animated in real time. Each instrument allows its player to deposit a different inexhaustible 'substance' across the screen by clicking and dragging. In *Aurora* this substance appears to be a shimmering cloud that disperses with time; in *Floo* it's soft-edged, growing tendrils; in *Yellowtail* it's brushlike strokes whose placement on the screen becomes a visual score for synthesized music.

Below: Levin's *AVES*.

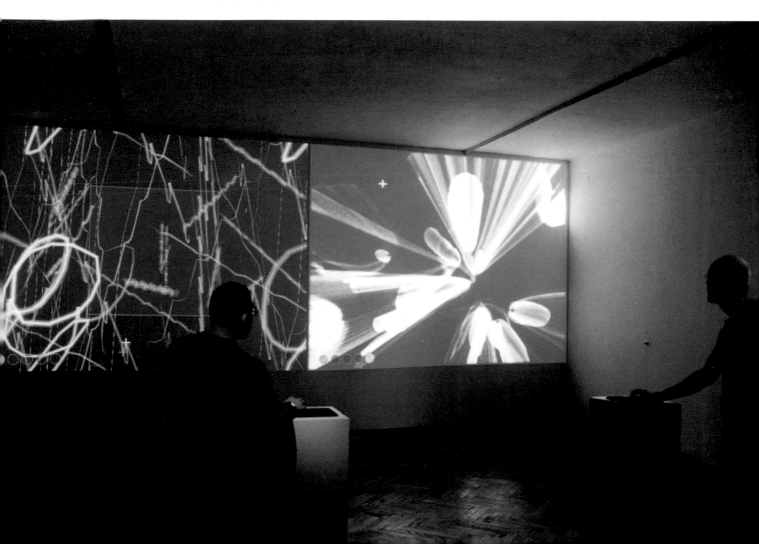

GRAPH PAPER ON ACID
Dextro and Lia, *Turux*

Opposite and below: Images from Turux.

At the other extreme from the lowly screensaver and keyboard are sophisticated animation suites like Macromedia Director, which offer a readymade, programmable toolkit with plenty of built-in features. Early interactive designers, however, restricted their use of this powerful tool to creating pulsing logos or morphing navigation bars for e-commerce sites. Seen in this context, *Turux* is a misuse of Macromedia's software only in so far as it demonstrates the raw visual horsepower of these tools when they're not yoked to some mundane purpose. Like Levin's *AVES*, each of *Turux*'s scores of interfaces allows users to click and drag their way to a dynamic abstract image; unlike *AVES*, *Turux*'s excessive animation is staccato or pointillist, governed less by organic growth than by chaotic irregularities. Clicking through a *Turux* work is like trying to plot points on a graph while dropping acid.

DEXTRO: A/TURUX-B

>110 ANIMATIONS, SEMI-AUTOMATIC
WWW.DEXTRO.ORG, WWW.TURUX.ORG   1995-2003

CD ROM, MAC (OS9/OSX) / PC   1024 x 768 MIN. (!) MONITOR, 24BIT COLOR REQUIRED

Code as Experience: Web

HyperText Markup Language is the lingua franca of all Web pages, a code so simple that most techies don't consider it programming at all. Yet the misuse of HTML tags can allow insights into online politics, community, and vision. Later on, we'll see how Internet artist Heath Bunting misused the anchor tag <a href> to comment on the politics of domain names. In the meantime, here is a brief primer of everything a Web-design class won't teach you about HTML.

Below: *Shredder.*

HTML HIJINKS

Olia Lialina, Darcy Steinke, Alexei Shulgin, Mark Napier and jodi

<frameset>

A fixture of first-generation Web pages, <frameset>s were supposed to allow one part of the page (such as a navigation bar at the left) to remain the same while another part (such as the content displayed at the right) changed based on the user's clicks. Olia

Above right: 'My Boyfriend Came Back from the War'.
Top right: *Form Art Exhibition*.
Below right: 'Blindspot'.

Lialina's hypertext story 'My Boyfriend Came Back from the War' undermines the intended purpose of frames — to produce a sense of stability as the user navigates through a Web site — by multiplying them indefinitely, nesting new ones within previous ones and subverting the navigation-to-content hierarchy, with the result that users aren't sure where to click next. Darcy Steinke's online story 'Blindspot' explores a similar misuse of frames, but here their proliferation is more deliberate and systematic. As the story unfolds from one pane to another, the irregular rectangles making up the <frameset> are gradually replaced by a blueprint of the apartment that serves as the setting and emotional anchor for the story.

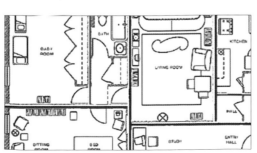

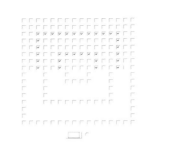

<button>

Another holdover from the Web's Jurassic period is the <button> tag, a stodgy gray rectangle used in countless online forms along with radio buttons, checkboxes, and input fields. Long reviled by Web designers for their clunky and inconsistent appearance across different browsers, these crude building blocks of HTML forms are elevated to the status of vocabulary for abstract art in Alexei Shulgin's *Form Art Exhibition*. The results of Shulgin's invitation to Internet artists are an uncurated set of Web pages built entirely with form elements: pages tiled over with submit buttons or pimpled with radio buttons, where every click leads to a new 'forest of signs'.

<div>

To view the Internet through one of Mark Napier's interfaces is to glimpse a landscape of unlimited visual possibilities. Napier's work is richer and more complex than the familiar print-inspired pages offered by corporate browsers like Netscape and Explorer. For example, his *Shredder* chops up any Web page into slivers of text and image, de-emphasizing the public face of a site while foregrounding such fine print as button icons and JavaScript code that make the site function.

When combined with **cascading style sheet**s, the <div> tag that *Shredder* exploits was originally intended to pin down the elements of a Web page so that designers could specify the same fixed page layout on different computer screens. *Shredder*, however, turns this page metaphor inside out by switching the placement of scripts and images to <div>s of its own making, thus revealing what Webmasters and designers have deliberately concealed.

JavaScript

If HTML is the skeleton of a Web page, JavaScript is the muscle. Unlike tags like <div> and <button>, which determine the location and style of static items on your screen, JavaScript is a fully functional programming language. Most Web pages employ it for superficial tasks like changing icons on mouse rollover, repositioning text or images in response to user clicks, and popping up new pages or error messages. JavaScripts can also handle sophisticated calculations or data processing, but some of the most successful misuses of the language focus on a single 'method' such as Math.random() or window.open().

One of the most notorious JavaScript methods is the ability to pop open a new browser window — a technique so overused by advertising companies and porn purveyors that around 2002 browsers began to offer the option of disabling this feature. While most popup and popunder windows are merely annoying, in the hands of Joan Heemskerk and Dirk Paesmans, the infamous glitch artists of jodi.org, they create absolute havoc. A visit to *oss.jodi.org* triggers a window.open() command that pops up a blank blue square. But the square is only visible for a fraction of a second, after which jodi's mischievous JavaScript executes a window.close() and reopens an identical blue square window a few pixels over. By looping this process in fast motion, jodi create the illusion of a square zigzagging across the screen, thus kludging an animation technique out of a handful of commands.

If the result were just a syncopated low-tech animation, *oss.jodi.org* would simply be an update on Jeffrey Kurland's *The Dotted Line*, a crude but compelling animation from the early 1990s in which mousing down on the browser's scroll bar animated a series of dots in the manner of Thomas Edison's

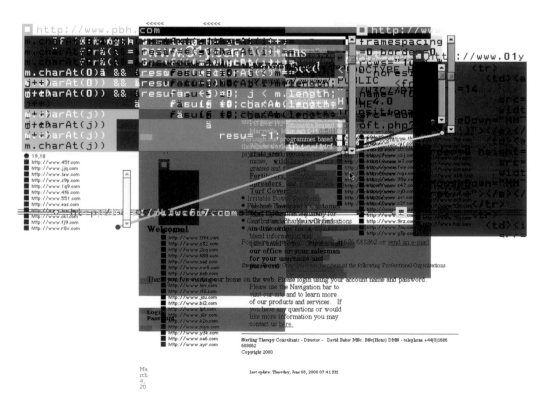

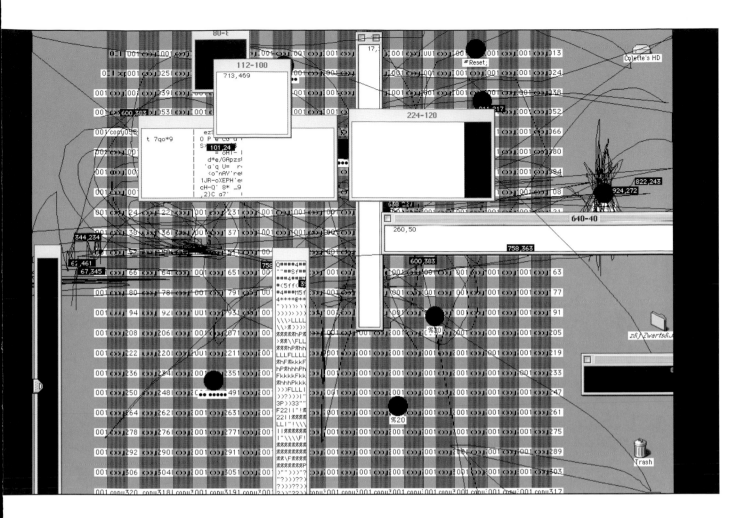

hand-cranked Kinetoscope. But jodi's runaway
animation has no hand-crank to control it; the
excessive popups stutter across the screen too
quickly for most mortals to catch and close them
manually. The only resort is to force-quit the
browser or shut down the computer — surely one
of the most perverse examples of narrative closure
in the history of art.

oss is only one example of jodi's cornucopic
misuse of code. Cascading sheets of green ASCII
text over a black screen, flashing 404 error
messages, proliferating form buttons and text
boxes — this is what awaits the unsuspecting user
who downloads one of their hacked games, inserts
one of their CD-ROMs, or visits their Web site.
Although much of jodi's work thrives on obfuscation
and illegibility,[53] *oss* is one of their most legible
works to date, for it misuses a single atom of code —
the window.open() method — and for this reason
it is also one of their projects most likely to agitate
viewers into reassessing their relationships to
their 'obedient machines'. Like the best examples
of software art, *oss* deflates the meme of a
seamless human-computer interface, exposing
ruptures where human and machine agendas do
not coincide.

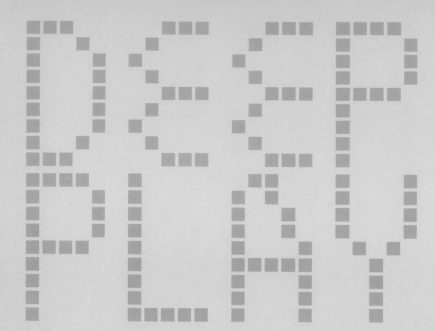

Cultural experience 'begins with creative living first manifested as play'.[1] While D. W. Winicott's words describe children's play, they also capture the creative energy of jaromil's elegant forkbombs and I/O/D's Web Stalker. Clearly, the kind of polymorphous perversity described in the first chapter requires sustained and engaged play with the tools, memes, and structures of digital technology. If this perversity is equivalent to the immune system's production of antibodies, then gameplay at its most profound mirrors the immunological moment when one of those antibodies latches onto a virus. In the physical body, this 'match' revs up the immune system and unleashes its power. In the social body, this match between artistic play and unarticulated cultural memes revs up the creative process and produces the kind of art we'll explore in this chapter.

But when does gameplay approach artistic expression? Some of the computer games we'll look at are clearly marketed as entertainment, yet the astute player can often discern a match between gameplay and deeper cultural dissonances. Avid players of *Grand Theft Auto: Vice City*, for example, might begin to sense that the over-the-top street crime in Liberty City, 'the worst place in America', is just a popular and playable version of the kind of corporate crime at the core of their own society.

Perhaps the measure of a game's relevance isn't any particular plot twist, theme, or game dynamic, however, but the extent to which it provides or reveals unarticulated technological memes for the player. Clifford Geertz's anthropological analysis of Balinese cockfighting sees in this violent sport an allegory of the entire social system of Bali, a kind of behavioral mirror of social power and stratification. Taking his cue from Jeremy Bentham's notion of 'deep play' as 'play in which the stakes are so high that it is … irrational for men to engage in it at all', Geertz describes the significance of the bloody fights and the irrational betting practices they engender:

> …[the cockfight] provides a metasocial commentary upon the whole matter of assorting human beings into fixed hierarchical ranks and then organizing the major part of collective existence around that assortment. Its function, if you want to call it that, is interpretive: it is a Balinese reading of Balinese experience; a story they tell themselves about themselves… Every people, the proverb has it, loves its own form of violence. The cockfight is the Balinese reflection on theirs: on its look, its uses, its force, its fascination.[2]

A similar statement might be made about the vast majority of violent computer games. Whether the enemies are aliens, monsters, dragons, or evil wizards, players clearly derive great pleasure from taking responsibility for defending themselves, a behavior not only taboo in Western culture but also very difficult to actualize given the elusiveness of threats to our survival. Whom do we blame for global warming? Toxic dumping? Decimation of species? Deforestation? Migration of jobs? Political marginalization? How can we articulate the ways in which we feel disempowered when the latest advertisements celebrate our infinite choices of car models, shampoos, or miracle drugs?

In games, we can enact our id rages on polygon prostitutes and mutant monsters. Or we can hone our skills in car-racing or skateboarding and become champions in a realm with easily defined rules and clear rewards and punishments. Either way, we regain some momentary, and virtual, control over our destinies. But can we exercise our newly acquired skills outside the box? Can we get the gamers out of the game long enough to discern the behaviors they are assuming rather than just being immersed in them? Such a moment of realization might be the difference between trivial and deep play, between killing time and working out social and cultural issues.

The moment of contact between art and technological or social memes is likely to occur in this kind of deep play, whether players become street versions of corporate butchers and robber barons (*GTA: Vice City*) or bickering schoolgirls trying to tear each other's hair out (*Sissyfight*). If something startles the player out of immersion and into reality, out of illusion and into insight, then we have a moment of arrest remarkably similar to the instant when an antibody latches onto a virus. Suddenly, a shift in the system (immunological or ideological) occurs, and nothing remains the same. Focusing on moments of arrest may seem counterintuitive to those who believe, like Henry Jenkins, that gameplay is about movement:

> those memorable moments don't simply depend on spectacle. After all, spectacle refers to something that stops you dead in your tracks, forces you to stand and look. Gameplay becomes memorable when it creates the opposite effect — when it makes you want to move, when it convinces you that you really are in charge of what's happening in the game, when the computer seems to be totally responsive.[3]

While this visceral immersion may be intoxicating, it's in fact the moments of arrest that can constitute game art as opposed to mere entertainment.

Although he didn't use the term, the German playwright Bertold Brecht championed the political value of arrest. Brecht felt that catharsis — the driving force behind most forms of entertainment from Aristotle to Paul Auster — would defeat any lasting social effect that art might have. In place of enthralling emotions like fear and terror, Brecht advocated a self-aware art form that would enlighten rather than engross. Arrest is the Brechtian moment when we become aware of the magic of the genre and cast a critical eye over what is happening.

If code is the magic of our time, then games are the magic shows that enthrall the masses, recently topping Hollywood in gross revenue. But in gameplay, the magical sense of control and movement Jenkins describes is illusory. While your avatar may be flying through cloud banks or smashing through police barricades, your bottom is still on your chair, your bladder is filling, your stomach is grumbling, and only your thumbs are twitching. Furthermore, while the game may give you the illusion that you are in charge, in fact that role is largely reserved for the game designer. In moments of arrest, the illusion is shattered and the Wizard found to be an ordinary man behind a technological curtain. < >

LIBERTY EQUALS GRAND THEFT
Rockstar Games, *Grand Theft Auto* **Series**

For pure, wanton, unmotivated violence, *Grand Theft Auto* reigns supreme among blockbuster games. Gameplay consists largely of beating prostitutes, pumping police and innocent pedestrians with bullets, and jacking cars to complete gangster missions. With each new release of the game, the weapons proliferate, the targets multiply, the sound effects get more realistic, and the music on the car stereo is modernized. In *Grand Theft Auto 3*, a revenge narrative supplements the free-for-all and helps drive the action. The premise is that you, the player, have been betrayed, then shot and left for dead at a heist. Now you are returning to reclaim your turf. Unfortunately, you return as a street thug and must work your way back up the crime ladder by completing missions — killing rivals, stealing cars, delivering packages. If you survive and evade enemies and arrest, you may regain some of your lost power in Liberty City.

When gamers describe *GTA*, they use terms like *freedom*, *depravity*, *variety*, *satisfaction*, *excessive violence*, *black comedy*, and *innovation*. The freedom comes not only from the easy violence but from the ability to ignore missions and roam the city creating your own adventures — stealing a taxi and pilfering fares, gunning down innocent bystanders, killing rivals and stockpiling their weapons, triggering a killing frenzy or gang war, and ramming busses through police blockades to your favorite soundtrack. (*GTA 3* has nine radio stations featuring popular tunes and original music as well as 'hilarious' talk radio and commercials.)

Liberty City is a fully rendered, fully destructible city. You can leave skid marks on the pavement, dents in your car, blood and mashed bodies on the sidewalk. And apart from competition from rivals or tracking by police, you are lord over this environment with nine lives to use up and millions of dollars to make. Arrest for multiple felonies and a string of murders only gets you a mild slap on the wrist: you lose weapons and points, and end up back on the street.

Given all this, it's not hard to understand why many countries have banned the game outright while others have decried it in their media. In Miami, Florida, a hundred-million-dollar lawsuit was filed by the family of a victim killed by two boys mimicking the game. Lawyers claim that the drive for profit from *GTA* endangers human lives. But the real danger of this horrific game may have less to do with the frenzied violence and underworld scheming portrayed in it than the critique it makes of the very institutions and bodies that seek to ban it. 'Every people … loves its own form of violence,' Clifford Geertz claims. If Balinese men love the cockfight, American males love violent computer games. If we follow Geertz's analogy, these games provide a reflection of America's violence, 'its look, its uses, its force, its fascination'. The violence Geertz examined was not murder and war but the abstract and arbitrary social arrangements that lead to profit and triumph for a tiny minority and to tragedy and loss for the great majority. Both cockfight and violent games produce a cathartic experience that helps players return to their lives purged of rage, fear, anger, and feelings of injustice. But neither is meant to draw attention to the problems with the structures it both represents and re-enacts; to look in a mirror is not necessarily to question what we see there.

Substitute 'corporate ladder' for 'crime ladder', however, and you get a shocking but revealing portrait of the typical American city: corporate bosses competing for 'blood money' in ways that endanger human lives, an ineffectual criminal-justice system, citizens with pent-up rage, and enough jazzy cars, missions (jobs, romances, vacation adventures), and music to keep us all playing the game. Mafia-like organizations often appear in neighborhoods for which the local economies and governments don't work. They arise as ways for local tribes to take care of their own.

FANTASIES WITH CONSEQUENCES
C-Level, Games

Despite the numerous clues that *GTA* provides both mirror and critique, most players interact with it on a behavioral level, acting out what they can't discern or articulate. But once game artists come onto the scene and start to mess with mainstream games, it becomes harder to ignore their implications.

One of these implications is the media's role in producing desensitized viewers. Many of us who saw the World Trade Center towers collapse or footage of the Madrid railway bombing had a hard time matching images to feelings. We see so much mediated violence, in ways that alienate us from the victims, that we can't reconcile what we see with what we feel or what we think we're supposed to feel. Three games produced by various members of the artist group C-Level[4] address this issue of disconnection.

Game enthusiasts often rate games by their ability to produce deeply immersive experiences, experiences so enthralling that they produce physiological reactions beyond the adrenaline rush — falling back from your chair when the tyrant in *Resident Evil II* crashes through the wall, or breaking into a sweat when you hear the invisible zombies in *Nocturne* shuffle by. So when art games like *Cockfight Arena* disrupt that video trance, we begin to get a glimpse of how games affect us. *Cockfight Arena* invites players to dress up like chickens, their game avatars. While they play, they also hold winged controllers and wear feathered

headgear. As C-Level explain, 'We saw this as a novel way to articulate the relationship between the person who plays the game, the avatar that stands in for them and the complex process of identification that occurs when you play a video game'.[5] C-Level compare the complex identification in gaming to that of fans watching a sports event or gamblers betting on a racehorse. By helping us to visualize this relationship, such games enable us to see the ways we identify, and yet maintain distance between, ourselves and our avatars. We don't mind expressing rage and inflicting pain, but we'd rather not have to feel guilty or suffer any consequences. After all, even if the emotion is real, it's being exercised in a fantasy world.

An even more visceral intervention is *Tekken Torture Tournament*, a PlayStation **mod** for *Tekken III*, a multi-player fighting game. In *Tekken Torture Tournament*, players strap electrodes to their right arms that emit shocks when on-screen avatars are injured during a fight. The shocks have a dual purpose: first, they provide a real-world visceral consequence for game events; second, they cause the player's arm to 'flex involuntarily', making it more difficult for him to fight his game opponent. The shocks are supposedly too mild to be dangerous, and some players reportedly get used to them and apparently enjoy pushing the game to its limits in the presence of excited spectators.

This game disrupts a number of expectations about consumer games. First is the obvious visceral consequence for actions engaged in during gameplay. The body is now responsible and vulnerable. For once, a genre that claims to be immersive and interactive really does engage the

Waco Resurrection.

One poster advertising *GTA3* enunciates this clear disenchantment when it describes the game as 'A new way of getting things done'. Another poster features an FBI agent seen from the back with the following prompt: 'Now get this punk outta here.'

The sheer glee that gamers feel when unleashing their pent-up feelings of violence is also telling. In a genre dominated by violence and missions to kill 'bosses', the frustration of players (read: workers) ought to speak beyond the confines of the game. They include postal workers and soccer fans, gang leaders and drug dealers, gun-toting high-school kids and splinter-group fundamentalists. There is room for all of the disenchanted, and the disenchanted have invested enough cash in the *GTA* series to make the games runaway best-sellers. As if that wasn't enough, the equation of Liberty and Grand Theft, of freedom and violence, ought to give us pause. Violence is often a strategy of self-defence, a way to protect ourselves. Games seem to give us a way to defend ourselves, but the real theft may be occurring under our noses rather than in virtual worlds. As long as *GTA* works as catharsis, it merely purges our emotions and then allows us to return, unchanged, to an unchanged society.

Right: *GTA3*.

body with physical consequences. Second, the complex identity formation of avatar/player adds a third persona to the performance: the spectator. While watching other people play games may be common in **LAN parties** and college dorm rooms, it's an often-overlooked aspect of the complete spectacle of gaming. The levels of identification and/or distance are complex, as complex as the 'realities' brought to us by our news media. It's no wonder we feel a schism between what we see and what we feel.

Game critic Dyske Suematsu has described this schism as a 'disconnect', explaining that

> while novels and films also produce feelings in us, those feelings are usually active. This is the difference between art and entertainment; the former is an opportunity to find our genuine, active emotions, whereas the latter manipulates our sensory perceptions to artificially induce emotions in us. This is why true art makes consumers work hard, whereas a piece of entertainment is served on a silver platter for easy consumption, essentially telling consumers how to feel. The reason why video games tend to invite criticism of disconnect is because most of them provide no opportunity for our active emotions to manifest themselves.[6]

According to Suematsu, *Waco Resurrection* is one art game that attempts to short-circuit that disconnect. It provides players with the opportunity to review the 1993 storming of the Branch Davidian compound in Texas that resulted in the fiery deaths of eighty people. C-Level see a connection between the Waco tragedy and the political situation in the US and Europe during the weapons inspections and war in Iraq: '[David] Koresh is both the besieged religious other and the logical extension of the neoconservative millennial vision. Our primary focus is the hypocrisy and contradiction that permeate the Waco showdown.'[7]

Waco Resurrection is a cross between a **first-person shooter** and an interactive documentary. Assuming the role of Koresh, players must battle US agents, respond to skeptics and upstarts (each player assumes the role of another Koresh), cultivate followers, and carve out a peaceful sanctuary in the midst of confrontation and crisis. To reinforce the documentary focus, the game incorporates audio samples of Koresh's voice and music, as well as footage from media coverage of the event.

It's important to note that none of the C-Level games presents a solution, or even claims to clearly identify social problems. Rather, the games provide spaces in which to engage in deep play around a structured experience. They work by disrupting the usual patterns of behavior and scripted interactions that limit mainstream games, thus forcing players — and, hopefully, the games industry — to become more reflective. These games work at the level of individual experience as it meets social crisis, and they do this by providing a safe place in which to engage in behavioral fantasy — perhaps the most powerful effect of immersive, interactive games. Part of *Endgames*, a series of works based on 'alternative utopias' and 'apocalyptic moments', these game mods and hacks 'incorporate elements of subjective documentary and experimental fantasy with game development technology to create a visceral gaming experience focused on extreme psycho-social phenomena'.[8]

Cockfight Arena.

Arrest

Immersion may be the hook by which C-Level grip their viewers, but — unlike most of their commercial counterparts — their games don't have the desired effect until that hook is set and the gamer is caught off guard, not by one of the game's monsters or Mafiosi but by one of its ontological or ethical dilemmas. While moments of arrest occasionally crop up in commercial games, even in such mainstream titles as *GTA*, the kind of work done by C-Level and their contemporaries offers hope for a more self-critical future for games. Games-focused art exhibitions like 'Cracking the Maze' (1999), 'Game Show' (Mass MoCA, Boston, 2002), 'Game On' (Barbican, London, 2002), 'Art Games and Breakout' (Siggraph, 2002), and '// Killer Instinct //' (New Museum of Contemporary Art, New York, 2003) remind us that the power of games can be harnessed for more than just juvenile power fantasies and feudal political scenarios. Currently, most games mirror the dominant cultural values of their largely privileged, usually American, male producers and designers. Geared to a generation of boys assumed to be the heirs of influence and power, they rarely reflect the experiences, values, or dreams of girls, women, or non-Western players, assuming the technology is even available to them. Most still re-inscribe conservative assumptions about gender, self-governance, cultural hegemony, and fantasy. Such games serve as catharsis for tensions in the culture rather than providing the arresting moments that would allow us to reflect on these tensions and begin to address them.

As long as the game industry remains concentrated in the hands of an even smaller group than Hollywood's film business, with even larger production costs and cycles, game values and designs are bound to remain conservative rather than genuinely creative. Some designers are attempting to shift some of the momentum from the hands of technicians to those of creators. And savvy players have begun tweaking **open-code game engines** to represent the kinds of worlds that correspond to their own fantasies, desires, fears, and values. Here we find the wellsprings of games as art.

A true transformation into art of the Internet age — the shifting of creative control from corporate to popular forms of self-representation — has yet to occur. The real question is whether gaming is a technology for centralizing or distributing cultural power and creative energy. As long as it continues to be centralizing, no matter how technologically sophisticated, it will remain firmly entrenched in the paradigm of old broadcast media rather than exploring the emerging one of distributed creativity launched by the Internet revolution. It remains to be seen if immersive technology can free us from corporate-defined culture or if it will merely deepen the cathartic trance. Part of the answer depends on how many creative hands have access to the tools and tropes of game design, and if those hands can place us under a different kind of arrest.

Opposite: *Cockfight Arena.*

City (E)scapes

Like Carnival, Mardi Gras, and gladiator sports, gaming has the ability to channel emotions triggered by conditions in the real world into a controlled space outside quotidian experience, a kind of cultural, in this case technological, black box. While this may prevent disgruntled employees from slashing their bosses' tires, it may also prevent them from joining and participating in their local union. If only we paid attention to the behaviors and fantasies we enact in game space, we might learn something about the tensions and contradictions in our real lives.

One complex experience we might be able to elucidate is that of living in large cities, where we frequently interact with total strangers and encounter novel experiences. Gameplay might teach us how to cope with the complex physical and social navigation required to survive in such places. Besides *GTA*, a number of games present different ways of conceiving or coping with city life.

URBAN POSER

**RockStar Games, *Midnight Club 2*;
Neversoft Entertainment, *Tony Hawk's
Pro Skater 4***

Midnight Club 2 follows the no-rules premise of other RockStar games but turns Los Angeles, Paris, and Tokyo into illegal street-racing scenes. The key game experience is driving souped-up vehicles, race cars, or motorbikes in an attempt to defeat your adversaries. Your goal is to hit as many checkpoints as you can on your way to the finish line by whatever means you choose — shortcuts, back alleys, direct routes — all the while ducking the authorities.

Another take on the city streets is *Tony Hawk's*

Midnight Club 2.

Pro Skater 4, the most recent in a popular series of skateboarding games. Most of the levels take place in quasi-realistic recreations of actual locations such as San Francisco, Alcatraz, and Chicago, but there's also the huge Kona skate-park and such places as a shipyard, a zoo, and a carnival. In these settings you can seek out targets and terrains to practise your 'double kickflip indy', 'bs nosegrind', 'fingerflip', or 'fakie pivot grind'. Like other city-based games, freedom of play is important. The objective is to interact with the environment in such a way that you can master the terrain. The player explores, learns, and discovers goals and completes them, all in a way that gives a feeling of freedom and control.

What may not be evident in these virtual urban worlds is the extent to which gameplay is actually quite limited. This is of course a technical issue; more freedom means more complex and more intelligent rendering. What these games manage to do so well is to tailor gameplay to the virtual environment in such a way that the player only imagines a certain range of behaviors — drug dealing or car-racing or skateboarding. When a player tries to stray from these activities, the constraints of the game — both physical and ideological — become more apparent. As game critic Benjamin Johnson has explained,

> Good interactivity does not require that I be able to do literally anything at any time... A good level designer provides clues as to how I should interact with the environment. If the clues are subtle and well done enough, I shouldn't even realize that I am effectively being lead around by the nose. When we notice a particular game isn't letting us do whatever we want, we say the game is putting us 'on a rail.' Reflexively, we seem to long for a game that grants us the ability to do anything we want. However, even the briefest study of the art of interactivity reveals that this is not what we want at all. We don't want to do everything; we want to do the right thing, or perhaps occasionally the cool thing.[9]

In sum, 'cool' or 'right' are values deeply embedded in game design.

As a *distributed-creativity* online discussion about this 'concrete playground' suggested, skateboarders in real cities grind down buildings and smooth out pedestels, reinterpreting the city architecture for their own purposes. In Dennis Mcnulty's words, they 'move beyond the surface of the technology to explore the cracks and ledges: to see past the intentions of the designers/manufacturers: to create something that is more than a demo or advertisement for the bleeding edge'. While skateboarders in Dublin are remaking the city by breaking the rules, skateboarders in a game are merely playing by them.

Tony Hawk's Pro Skater 4.

WALKING ON THE EDGE
Stephen Honegger, *Margin Walker*;
Jim Monroe, *Liberty City*

Margin Walker.

A few art games challenge the illusion of freedom produced by good game design by trying to perform actions outside the scripted plot lines. Stephen Honegger's *Margin Walker*, for example, exploits a glitch in a PlayStation golf game to allow the player to explore the margins of the terrain, which features mountains and lake vistas not normally seen by golfing players.

Similarly, Jim Monroe's movie of his trip through *GTA3*'s Liberty City makes the declarations of 'freedom' in this game seem naïve at best. First, he constructs different 'skins' which allow him to play characters of his own design. He dons a 'Canadian tourist' skin complete with camera, eschews the temptation of driving around in cars, and attempts to 'tour' the city on foot: 'If you really want to see it you should walk around …' What he discovers, beyond confused or incommunicative pedestrians, are secret rooftop vistas and a green park or forest on the city's outskirts. 'Another thing I love about the city was the lack of advertising,' the 'Canadian tourist' says, wondering if it was difficult to find companies 'to get behind such an extreme game'. Given typical game scenarios, some moments in the movie are hilarious: 'Yeah, it was just great to get away from the city hustle and bustle and just hang out in the trees.' Of course, this player 'tourist', unwilling to jack a taxi and kill the driver, can't get one to stop for him in the pouring rain and so ends up running all the way home. The next morning finds him walking a different margin, this time in 'street priest' skin, attending a homicide and snatching up stray dollars from the street like all the other pedestrians who've spied a stash of lost goods.

BOTTOM LINE
Matthew Lee *et al.*, *Dopewars*;
Stephen Honegger, *Three Hour Donut*

Three Hour Donut.

Dopewars takes an opposite tack to reflect on the *GTA* series. It's a drug-trading game whose sole objective is to get as rich as possible in thirty days. 'Buy drugs low and sell them high — but watch out for the cops.'[10] Not only does this game reduce *GTA* to a single, rather boring action, but it equates drug dealing with stock trading, reinforcing the parallel between the underworld and the corporate world hinted at in *GTA*.

Some game mods, rather than challenging game illusions, exaggerate the primary action, distilling a

game to its essential gestures. Honegger's *Three Hour Donut* is PlayStation's *Driver* executing one repeated 360-degree spin for 180 minutes of a VHS tape. Monotonous, repetitive driving. Going in circles. Take that and dress it up with points, contests, and levels, and you get a video game.

CRITICAL GESTURE
Alex Galloway, *Prepared Playstation 2* and *Time-To-Live*

Time-To-Live.

Two game hacks produced by Alex Galloway also distill mainstream games to an emblematic moment. Though their immediate effect is humorous, these hacks also stake out a virtual no-man's-land where gamers and game designers alike seem to have lost control. *Prepared Playstation 2,* Galloway's hack of *Tony Hawk's Pro Skater*, traps a skater in a particular physical loop, for example getting caught in a pit or wedged between a corner and a bench.[11] The skater almost escapes the loops but not quite, so there's a kind of snare which is hilarious at first but which, after a while, begins to feel like an existential trap, a kind of skater's 'eternal return'. Another hack creates a pit carved and studded with so many obstacles that it would be impossible to skate it in any meaningful way. The skater always crashes and falls.

Such unintended 'traps' exist in other games as well. In the 1990s flight simulator *Hornet F-18A Classic*, setting 'crash disabled' in the game preferences may seem like a good idea for a novice pilot, but this setting can force the plane to skid along the ground, bouncing and smashing everything in sight but unable to either take off or come to a stop. When game physics take over, you get an experience of who (or what) is really in control. Equations deep in the code that engender game physics may create the illusion of freedom, but when these laws take over, they feel as inevitable and constraining as gravity.

Galloway's *Halflife* hack, *Time-To-Live*, takes another twist on the wildly popular **first-person-shooter** game by playing with the laws of game physics, in this case producing smoke and earthquake effects from the simple swing of a crowbar. In the original *Halflife*, Gordon Freeman's mission is to combat aliens released by an experiment gone awry and also escape the Federal agents sent in to 'erase' the entire incident. His only strategy is deception and aggression. He must strike before he is struck. Galloway's video loop of a player triggering virtual pyrotechnics with the smack of a crowbar distills the complex motives behind the aggression to a single repetitive gesture, one that accurately captures the behavioral experience of many first-person shooters. Shoot an alien, swing a crowbar, toss a grenade: that is the behavioral limit of game interactivity. Of course, Galloway's additional feat — to code the smoke and fire — is both another level of agency and a reminder that the real power in games lies in hands of designers not players — and of the hackers and modders who mess with the rules rather than playing by them.

Violence Comes Home

All effective immersion experiences in games are based on a willing suspension of disbelief. But there is a difference between those games that create believable but clearly fictional worlds and those that attempt to simulate real experience. Simulation games depend on the extent to which they can approximate their real counterparts. *Tony Hawk's Pro Skater*, for example, attempts to reproduce the exhilaration of skateboarding, albeit with a game control. Sid Meier's *Civilization* tries to reproduce the experience of empire-building. Car-driving and military-aircraft games challenge your driving and piloting skills. *The Sims* challenges you to build a virtual family or city that works. But the 'realism' of these genres pales beside that of war games produced either for entertainment or for official training.

At one extreme are the simulation games used by the US military to recruit soldiers or train troops and commanders. When a game scenario overwhelms the player's sense of the real, however, lives can be lost. Critics have argued that it was exactly such a 'simulation mindset' that led the commander of the USS *Vincennes* to order missile fire that mistakenly shot down an Iranian passenger plane in 1988, killing 290 civilians.[12] To these critics, such events raise serious issues about the extent to which game scenarios should be used to train military personnel.

Since effective gameplay relies on the player's willingness to simultaneously conflate and distinguish the virtual and the real, the question of ontological slippage is important. In the case of child's play, this slippage is common and necessary, though the negotiations between the made-up and the real are far from simple, as we can see in this 'war game' between a five-year-old boy and his three-year-old sister:

Boy: I'm going to kill you.
Girl: He's going to kill me.
Boy: I'm going to kill you.
Girl (to parents): He said, he is playing a killing game.
Parent: Do you want to play a killing game?
Girl: I want him to play a killing game.
Boy whacks girl on the head with a plastic plane.
Girl (crying and howling): He hit me!!
Boy: Ok! Ok! I'll give myself a timeout. (He sits in the chair.)[13]

This scene reminds us that while it is critical to keep reality and play distinguished at one moment (the boy doesn't really want to kill his sister; he must be 'playing' a 'killing game'), for the game to 'count' it is equally important that the players conflate them at another (the boy knocks the girl on the head to show this is no mere verbal tease but a real engagement). When both players see that the conflation of game and reality has gone too far, they stop and the offender is reprimanded.

Both game critics and designers have argued that even with simulation games, players are easily able to distinguish game and reality. First-person shooters don't result in mass murders at high schools, they argue. But as the children's interaction just described suggests, the fall from games into reality can be precipitous — broken only by an arresting moment, like getting hit on the head by your brother. A look at some war games will help us ponder this more deeply.

BACK DOOR DRAFT:
AN ALL-VOLUNTEER ARMY
US Army, *America's Army*

Inspired by the number-one online action game *Counterstrike*, an anti-terrorist game based on the *HalfLife* **engine**, *America's Army* promises players authentic state-of-the-art military experience while training for and combating terrorism in simulated missions. A free, downloadable online game, it attracts its share of Army recruits. *America's Army* boasts two kinds of gameplay: 'Operations', a first-person action game, and 'Soldiers', a goal-based role-playing simulation. 'Operations' allows multiple players — up to thirty-two — to join the same 'virtual' unit. Training missions teach recruits by subjecting them to the Army's obstacle course at Fort Benning, Georgia, and to parachute training, and to familiarizing them with authentic military equipment. Communication and teamwork are crucial to success.

The updated *America's Army: Special Forces* continues the recruitment **adver-gaming** with an additional challenge: the opportunity to earn Green Beret status by completing special missions. The website boasts a slew of realistic features, including 'Authentic U.S. Army experience — Realistic depiction of the values, units, equipment and career opportunities that make the Army the world's premier land force — continually updated to incorporate new occupations, units, technologies

and adventures'. But the line between realism and doctrine becomes blurred with the final feature, which guarantees 'Accurate Soldier behavior — Players are bound by the laws of land warfare, Army values (honor, duty and integrity) and realistic rules of engagement'. This claim, while a good recruiting tool, ought to raise an eyebrow about the 'authenticity' of the game, especially its ideological position supporting the use of force by the world's superpower against small groups of resistance fighters. Whose freedom is being defended? Why? At what cost? Against whom? And why spend over $6.3 million turning this message into an interactive experience?

America's Army is an ingenious tool for aligning an acceptance of the rules of gameplay with acceptance of an implicit political agenda. Both forms of surrender require a willing suspension of disbelief – and the absence of any moments for reflection that might arrest it.

America's Army.

TOUGH, BRAVE, OBEDIENT, AND IN THE DIRT
Institute for Creative Technologies, *Full Spectrum Warrior/Command*

'Only one type of soldier is prepared for battle,' the trailer for another military-tactics game barks. 'He is a Full Spectrum Warrior.' *Full Spectrum Warrior* trains soldiers for command and control of a US Army light infantry squad, while its counterpart, *Full Spectrum Command*, trains company commanders.

Gameplay is set in Eastern Europe as part of an urban peacekeeping mission and involves squad-based tactical action. Players move between two fire teams attempting to accomplish their missions while protecting their troops. The designers claim a number of features that make this military tactical-action game authentic: 1. It's based on actual US Army infantry doctrine; 2. Its advanced **AI** simulates the behavior of soldiers in intense combat conditions; 3. Rules of engagement simulate real-world conditions; 4. Weapons reflect those currently in use by the US Army; 5. Soldier animation is based on live footage of combat veterans.

Developed by the Institute for Creative Technologies in consultation with experts at the Army Infantry School at Fort Benning, and based on a game commissioned by the Army for similar purposes, *Full Spectrum Warrior* attempts to create 'training simulations that are intended to have the same holding power and repeat value as mainstream entertainment software'. Why the designers felt that war training would be readily consumed as entertainment is unclear, though Western media have been conspiring to reduce war to entertainment for some time now. But the difference between passively conflating the two on TV and actively engaging in war as immersive experience ought to concern us. Given the accurate replication of actual battle drills and small-unit tactics used to train soldiers, should we expect to see a new generation of trained troops strutting through American high schools, right past the gun checkpoints? If these games are effective as training, what's their effect as entertainment?

Of course, training soldiers is not just about developing combat skills; it's also about 'indoctrination'. Army doctrine in this game is quite clear: The real heroes are infantrymen (*not* - women) standing side by side, representing the most powerful nation on earth, and fighting for a just cause: 'The U.S. Army is the most powerful ground force in the entire world. The backbone of a ground invasion is the U.S. Army Infantry'; '*Full Spectrum Warrior* puts you in the dirt with your men, where danger lurks around every corner'; 'We've got a job to do, folks. Move out!'[14] Tough, brave, obedient, male soldiers dedicated to their 'job' embody the values of the military in this game and also make up the superpower strength of the US. What force could challenge such might? Only the likes of Mohammad Jabbour Al Afad, leader of the Zekistan rebellion against the Soviet Union, and suspected world terrorist. Game history explains that he hails from wealthy, neglectful Lebanese parents, was educated in the UK and US, led rebels in the Afghan uprising against Soviet Russia (having benefitted from CIA training), and — having avoided capture by the Soviets — ended up in Zekistan among a small group of guerillas. Such is the face of the enemy. Ironically, an enemy the US helped to create. What, then, are sixteen- and seventeen-year-old gamers learning here?

Whatever it is, it has the opposition worried. In a global scene dominated by powerful media, wars are often won by headlines and rumors. Palestinian and Lebanese digital artists are responding in kind to *Full Spectrum Warrior*'s ideological missile.

Below and opposite: *Full Spectrum Warrior/Command.*

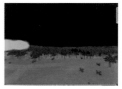

COUNTER-COUNTER STRIKE
Hezbollah, *Special Force*

Hezbollah's *Special Force* responds to *America's Army* and *Full Spectrum Warrior* with a military first-person shooter that attempts to represent the history of the Muslim resistance to the Israeli invasion of Lebanon in 1978 and 1982, and their withdrawal in 2000. Players begin with a training simulation, practising their shooting and grenade-launching skills against pictures of Israeli political and military figures such as Ariel Sharon. They replay the conditions that faced the original Hezbollah fighters breaking through Israeli positions in southern Lebanon, honoring pictures of real-life 'martyrs' killed at the same spots and eventually fighting Israeli troops and obstinate settlers. Arab game designers, concerned with the messages being conveyed to young Arabs via Western games that portrayed them as terrorists and victims, felt they needed an alternative, a game to show Arabs how to defend their homelands and defeat their enemies.[15] *Special Force* went on sale in early 2003 in Lebanon, Syria, Iran, Bahrain, and the United Arab Emirates and sold out its initial run of a hundred thousand copies in its first week.

Right: *Special Force.*

THE HOME FRONT: A NEW HERO
Dar al-Fikr, *Under Ash*

Like *Special Force*, the Syrian game *Under Ash* attempts to reclaim a space in which to recount its own history and thus to educate Syria's youth. *Under Ash* tells the story of Ahmad, a young Palestinian who confronts the Israeli occupation of Palestine during the first *Intifada*. Ahmad begins his resistance by throwing stones at invading soldiers and ends up by shooting at Israeli settlers. The game charts this escalation of violence on both sides. Like *America's Army*, it is a free download. The urgency of adding an Arab voice to the historical record as well as to media representations of their story comes through in its Web-site description:

> A nation in Palestine is being uprooted: their houses are being devastated, their establishments are being destroyed, their lands are being occupied, their trees are being pulled out, their property is being confiscated, their cities are being besieged, their schools are being closed, their sanctuaries are being violated, their sacred structures are being made permitted, their children are being beaten, their hands are being broken, their bones are being crushed and they are imprisoned, tortured and slain. They are even prevented from crying and moaning. The whole world is plotting to ignore them. None hears them moan. None sees the trains of their martyrs. None says a word of

support to their rights.[16]

In all of these war games, the target audience is clear: young males, either potential inheritors of structures of power and oppression, or warriors of resistance. There are children here but no weeping girls, no protesting women, no negotiating elders. The implicit assumption that history belongs to the struggles of young men, and that the future lies in the hands of boys twitching their figures on game consoles — an assumption shared by all sides — is far more devastating than the violence of local conflicts portrayed. The writing out of girls and women from power — from history — underlines the depth and pervasiveness of the games' violence. This violence is in no way redressed by switching the gender of the warriors without changing the plot, as American game designers and military commanders are fond of doing. While *Special Force* and *Under Ash* bring necessary balance to a gaming world dominated by American viewpoints, the real innovations may come from those game designers who can imagine a future in which all humans can contribute to our memories of the past and to a vision of our possible futures.

Under Ash.

MISREMEMBERING ZION

Eddo Stern, *Sheik Attack*

Careful, we're building here (x3)

A number of artists have offered their takes on war gaming. Eddo Stern's *Sheik Attack*, a '**machinima** documentary', weaves 'capture' scenes from gameplay (*Settlers III, SimCity, Command and Conquer, Nuclear Strike*, and *Delta Force*) and Israeli pop songs to produce a nostalgic and horrifying account of 'the blood of sheiks and a mis-rememberance of long lost Zionist utopia'.[17] The film, which captures the feel of both games and live news events (and thus indexes the uneasy conflation of entertainment and news reporting), charts the development of the State of Israel from its settlement in the 1960s, through the emergence of cities, to the escalation of conflict into war, and, finally, to the current political stalemate in the Near East. *Sheik Attack* disrupts the ideologically constructed nostalgia for an ideal Israeli state by juxtaposing scenes of stunning beauty – the aesthetically rendered landing of an assault helicopter — with scenes of stunning violence — cold-blooded shootings in civilian and domestic spaces. The contrast of an idealized vision of a homeland, lulling nostalgic music, and aestheticized violence raises questions about the uses of the media and nostalgia in the formation of ideologies taken as 'natural' or 'historical' truths. More current works by Stern such as *Vietnam, Mon Amour* and *Redball* use the technologies of computer and pinball games to explore ideological issues surrounding

both the Vietnam War and the demise of the USSR.

Reflecting both his stint as a soldier in the Israeli Army and his experience as a game designer and player, Stern's works suggest that the structures and content of gaming can be harnessed for more complex cultural purposes than just raking in mega-profits by catering to the fantasies of adolescent boys or the ideologies of superpowers. In 'The Cultural Study of Games: More than Just Games', Matthew Southern comments on the need for games to mature in precisely the way they have in Stern's hands:

> Whereas a flight game might … fly over exactly the contours of the ground and buildings as in reality, like the Western news, it won't often dwell on the atrocities caused by warfare … These video games based on genuine contemporary conflict, where the point of view is always a military one … play a part in the obfuscation of the real conditions… If games are to mature, then the themes explored must address the lack of any serious political enquiry.[18]

Top and right: *Sheik Attack.*

RAW DATA AND REAL VIOLENCE
John Klima, *The Great Game*

John Klima has produced a different take on military gaming with *The Great Game*, 'A War Game (Sort of), but You Can't Control the Action'.[19] An avid gamer since his youth, Klima marshaled his coding abilities to produce a game interface for the post-9/11 war in Afghanistan. *The Great Game* relies on daily US Defense Department briefings to produce a 3D game-like map of the conflict. Over bumpy brown terrain, Taliban holdings emerge as green icons — bases, cities — while US bases and weapons appear as bright blue. In this non-interactive game, movement forward occurs as time passes: each day's data produces new visual configurations, and viewers can see one day after another as they watch the game load and progress.

The Iraq expansion pack — 'Now Anyone Can Be a "Blow-dried Armchair General"' — picks up the trope of game mods and applies it to the escalating violence of a follow-up war in Iraq. The effect is eerie and chilling. Given the early media blackout Americans experienced during these wars — as opposed to the made-for-TV-drama of the Gulf War — this reduction of conflict and carnage to a game

board only reinforces the terrible distortion imposed by the media on 'reality'. The intelligence data collected by Klima as raw numbers fails to give a sense of the stakes, the suffering, and the cost of this war. When conflict can so easily be turned into information, downloaded as data, and coded as entertainment, we know that the Information Age harbors serious threats to our sense of reality. Klima's war games are a wake-up call. If the medium is the message, this is one message worth listening to.

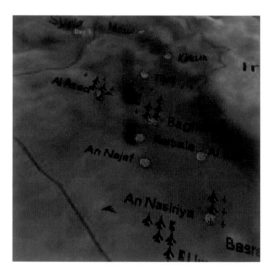

THE ENDS OF WAR
Orson Scott Card, *Ender's Game*

If *The Great Game* forces us to rethink the effect of the media on reality (and vice versa), *Ender's Game*, a novel about the effects of war games on a young boy, pushes the point even further. In Klima's game, it's the disjuncture between real war and war games that feels so queer and destructive — a disjuncture invisible in the military games currently on the market. *Ender's Game* erases that disjuncture completely so that war gaming becomes a method of waging war using the gaming skills of a reluctant six-year-old genius named Andrew 'Ender' Wiggin.

After two near-fatal attacks by aliens, called 'Buggers' for their resemblance to insects both in their appearance and in their 'hive' mentality, Earth faces a third attack. To defend itself, it trains young boys in a series of war games. Though Ender tries to resist the militarization of his psyche, the suppression of his compassion, and the tapping of his aggression, in the end he is deftly manipulated into become the very thing he abhors: a killer. What Ender doesn't realize is that as he progresses through ever more complex games, he shifts out of virtual reality and into real war: his games turn out to be command sequences for the actual Earth Starfleet. And when he wins the final game, it transpires that his game-violence has wiped out an actual alien species. Ender comes to understand that the defensive war to save humanity was a lie told by the power élite in order to stage a pre-emptive war against a species it could not understand.

In addition to the moral complexity of the story, *Ender's Game* suggests a complex reading of the effects of game technology on our young.[20] On the one hand, they develop confidence in their skills in the virtual world; on the other, they are oblivious to the ways in which adults use this technology to manipulate and enslave them. This manipulation of children for warfare is no mere sci-fi fantasy, as Amy Harmon's research has revealed:

> The possibilities of networked computers, combined with an increasingly remote-controlled military like the one Defense Secretary Donald H. Rumsfeld has vowed to build, has spurred interest in adapting the architecture of multiplayer games like Everquest and Ultima to create a 'persistent world' for training and perhaps more. One notion involves a scenario quite literally torn from the pages of a science fiction novel, in which a virtual training system becomes the actual means of waging war … '"Ender's Game" has had a lot of influence on our thinking,' said Michael Macedonia, director [sic] of the Army's simulation technology center in Orlando, Fl, which plans to build a virtual Afghanistan that could host hundreds of thousands of networked computers. 'The intent is to build a simulation that allows people to play in that world for months or years, participate in different types of roles and see consequences of their decisions.'[21]

In *Ender's Game*, war games not only wipe out an entire alien species but also destroy the children lured into playing them. The parallel to both the war in Iraq and resistance movements is chilling. The message that war always destroys — if not outright, then by forcing you to turn into your enemies — links this ominous tale to the efforts of both the US military and 'terrorists' or 'resistance fighters' to use children as cannon fodder.

PAWNS OF THE WORLD: UNITE!
Ruth Catlow, *Rethinking Wargames*

3 Player Chess.

While the artists' games and narratives we've just described are critiques of war gaming, other projects offer alternatives. *Rethinking Wargames*, Ruth Catlow's online Net-art project, 'calls upon "pawns to join forces to defend world peace", using the game of chess to find strategies that challenge existing power structures and their concomitant war machineries'.[22] The inspiration for this project was the growing global peace movement that became visible during the 2003 protests against the impending war in Iraq. At that time, Catlow posted a reconfigured chessboard on which all of the pawns united, along with a simple question: 'Under what conditions could the pawns in this game win?' Catlow's rationale was that conventional chess describes a political hierarchy in which the goal is for one tribe/color to dominate the other. Members of the hierarchy include royalty, nobility, clergy, and military who deploy pawns in their quests to achieve supremacy. *Rethinking Wargames* seeks to challenge the ideology implicit in this despotic structure and to invite democratic constructions of power.

A number of alternate strategies have been proposed, including *Activate: 3 Player Chess* and *Carol's Chess*. In *3 Player Chess*, developed by Catlow with programmer Adrian Eaton, the game proceeds as usual except that pawns intercede to prevent the 'nobility' from capturing any of their enemy. With each successful round of play, grass begins to grow over the black-and-white battlefield, so that if the pawns are successful at preventing war and violence between the nobles, the black-and-white territories evolve into a grassed-over commons without boundaries. The parallel to recent political events is unmistakable. While initially unsuccessful, the six-million-member world protest against the conflict in Iraq launched a global peace movement uniting ordinary people against their leaders. In

Carol's Chess, the square board is replaced by a circular one of concentric rings that looks like a dartboard. All players begin in the inner rings, and the goal is to move to the outer ones in such a way that each player has one of the opposing colors beside it by game's end. No players are captured or defeated; all movement is from center to periphery. Diversity and peace are the final outcomes.

3 Player Chess at Urban Olympics, Bristol, UK, 2003.

BRAVE NEW WORLD GAME

Natalie Bookchin, *agoraXchange*

A more radical rethinking of war gaming can be found in Natalie Bookchin's *agoraXchange* project. If war emerges as politically and economically motivated conflict between nation-states, what happens when you eliminate the power and support of nations? This is the question behind Bookchin's project. Launched at London's Tate Gallery in March 2004, *agoraXchange* is an online forum for culling ideas, rules, designs, code, and gameplay for the formation of a multiplayer game designed to challenge the current world system. Participants are asked to reflect on the four decrees that form the new political order. They include: 1. Citizenship by choice not birth; 2. No inheritance; wealth is redistributed at death; 3. No marriage, or no State jurisdiction over kinship relations; 4. No private land rights but lifelong leases for non-harmful uses of land to individuals and organizations. Selections from the manifesto describe the premises behind this collaborative effort to recreate the State using game technology:

> We put forward agoraXchange to elicit collaboration for challenging a world in which myths about birthright result in violence and suffering within and among nations and families. We urge eliminating the laws responsible for nation and marriage because we believe that these institutions misshape our material and psychic lives and constrain the imagination in ways that stunt us all.
>
> We are disturbed by the familiarity and even acceptance of war among much of the world's population, where each day on average hundreds will die from bombs, guns, machetes: over six million dead in wars since 1989... We also believe human beings deserve an earth that has air that is not toxic, water that is uncontaminated, and an infrastructure that affords everyone basic education and health care.

Finally, we see the travails of war, hunger, restrictions of movement, environmental degradation, the lack of compassion in our political institutions and in our families, as largely rooted in laws that use birth for assigning us our place in life... It is the laws giving us inheritance and kinship that determine whether one will have access to the hundreds of trillions of dollars in wealth from estates or whether one will grow up in poverty. It is marriage law that produces the family tree, whose roots are always national.

> Our present political institutions are not natural or inevitable, but an experiment gone awry, a utopia for the paranoid.[23]

While *agoraXchange* differs dramatically from the other politically motivated structures that have produced the war-game genre, it embodies a similar belief in gaming as a technology well adapted for producing specific values and behavior. Its slogan, 'Make the Game, Change the World', echoes the objective of Buckminster Fuller's 1969 *World Game*:

> To make the World work
> For 100% of humanity
> In the shortest possible time
> Through spontaneous cooperation
> Without ecological offense
> Or the disadvantage of anyone.[24]

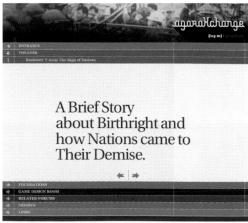

agoraXchange.

Gender Bending

In its raw form, gender can be arresting, as the hit counts of porn sites readily attest. In the context of gaming, however, gender more often serves as a character embellishment meant to drive rather than halt the story. Yet without moments of arrest, games that invoke or rely on gender as a plot device usually fail to transcend stereotypical roles for male or female characters.

While gender may be a structural element of Romance and Germanic languages, it is not ubiquitous in human cultures. The Wabanaki Native Americans of the north-east, for example, structure their languages not on a male/female difference but on an animate/inanimate distinction. In this light, our fascination with gender looks more like Manichean pathology than biology. Whose fantasies are we enacting and why? Why the obsession with a woman warrior? A killer Eve? A vicious school girl? A terrorist cook? While we clearly need to continue to 'trouble' gender, does our fixation on it (or its omission) break us out of this pathology or merely re-inscribe a paranoia? Fortunately, most of the gender-bending games that follow offer more oblique insights into our current cultural dilemmas than any straight reading of gender allows.

Left and opposite:
Tomb Raider's Lara Croft.

FEMME/BUTCH FATALE
Eidos Interactive, *Tomb Raider*

In 1996, Eidos Interactive released an adventure game that would alter the course of gameplay and design: an adventure game/**third-person shooter** with a powerful, athletic, gun-toting, *female* protagonist. *Tomb Raider* placed Lara Croft front and center on screen and off. Object of fascination and desire for both male and female gamers, hailed as gaming woman of the year, and derided as the latest celebrity bimbo, Lara Croft aroused gamers and critics alike. Between 1996 and the end of 2000, Eidos Interactive released five versions of Lara Croft adventures games. During this time, Lara herself went on to become a multi-genre heroine, breaking out of the confines of an enclosed game industry with moves as varied as those of her character: exploding onto magazine covers, leaping into concert with U2, charging into a Hollywood hit movie with Angelina Jolie in the starring role. How did the introduction of a female protagonist inaugurate a blockbuster game series and launch a game-publishing empire? Why was this particular spin on gender so popular?

A bored aristocrat bent on adventure, gun-toting, acrobatic, sexually alluring Lara exudes power. With seemingly infinite resources, cunning, and curiosity, she ventures into the most forbidding territory, from ancient Egyptian ruins to Atlantean caverns, from the wilds of Antarctica to the Great Wall of China. Her quest for lost treasure produces gameplay which is an innovative mix of adventure, puzzle-solving, and weapon-firing. Success depends on the player's ability to make Lara leap, swim, roll, grab, crawl, sprint, somersault, dodge, and run at just the right moments, all while firing her endless supply of ammo.

Lara is clearly a 'non-consensual fantasy engine',[25] but whose fantasies is she enabling? Scantily clad and well endowed, she may satisfy male sexual fantasies, but that appeal also spells a certain kind of power for female players, especially if it remains a taunt rather than an offering. Of course, male players can control Lara's body through the game, but what they do with that body is pretty much limited to feats of athletic prowess or aggressive triumph over enemies. For players of either gender to experience a sexualized female as agile, mobile, and powerful is to recode the meaning of the feminine body, perhaps even to expand the arena of erotic sensibility from the genital to the muscular.

If such freedom of movement, such agility, such power were to translate into real-world expectation and activity for women, it might do a good deal to counteract the advertising industry's imagery of women as anorexic waifs. Lara Croft owns weapons and uses them freely, not merely to defend herself but to satisfy her desires. She travels alone and confronts her enemies with cunning and equanimity. She has a vast fortune and hired help to do her bidding. Given such an array of resources and the mission to 'find your lost treasures', it's hard to see how any woman could resist this enactment of fantasy. Perhaps most important is the fact that a female character and player can pursue her own adventure, that a female gamer can begin to identify with this fantasy agent. Another iteration of soft porn? Perhaps. But this sexy bitch is available to men only to the extent that they complete her adventure. And, unlike most porn narratives, Lara's adventure has nothing to do with submission. Play her if you like, but it's her game, and her treasures, that matter.

The *Nude Raider* game mod that produces a nude 'skin' for Lara throws one more pebble into the gender pool. Does this naked Lara foreground the power of the game's scopophilic attraction? Or is *Nude Raider* an attack based on discomfort with Lara's perceived power? Why, in any case, do we insist on undressing our heroines?

Like Xena, warrior-princess, her scantily clad TV counterpart, Lara troubles the clear edge between masculine and feminine. Xena turns out to be a mother, a condition suggested by Lara's breasts, unrealistic on any body except a nursing mother's — but in the world of *Tomb Raider*, there is no child because there is no reproductive sex. Perhaps the presence of a child would provoke too great a gender clash with the hero narrative of adventure and destruction. It may be easy to play the adventurer without children, but liberating mothers is a goal that decades of feminist research have failed to accomplish. Xena may literally be able to juggle an infant in the air as she slashes her enemies' limbs, but most feminists-turned-mothers find themselves in a completely new cultural battlefield once the care of children interrupts their battles for gender equality. Xena also has a female side-kick, male lovers, and friends of both genders to help her in her quests. Finally, her quests are not self-serving but responses to oppressed or downtrodden neighbors. Despite the immersive experience, Lara's quests pale by comparison.

Perhaps a more liberating strategy would be to enable men to play roles often reserved for women, for men to care for, nurture, or educate the young, or heal others' injuries, or encourage other's quests at the cost of their own. Perhaps narratives of sex and reproduction can be cast as powerful and exhilarating adventures — as they are in real life.

There are emerging hints of these kinds of behaviors in many quest-based adventures or **Role-Playing Game**s (RPGs). Games like *Final Fantasy* and *Xenogears* require cooperation, support, and healing powers to advance their respective quests, as do the more battle-minded *Everquest* and *Warcraft*. But healing almost always occurs in the context of battle as one more weapon to wield against the enemy. Moving beyond a mindset that imagines the world in terms of embattled binaries, whether self/other, friend/foe, or male/female, may be more important structurally than any permutations we make to the terms that populate those binaries.

Opposite: *Final Fantasy X, Final Fantasy X2*, and *Xenogears.*

Right: *Tomb Raider.*

MOTHER OF ALL EVIL
Square Soft, *Parasite Eve*

In 1998, a few years after the first release of *Tomb Raider*, Square Soft released *Parasite Eve*, another hybrid genre with a female protagonist. A blend of action, horror, and RPG, *Parasite Eve* combines the creepiness of *Resident Evil* with the earnestness of a *Final Fantasy* quest. Dubbed a 'cinematic RPG' by its makers, *Parasite Eve* follows its heroine as she battles a foe able to incinerate humans by cranking up their mitochondrial energy. Immune to the weapon, a young New York cop, Aya Brea, must find a way to save her fellow humans. This heroine is tough and realistic with an occasional sense of humor, especially in the sequel, *Parasite Eve 2*. Perhaps the most important development with this release is the lack of surprise or attention to gender triggered by the female protagonist. Is this because Lara Croft's novelty has worn off, leaving females to play in the terrain of male fantasy?

Aya Brea's nemesis, Eve, host to the mutated mitochondria, is also a woman. She joins other perversely populating female monsters like the mother-creature in Ridley Scott's film *Aliens*. A mother figure as destructive force, an Eve who ends life rather than originating it, may say more about another set of male fantasies — those driven by fear — than it does about women. Sexual reproduction and the cultural role females have played in that arena haunt these game environments, whether as devaluations of sex or as the demonizing of reproductive power. Furthermore, the fact that this Eve was a dead woman whose resuscitation by her mourning lover triggered the virus couples fear of sex with the Frankenstein-fear of technology gone wrong. The issue is less whether females have lead roles (one wonders if two females battling it out is any less a male fantasy than two lesbians getting it on) than whether these are the kinds of roles that women would choose to play in their own fantasies. It may well be that those who control the spaces of cultural fantasy are those who end up with political control as well.

Below: *Parasite Eve*.
Opposite: *Final Fantasy X*.

キマリ：力を示せばいいのだな

DRAG QUEEN, FRAG QUEEN
Nintendo, *Metroid Prime*

If Lara bursts onto the game scene to satisfy the voyeuristic player, and Aya Brea slips into a *noir* horror game to reassure the paranoid one, then Samus of the highly acclaimed *Metroid Prime* sneaks in the back door to startle the sexist player. Essentially a biogenetically engineered bounty hunter, Samus searches the planet Tallon IV for ancient Chozo artifacts. To survive, and to defeat her many and varied enemies, she must be as proficient an explorer as a warrior. This means that gameplay has as much to do with deciphering complex and convincing terrain as it does with blasting jellyfish-like enemies or Zebesian space pirates. Covered by impressive red and gold armor, Samus plays like a man — so much so that players who take her for one are often shocked at the end when a scantily clad Samus is revealed as 'reward' for the male player. To have to confront feelings of identification with this tough female character without being able to demote her to the role of sexual prey could have elicited a deeper and more powerful effect on both male and female players. Instead, as many reviewers have hinted, male players who know the secret often rush through gameplay to catch a glimpse of the woman beneath the armor.

Still, two unusual features in *Metroid Prime* break the typical masculine shoot-'em-up pattern:

the inclusion of text critical to solving the mystery and the use of visual perspectives or points of view. Like *Myst*, *Metroid Prime* stuns with spectacular scenery rather than strict storyline, but freedom of movement is tied to the solving of a mystery that requires a significant amount of reading, some more scientific than narrative — a rather unusual demand for what at first appears to be a first-person shooter. For example, upon finding the journals of the space pirates, Samus can read about their creepy genetic experiments as well as witness the damage she's inflicted on them. Another way to gain intelligence is the clever use of three different 'visors', or heads-up displays, each of which gives her a different kind of information or view of her environment. The 'default' combat visor provides a clear view of her surroundings as well as easy targeting of enemies, while the scan visor allows her to gather data about alien creatures, space anomalies, or environmental details. Information acquired via scan is automatically recorded in Samus's log in clear, coherent language that can be accessed at any point during gameplay.

These innovations in 'intelligence' and point of view signal a more complex, less stereotypically gendered game space. They may be even more important innovations than the revelation of a female protagonist at game's end, for they remind us that reality is complex and multivalent, requiring as much brain as brawn, and, most importantly, that survival may be a result of being able to recognize and respect more than one perspective.

Metroid Prime.

SAVING A LOST WORLD
Funatics, *Zanzarah*

Zanzarah.

With *Zanzarah*, released at the end of 2002, the heroine stepped out of the closet of game culture and sex stereotypes and into her own adventure. Unlike *Tomb Raider*, there's no sense of being ogled by the player despite the similar third-person perspective, and unlike *Metroid Prime*, all the heroism accrues to a female from the outset rather than to a woman who must hide her gender to the end to be effective. The official website promotion speaks in clear defiance of the heroic tradition:

> The legends speak of a long forgotten prophecy ... of a gleaming hero, and of perilous adventures ... of sinister powers, strange worlds and hosts of fairies ... but they say nothing of a girl with more heart than muscle ... but then, even legends can sometimes be wrong.[26]

To reinforce the departure from the ego-inflating heroes of traditional gameplay, the protagonist, Amy, is an ordinary young woman living in London. After a disastrous eighteenth birthday and a fight with her parents, she flees to her room with a sense that there's something horribly wrong with the world. Her fears are well founded. Finding a rune in a box, she is transported to Zanzarah, an alternate world of fairies, elves, dwarves, and other strange creatures, where she learns that past persecution of these magical beings by rampaging humans drove them to another realm. But some fairies are beginning to fight among themselves, and there are signs of impending ruin unless Amy can find a way to fulfill the prophecy and help them. Her task is to heal the breach between the two worlds by collecting, training, and battling with fairies.

However, what begins as a quest involving puzzle-solving, learning about other beings, and deciphering mysteries quickly devolves into a skill-building, fairy-collecting battle system more reminiscent of *Quake III* than a legend-busting adventure. Perhaps this is merely an atavistic return to the adrenaline-pumping scene of game battles, though clearly in a different kind of drag — one that substitutes stunning scenery and pretty elves for blood-letting and gore. Clearly, women experience rage, aggression, and fight impulses just as men do. What isn't clear is whether these different forms of battle extend the range of possible human response or are merely the same Manichean binary dressed up in fancier clothes. That Amy is trying to save the world puts her in the same moral realm as the Bushes and bin Ladens who demonize their enemies in order to justify the high moral ground they occupy.

If both women and men need to exorcise rage in their chosen forms of entertainment, perhaps our own world is in as much danger as that of *Zanzarah*, and perhaps Amy's (and the player's) feeling that all is not right ought to be taken a bit more seriously. Despite the high production values, intriguing Enya-like soundtrack, and stereotype-busting storyline, *Zanzarah* lacks the commitment to complex character development, coherent and rich narrative, and psychological depth that marked its model and predecessor, *The Longest Journey*.

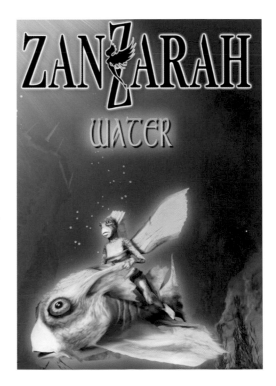

HERSTORY HEALS HISTORY
Funcom, *The Longest Journey*

Produced in 2000, two years before *Zanzarah* and *Metroid Prime*, by the Norwegian developer Funcom, *The Longest Journey* staked out completely new ground, earning superlative reviews from adventure gamers around the globe. 'It makes every other game you've ever played seem unimportant and trite,' one reviewer noted.[27] '...[It]'s an interactive epic legend with a story that rivals anything Hollywood could do. It is probably THE best game (and story) I've ever come across, not just in the adventure genre, but in all genres of PC gaming,' enthused another.[28]

Right, below, and opposite:
The Longest Journey.

The Longest Journey features a fully fledged, fully believable heroine who turns the paradigm of the war hero on its head. Like *Zanzarah*'s Amy, April Ryan is an ordinary eighteen-year-old, in this case an art student struggling to make a life for herself in the industrial wasteland of a twenty-third-century metropolis. She lives alone in a boarding house, having escaped a domineering father and passive mother only to encounter a brutish neighbor. During the day, she waitresses in a café to support herself and pay for art school, but at night she's a victim of disturbing dreams. When dream events begin to infiltrate waking life, April realizes that something is terribly wrong. She discovers a world of science and technology called Stark, and another of magic and enchantment called Arcadia, as well as a force called Balance that keeps the two worlds in harmony. Apparently, the guardian of Balance has vanished,

disrupting the harmony and plunging both worlds into Chaos. As a 'shifter', April has rare access to the two worlds, and while she does not control the timing or nature of the shifting, she can use it to try to heal the breach between them and restore Balance.

As she travels to exotic lands, April meets a host of unusual characters, including Abnaxus, a Vener who lives across time rather than space; the crazy Burns Flipper, a curmudgeonly hacker who's lost his legs and thus speeds around in a hover car; and a talking bird called That Damned Bird. April has the ability to interact with these other characters in convincing and appropriate dialogue. From Arcadia's Vestrum Tobias, she can learn religious philosophy, from the Bandu she can learn about digging and shaping the earth using her will, from the librarian Minstrum Yerin she can get access to essential books. Most non-playing characters have something to offer April in her quest. These encounters teach her about the foreign worlds and also about herself, since her quest is at once a personal and a political journey. She uses a conversation log to keep track of her encounters, and of video replay to revisit scenes relevant to the plot. Throughout the story, she also carries a diary filled with details garnered in her travels.

While its graphics, sound, and adventure gameplay all score at the top of the charts, what distinguishes *The Longest Journey* is narrative sophistication. April begins her quest as a naïve country girl and undergoes a transformation. She has meaningful, spoken interactions with other characters that are linked to the complex plot. There

are Brechtian hints that she's aware that she's a game character, and also aware of your presence as a player, thus stimulating critical analysis during gameplay. Despite the fantasy worlds through which she travels, there's an attempt to present a realistic future world, including lesbian colleagues, domineering fathers, and helpful children. All of these are details of storytelling underdeveloped in most computer games, and they transform a tale of a simple young woman into an epic adventure. This model of heroism is one earned not by blasting enemies but by confronting struggles which teach wisdom, by encounters which require listening and learning, by moral dilemmas which require elucidation. This is the heroism of an ordinary life transformed by service to others. In many ways, April recalls *Halflife's* Dr Gordon Freeman without the lethal weapons, just an ordinary citizen whose acts of courage help to heal and save her corner of the world.

Computer games can't be reduced to print storytelling. Their immersive effect depends on graphics, sound, and gameplay as much as on story. But good storytelling in any medium is immersive and transformative. It has the power to create, critique, and alter worlds, and this power provides us, as in *The Longest Journey*, with a space in which to engage in deep play.

GENDERED CODES
John Klima, *Jack & Jill*

A number of digital artists have attempted to trouble notions of gender in gaming as well as to reveal the narrow range represented by many games. One example is John Klima's *Jack & Jill*. Commissioned for the Whitney Museum of American Art's 'CODeDOC' exhibition, *Jack & Jill* is a simple game based on the nursery rhyme. In the rhyme, both children go up the hill to 'fetch a pail of water', but once the water is in the bucket, their roles change: Jack falls down and breaks his crown while Jill comes tumbling after. In Klima's game version, written in **Visual Basic**, the roles become interchangeable depending on variables in the code. Since the 'CODeDoc' project was commissioned specifically to foreground the code that creates an artwork, we can see the technology that leads to the gendered game roles. We can also see how easy it is to slightly alter the code so that the stereotypical roles can be reversed. Klima's do-while loop contains the following code, which also serves as cultural commentary:

```
If YourAttitude = CHAUVINIST Then
If Fetch(pail, jack, jill) Then GoUpHill jack, jill
If FellDown(jack) And BrokeCrown(jack) Then
TumblingAfter jill, jack
ElseIf YourAttitude = FEMINIST Then
If Fetch(pail, jill, jack) Then GoUpHill jill, jack
If FellDown(jill) And BrokeCrown(jill) Then
TumblingAfter jack, jill
```

In other words, if you're a chauvinist, then Jack will lead and Jill will follow, while if you're a feminist, Jill will lead and Jack will follow. Of course a do-while loop will repeat a statement until the original condition, or 'test', proves false. But Klima includes variables which can affect the original conditions and make the original test false, as we can see in this **if-then statement**:

```
If ChangeItIf(SlimChance) Then
If (Leader.EmotionalState = INDECISIVE Or
Leader.EmotionalState = RELUCTANT) And
```

Jack & Jill.

```
ChangeItIf(Leader.Desire) Then
Leader.EmotionalState = WILLING
ElseIf (Leader.EmotionalState = INDECISIVE Or
Leader.EmotionalState = WILLING) And ChangeItIf(1
– Leader.Desire) Then
Leader.EmotionalState = RELUCTANT
ElseIf (Leader.EmotionalState = RELUCTANT Or
Leader.EmotionalState = WILLING) And ChangeItIf(1
– follower.Desire) Then
Leader.EmotionalState = INDECISIVE
```

The decision about who leads can change on the 'SlimChance' that the leader's emotional state — 'indecisive' or 'reluctant' or 'willing' — changes. In a humorous and direct way, Klima has represented the way in which simple yet hidden codes influence behavior and the fact that changes in the programming code are easy to make. His program also suggests that to a large extent changes in behavior appear to be dependent on who the current leader is. Since Klima begins with a gender binary (Jack/Jill), his options remain caught in dualistic thinking. But a quick perusal of the code suggests that narratives with three or more alternatives are equally possible by simply adding functions, variables, or 'if' and **'else if' clause**s. If coding computer games has largely been in the hands of men, then the code behind both gender stereotypes and game design is likely to be caught in outdated do-while loops until someone is willing to alter it. Blaming the market for failures in coding — both cultural and computer coding — seems hopelessly naïve given Klima's easy exposure of the structures behind the Jack-and-Jill tale.

MUTINY IN THE KITCHEN
Josephine Starrs and Leon Cmielewski,
Bio-Tek Kitchen

Bio-Tek Kitchen.

Bio-Tek Kitchen patches the *Marathon Infinity* game engine so that instead of blowing up aliens to a spooky soundtrack with 'awesome killing sounds', the players 'clean up the filthy kitchen laboratory of a home biotech enthusiast using weapons such as dish cloths and egg flippers'.[29] Mutant vegetables like giant corn and flying tomatoes, supposedly produced by genetic nouvelle cuisine, attack the player, who must defend him— or herself with a limited arsenal of kitchen utensils. During the course of the game, the player learns about a 'world wide corporate conspiracy to take over the entire food chain'.

While the transformation of a game described as an 'enjoyable mixture of raw carnage and intelligent puzzle-solving' to a battle between egg flippers and tomatoes is at first hilarious, it doesn't take long to realize that the gameplay for both the best-selling game and the ridiculous **patch** are very similar. Once the veneer of macho bloodletting and high stakes is removed, the gameplay is exposed as rather trivial.

ARRESTED DEVELOPMENT

Eric Zimmerman, *Sissyfight*

Sissyfight.

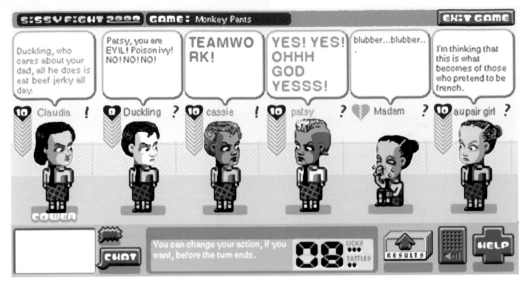

Eric Zimmerman's *Sissyfight*[30] troubles gender by moving aggression from the battlefield to the schoolyard. Described as an 'intense war between a bunch of girls', *Sissyfight* combines the live strategy game with virtual community. The goal is to attack other players' popularity and damage their self-esteem until they are humiliated enough to cower in a corner and cry. You begin by creating and naming your character in the 'dressing room', then choose a school, enter the 'homeroom' to scout the action, and finally pick a 'schoolyard' fight. Your 'weapons' include grabbing, scratching, or teasing — all of which erode the ten self-esteem points with which each player begins — while your defense is limited to cowering, licking a lollipop, or tattling on others. Since actions are more powerful if performed by more than one player, and since up to two players can win, there's a clear advantage to forming alliances and making friends. Once all players except two have lost all self-esteem points, the round ends with winners and losers whose scores are permanently recorded and available anytime during play.

Players call the game fun, addictive, and intensely social, and many claim they have formed real relationships through gameplay. Unlike the fantastic or futuristic settings of many shooters or military-strategy games, *Sissyfight* is based on experiences familiar to most players. Its humor and playfulness allow players enough distance to engage in relationships of competition and cooperation. *Sissyfight* clearly demonstrates that aggression, competition, and triumph are common across gender, and that the aggression we see on the battlefield is no stranger to the backyard.

Indeed, *Sissyfight* offers us a reading for the current state of gameplay. If we can connect the difficult real-world battles that trouble our children to their fascination with computer games, perhaps we can learn something about how we are failing them, and how they are trying to cope with these failures in the fantasy realm of games. If we read their play as deep, we will see a dark reflection in this particular technological mirror — one that reveals a struggle for safety, agency, and respect that goes beyond the gender divide, and certainly beyond the boundary of the game box.

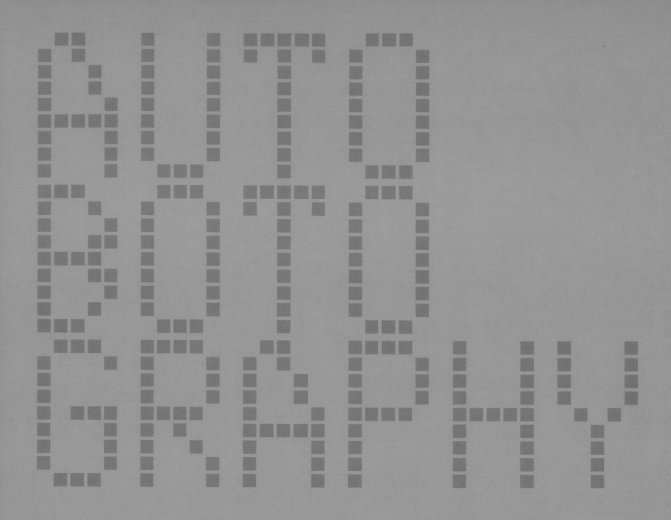

AUTO BOTO GRAPHY

The third stage of immune response occurs when lymphocytes alert the immune system to the presence of foreign antigens. In order to do this, they must distinguish between what belongs to the body and what is foreign. An error in this identification could easily lead to fatal vulnerability or suicide. But because lymphocytes are born in bone marrow alongside red blood cells, they learn to distinguish self from non-self at an early stage of development. When it is mature, a lymphocyte matches the shape of its antibody to the shape of the antigen, revealing something that was previously unknown to the body. Though the antibodies cannot precisely say what they have found, their revelation triggers the execution of code to protect the body.

While antibodies' main job is to reveal non-self, they also reveal aspects of the self which remain hidden.[1] Digital art can do the same thing. This is the space of autobiography, where the relationship between individual and society, self and other, is articulated. But autobiography 'has not always existed, nor does it exist everywhere', Georges Gusdorf reminds us in his landmark study *Conditions & Limits of Autobiography*.[2] In fact, autobiography is a particularly Euro-American preoccupation, rarely found outside this culture: 'This conscious awareness of the singularity of each individual life is the late product of a specific civilization. Throughout human history, the individual does not oppose himself to all others … lives are so thoroughly entangled that each of them has its center everywhere and nowhere.'[3] Philosophies of India and China express caution about the 'evil illusion' of personality and seek salvation in release from the ego. Yoruba and Native American cultures name children after dead ancestors who return in spirit to inhabit the newborn, forming a cycle of life based on community and continuity. The grafting of Christian validation of every life onto the Classical tradition of examination produced St Augustine's *Confessions*, however, and launched a genre of self-examination that persists in current digital practice. Writers since Augustine have used events in their own lives as inspiration for new forms of narrative, but never before has a technology automatically rendered such details in a form that can be witnessed instantaneously across the globe. In projects such as *life_sharing* and *jennicam*, privacy has become a commodity easily traded for artistic capital. Many have wondered if setting up a video camera to record your most quotidian acts or open-sourcing your hard drive are exhibitionism or art.

Even in the Euro-American literary tradition, there is a good deal of controversy about the nature of autobiography – whether it is a distinct genre, whether it can capture 'truth', or whether it is even possible. For Wilhelm Dilthey, autobiography 'occupied a central place as the key to understanding the curve of history, every sort of cultural manifestation, and the very shape and essence of human culture itself'.[4] If history offers us an abstracted chronology of events, or a record of the public actions of famous men (and, more rarely, women), autobiography offers a glimpse of an individual life. Roughly translated from its Greek roots, 'autobiography' means 'self-life-writing'. But none of these terms is easily fixed. *Autos*, or 'self', has been fractured by psychoanalysis, deconstructed and multiplied by post-Structuralism, and dispersed via digital avatars. *Bios*, 'life', has been rendered equally problematic by the attempt to turn it into art. Formless, chaotic, resistant, life mocks our attempts to give it shape, meaning, or structure. *Graphe*, usually translated as 'writing' but in fact more accurately 'to mark', suggests a trace produced by some technology. But what does this trace

capture or bring into being? Since Werner Heisenberg, we've known that any act of observation changes what is observed. In what ways do digital autobiographies change the observing subject? Since Foucault, Derrida, Barthes, and Lacan, we've known that the text of autobiography takes on a life of its own, that there is no fixed self which precedes the activity of writing, nor one after the text is complete. For post-Structuralists, the self is always a fiction, and so is the life.

Despite these paradoxes, the Internet has spurred a resurgence of autobiographical practices. One reason for this proliferation may be that our stories have been taken from us, repackaged, and sold back via broadcast media for so long that we are eager to get them back. But this autobiographical urge is not a simple matter of putting new tools into the hands of would-be writers and artists. For every netizen eager to tell all to a world-wide audience, there is another who warns about the abuse of surveillance and the violation of privacy. If the technologies of the Internet and policies like **Total Information Awareness** and **ECHELON**[5] make us wary about revealing personal information lest it be used against us, how can we account for the massive outpouring of autobiographical data – as text, image, code, or video – online? To whom do our stories belong?

Many of us who followed the *jennicam* model first became active agents online by publishing **home pages**: a CV, an album of family photos, a diary of experiences for friends to read, a list of favorite links. While not exactly in the form of conventional autobiography, all of these publications might easily be recognized as expressions of a new digital self. Since these early experiments in homespun HTML, new documentary tools have flooded the Web, including Webcams, **blogs**, and **Flash** and QuickTime movies, resulting in a veritable tidal wave of self-revelation. Many of these tools are so easy to use that they seem at times to write the stories of our lives *for* us – suggesting the term *autobotography*, the digital self as revealed by bots, or computer programs.

What do these autobotographies reveal? Details of individual lives? Erotic play? Coding virtuosity? Submerged character traits? Perhaps. But, more importantly for this study, autobotography reveals the relationship of individuals to their new contexts or communities of the Internet age, and to the technologies that are being wielded to construct new subjectivities. McLuhan reminded us that the new powers we assume as we wield new tools entail a corresponding loss. If technology is a narcissistic mirror, it is one that extends our abilities in one dimension only to anesthetize and amputate our faculties in another.[6] Autobotography provides us with images of who we have become in front of this new mirror. The most powerful autobotographies help us to see both ourselves and the mirror; thus they disrupt the new technology's narcotic effect. Autobotography at its best reveals technological memes that describe how we are being inhabited by our latest tools and how our tools are embodying us.

'We are all chimeras,' Donna Haraway has written, 'theorized and fabricated hybrids of machine and organism; in short, we are cyborgs.'[7] This cyborg construction characterizes much of the work in this chapter: lives captured by video camera, egos embodied in hard drives, analysts in the form of algorithms. The boundaries between human and machine are being renegotiated. For the 'bot' in autobotography has infiltrated not just *graphe* but also *bios*, and it is the job of autobotographers to chart the new edge between self and society, flesh and machine. **< >**

SELF-DISCLOSURE

Jennifer Ringley, *jennicam (www.jennicam.org)*

In April 1996, Jennifer Ringley, a junior in college, bought a video camera on a whim, then decided to connect it to the Internet so her mother and friends could, in her words, 'keep tabs on me'. Intended to be a short-lived experiment, it lasted seven years before closing down at the end of 2003. '*jennicam*: Life, Online' was a digital portrait of the 'real life' of a young American woman. In her words:

> Except for camera shy guests … and places the cameras can't reach, I cut nothing. I am not always at home, sometimes you may see an empty house for hours or longer at a stretch… That's life. You may see me working at my computer, watching television, or being intimate. You may see nothing but animals or walls all day long. The point is, it's not a 'show'. Do not expect to be entertained. What I do is not exactly 'exciting' enough for television. What you'll see is my life, exactly as it would be whether or not there were cameras watching.[8]

jennicam.

A clear counterweight to Reality TV, *jennicam* ran without camera crews lurking behind bushes or on rooftops. There was no script, no contest, no prize. It portrayed what seemed to be unedited, unshaped, authentic life. The only selection made was what the cameras could see. And yet, it was mediated, like all

other autobiographies, by the technology used. Here, the life was either streaming video for 'members' or a series of stills for non-paying guests. But that video was framed in a browser window introduced by a menu of other materials, including tech notes describing how Ringley installed her set-up, a chat space, fridge poetry, desktop screen shots, favorite links including SETI @home, a journal, two galleries, and assorted other information. While we might have seen Ringley in a bathrobe, we also knew she was a geek, writing her own scripts, editing her pages in **pico,** and reading her mail in **pine.**

If text-based autobiography reads like a narrative, this project read like a collage. You are left to browse through the digitized materials of Ringley's life and draw your own conclusions. Beyond the framing, and the introduction and concept, there is no attempt to distill a meaning. That is left to the viewer. What kinds of revelation can be discerned here? What do we learn about Jennifer Ringley, the lovable geek, or about the tech she used to construct her life?

First, her loyal fans will tell you that a young woman's life looks nothing like *Buffy the Vampire Slayer.* Compared to Buffy's escapades, our own little dramas of who gets to take out the trash seem petty and insignificant. But when we see Ringley curled up on her bed at 10.00 a.m., we don't feel so bad about sleeping in. When we see that she doesn't look like Britney Spears but still has an erotic life, we can reclaim our own erotic adventures. Ironically, the most revelatory moments in *jennicam* are when nothing seems to happen. We see an empty chair for five hours. No special effects, no violence, no explosion, no bared flesh. For those curious enough to sit with the silence in the way John Cage asked us to,[9] there is revelation.

Despite this stillness, *jennicam* manages to produce an entire community of loyal fans and supporters. Some argue that the site was supported by voyeurs, but the question remains: Why did they choose *jennicam* over more graphic, so-called 'amateur' porn sites, especially since nakedness was neither common nor fetishized? Furthermore, while early shots did feature the soft lighting and flattering poses of soft porn, over time the images got starker and less flattering. But, apart from the fact that visual depictions of semi– or unclad women have difficulty being produced or read outside the ad/glamour/porn industries, these criticisms could be leveled at any act of self-revelation. After Madonna's *Truth or Dare,* and despite its clearly manipulated story line, there ought to be much less surprise about women's impulse to take control of their self-representation, clad or not. And, unlike spin-offs such as *WeliveinPublic*, which are much more self-conscious and thus begin to look more like Reality TV, *jennicam* retains the feel of a glimpse into an ordinary life. When so many of our self-representations are so clearly mediated, it is

CITIZEN SURVEILLANCE

Stephen Mann, *WearCam*

If exhibitionism is at one pole of autobotography, paranoia is at the other. While many autobiographical projects warn us about the downside of surveillance, computer scientist Stephen Mann wrests the technology from institutions and puts it into the hands — or on the foreheads — of ordinary citizens. Originally used for personal documentary, Mann's *WearCam* wearable camera not only grew in sophistication over the two decades of its development (1980–late 1990s) but shrank in size. Now the '"existential computer" invention comprises a complete multimedia computer, with cameras, microphones, and earphones, all built into an ordinary pair of eyeglasses'.[10] If this counter-surveillance project is autobotography, what is captured is not the interior life but the life that surrounds the *WearCam* user. In 'Shooting Back', a meta-documentary, Mann

confronts a clerk in a department store with questions about their own surveillance cameras before revealing his. The 180-degree turning of the camera panics the clerk.

WearCam redresses the imbalance between ordinary citizens and institutions which deploy cameras. '*WearCam* gives the nomad a form of personal protection once available only to establishments,' Mann has written.

There is already in place a natural tendency to behave in a dignified manner in the presence of others, so it is really the cameras of the establishment that pose the gravest threat to privacy ... a community of *WearCams* gives rise to a more distributed form of crime reduction than a network of cameras wired into the police station or the like.[11]

When *WearCam* users form small support groups, the power of 'reverse surveillance' is amplified. Mann's proposal for a 'SafetyNet' enlists a community of remote users transmitting images

Stephen Mann and *WearCam* crew.

refreshing to see new-media technology used to reclaim the *quotidian* aspects of who we are when we're at home.

Despite its apparent 24/7 omnipresence, *jennicam* inherited some of the deficiencies of text- or film-based autobiography and created some new ones along the way. First, Ringley's autobiography was partial, both in duration (seven years) and in context (we didn't see her at work). Second, while her gallery of images, videos, and text was certainly forthright, it was limited as an artistic shaping. There was very little reflection — a critical aspect of autobiography — and little attempt to discern or produce any kind of meaning. Third, what we saw was mostly surface: video, fridge poetry, desktop screenshots. We didn't see hard-drive contents, or the workings of Ringley's unconscious, or the complexity of her relationship to her friends, parents, or community. Despite this partiality, a trait all autobiography shares, the portrait we got of a young woman's life made for a refreshing change from the cover girls of *Self* magazine.

jennicam.

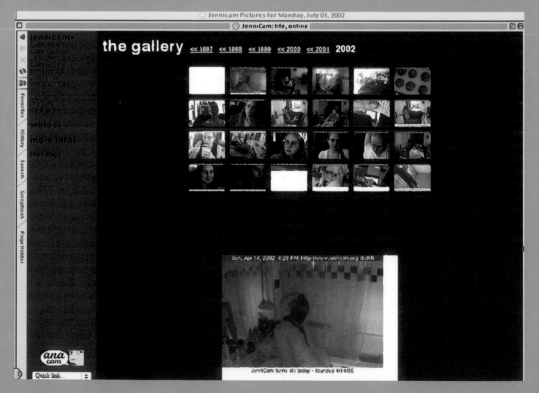

to each other. If one *WearCam* user signals distress, she can alert her remote partners who can then send assistance: 'Instead of relying on some distant and unaccountable force to keep watch over the society, individuals form small social networks that function much like small towns in a global neighborhood watch.'[12] But can communities be depended on to support their 'distant' neighbors? While the *WearCam* might redress the balance of technology and power as far as surveillance cameras are concerned, do we really want this technology in the hand of fundamentalist Christians or tyrannical bosses? Do we want more policing of our quotidian actions? The tactical gesture of revealing the violence of surveillance by putting it into the hands of ordinary citizens is a powerful critique. But it's not clear that arming citizens with surveillance gear will be any more liberating than arming them with pistols, if all they do with them is shoot each other.[13]

Stephen Mann and *WearCam*.

The Edge between Self and Society

Life captured by video-cam or Web page is mediated life. We are becoming more cyborg
than ever, as these technologies penetrate more deeply into our private lives. But for
every new venue of self-expression, or every gain in technological power, what are
we giving up? Do we regain in community, or democracy, or openness what we lose in
privacy and possession? To what extent do we control the contexts and conditions in
which we reveal or conceal our selves in this new technological climate? Can we derive
the benefits of community and egalitarian culture if we are willing to put our lives
on(the)line? Can we protect ourselves from government surveillance and corporate
marketing when we don the cameras on our own foreheads? Blogs, auctions, and
other automated forms of self revelation each shed a different light on these kinds
of questions.

The selves revealed in autobotographies often seem fleeting or elusive by
comparison to our pre-Internet concepts of subjectivity. Yet contemporary theories
of subjectivity that stress performance (Judith Butler), or an 'event-scene' on the
border of material and virtual zones (Deleuze and Guattari), as the constitutive moment
of subjective experience anticipate these net expressions. While digital technology
may have facilitated self-expression and self-examination, it has also provided us with
examples of these elusive new subjectivities, from performances of masculinity and
femininity freed from biological sex, to explorations of the boundary between physical
bodies and virtual selves. More importantly, digital artists have given us alternatives
to market-based, self-promoting individualism by reminding us of the communities
and networks upon which any experience or expression of self is based.

Indeed, autobotography's merit as art might be linked to the many new
ways of being in the world – virtual or material – that they offer. Because of their
experimentation with the question of what life is – individual, virtual, digital, artificial,[14]
social – these practices offer us clues which might enable us to champion the sanctity
of our small existences, and our local relationships, against the huge institutions that
exploit them for short-term profit.

Viewed in this light, *jennicam* is fresh and immediate but also superficial and
transient. To delve beneath the surface of everyday life, autobotography must connect
to deeper meanings and structures. Unlike most autobiographies, autobotographies can
influence economic and political realities. Autobotographies that dupe a museum into
accepting synthetic artists or force eBay administrators to amend their ethics policy
offer more than a new medium for self-examination. As we will see later, a single
revelation in the Internet age can ripple across electronic and cultural networks to
provoke change outside its own backyard, just as a single activated lymphocyte can
wake up a body's entire immune system.

EDGE STUDIES

Blogging Subjects

Although journals and their digital reincarnations fall short of the kind of reflection and conscious shaping typical of autobiography, they do provide outlooks on contemporary experience through some novel lenses. Because of the acute awareness of audience in most online digital work, self-censorship is a constant issue. Writers of **Weblog**s, or bloggers, can be cautious about not revealing their true names or private information about themselves or loved ones. They ponder whether to conceal what isn't flattering. They read and respond to fan mail, clear out **spam**, give advice to like-minded peers, and link all over the Net to try to anchor themselves in a set of meanings which are comfortable to them. This network of links has become *sine qua non* for most online autobiography and a powerful tool for exploring the network of other lives related to the blogger. Even more than print, digital formats can represent individual lives as part of a web or network of other lives, thus challenging the powerful Euro-American myths of autonomy and individualism, and reinforcing community and connection.

While most sites are focused on the immediacy of experience, individual or networked, a few have begun to 'blog the past', and thus attempt to incorporate self-reflection and conventional narrative shaping. Typically, all of these electronic diaries rely heavily on text for self-representation. Like the narratives themselves, the look of blogs can be raw or refined, depending on the degree to which the blogger has tweaked their **stylesheet** to bring a distinctive look to their blog. Whether diarists use an automated tool like **Moveable Type** or generate their own unique narrative forms, diaristic autobotography can reveal a variety of different selves depending on who is doing the revealing.

Right: *Journals.*

THE SUBJECT OF LANGUAGE
Ralph Moore, *Sentence*

Sentence.

One of the more self-conscious and self-reflexive digital self-presentations is the Web site *Sentence*. '*Sentence* is my mind,' writes author Ralph Robert Moore. This is a post-Structuralist analysis of subjectivity (a sentence's subject = a psychological subject), as well as a comment on an autobiographical/literary project (a Web site is my mind). Moore's site opens with his blog, in typical reverse chronology; there are also sections to promote and sell his fiction and essays, as well as a gallery and 'interactive features', a section that invites viewers to share some of their own stories. What distinguishes this site from its many peers is a clear and sophisticated attempt to be self-critical about the practice of autobiography:

All autobiographies are false, whether they're lines on a face, an airplane or bar conversation, or structured sentences. We're born with two mysteries: the mystery of life and the mystery of ourselves, and we don't solve either in the short gaming time we're given. All we can do is guess. What follows is a read of my life. Throughout, I've tried always to be honest. When it suits my purposes. Because so much material has to be left out of any autobiography, in order to show patterns, I cannot give the truth of my life, but rather only a sense of my life.

In contrast to shoot-from-the-hip blogging, this measured prose and carefully constructed portrait feels more artificial and thus raises the central dilemma of the genre: Is the 'truth' better captured by unselfconscious reportage, or is there another kind of 'truth' which can only be captured by an exercise of fictional techniques? Is the unconscious more likely to be revealed by reportage or fiction?

UBIQUITOUS DIARY
Jason Pettus, *Journals*

Like Moore, Jason Pettus hails from a literary background, specifically Chicago's underground writing scene. His 'electrostatic journal' has run through at least eleven versions, including visual updates as well as reconceptualizations. In one version, for example, Pettus evokes the metaphor of the Internet as electronic frontier with a launch page whose exaggerated fonts imitate an old 'Wild West' playbill.

Rather than just providing an account of daily activities, Pettus's work usually hones in on a particular topic and explores it in monologues which run for several screens. You can read about his latest encounter in a bar, about him filing his tax return, getting teeth pulled, having sex with a couple, traveling to Germany, applying for jobs, visiting his parents. Through it all run ruminations about writing novels, poetry, blogs, essays, or whatever else he's wrestling with at the time.

In addition to the topic-driven journal, there are links to other aspects of Pettus's life: a typography foundry, a 'slacker chef' page, essays, reviews, fiction, novels, **hypertext** fiction, photos, wireless diaries, and books for sale in print and digital format. One of his special projects, 'Ten Stories', was a heuristic for writing ten science-fiction stories in a year. Each month Pettus 'released' a story, got feedback from his audience, then revised what he'd written. At the end of the year, he published the stories on his web site.

Does this compendium of fonts, stories, journals, photos, and links constitute an autobotography? Is Pettus writing about his life, or is he living a life he thinks might be interesting to write about? It's not always clear which way the influence goes. And the materials brought together, though largely choreographed by the author, often include other perspectives or unusual items. What about his excerpts from other peoples' novels? Videos of poetry slams? Mission statements for a conference he plans to direct? Reviews about his work from *Artbyte* magazine? What happens to the genre when the shaping of the raw data is mostly technical — organizing the material into different parts of the Web site — rather than conceptual — organizing it into a narrative structure? What happens when the self becomes just another object of promotion? Like many other autobotographies, Pettus's site encourages us to consider whether self-promotion reveals who we are or merely constructs more ad copy.

Moore and Pettus raise one final question about the relationship between seemingly informal blog writing and the more formal genres such as novels and short stories. Both authors ruminate about the tensions between the two, a tension well articulated on **cyberpunk** author William Gibson's own blog:

> I've found blogging to be a low-impact activity, mildly narcotic and mostly quite convivial, but the thing I've most enjoyed about it is how it never fails to underline the fact that if I'm doing this I'm definitely not writing a novel — that is, if I'm still blogging, I'm definitely still on vacation. I've always known, somehow, that it would get in the way of writing fiction, and that I wouldn't want to be trying to do both at once. The image that comes most readily to mind is that of a kettle failing to boil because the lid's been left off.[15]

Ironically, Gibson's own highly crafted novels opened our imaginations to the virtual space that blogs now inhabit — it was he who coined the term *cyberspace* — even though he wrote a number of them on a manual typewriter. Perhaps the hurried, push-button culture of blogs is incompatible with profound leaps of the imagination such as Gibson's, which take years to perfect. It may be too early to tell whether he's right that blogging is an easy way out of the lonely task of honing prose, or whether we are just in the infancy of this more immediate, and potentially more collaborative, kind of writing.

BLOGGING A BIRTH

Ada T Norton

While blogs have been used to publicize the most private aspects of people's lives, most have been written after the events described were over. Imagine blogging meal preparation, a conversation, or sex while it is happening. Imagine blogging the birth of a child. That's exactly what happened during the birth of Ada T Norton. 'I've just had my next dose of castor oil. Woot!' the blog begins, clearly in the voice of the birthing mom. But as you would expect, she's not the only one blogging. The next entries reveal her accomplices: 'we're into contractions. Much pain. [gilbert]' This is indeed a strange entry and suggests a bit of the disruption caused by documenting an experience as it happens. First, it's not the mother writing. Second, there's a bit of a stretch in the 'we' that's in pain. No-one who's been through labor is likely to concur that the pain is shared with bystanders, no matter how intimate they might be. Curiously, this extreme case of blogging

immediate experience does suggest some of the ways in which the act of representation can influence experience. Writing about birth turns it into a shared experience in which a 'we' is in pain, and other characters (tagged as gilbert, dyson, danny) tell about the event as though it's their own experience. While it would be interesting to get an account of a birth from four different perspectives, that is not quite the same as describing a birth as though it was one perspective shared by four bloggers.

In this birth blog, four subjects claim the linguistic subject position 'we', perhaps signaling the peculiar confusion of subjectivity experienced by a birthing mother: first, because it's not clear at which point there is one organism or two; second, because labor — which is both voluntary and involuntary — casts doubt on the assumption that a mind or ego controls the body. What this experiment makes clear is the slippage between self and self-representation, between action and documentation. It suggests some of the difficulties encountered when the subject tries to occupy both the written text and the body at the same time.

Ada T Norton.

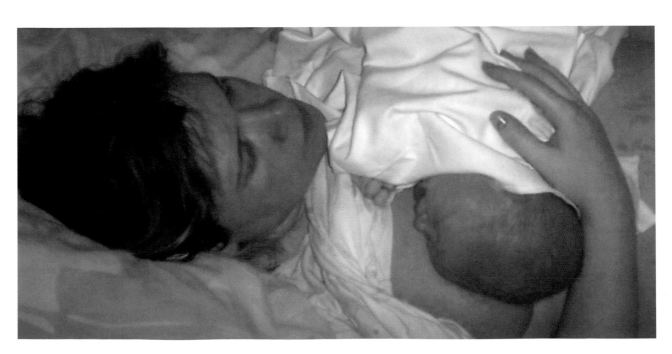

Moving Self-portraits

Blogs have inundated the Web with self-portraits, journals, Web diaries, compendia of adolescent rants, and adult mid-life crises. But the lure of becoming a celebrity often overshadows the quality of much autobiographical work. Where you get relatively open presentation of material, like the links in Jason Pettus's site, the writing, while energetic, is often naïve. The topics are serious enough: his father's suicide, sex tips, and articles written about the effects of globalization in Honduras, as well as attempts to tackle complex issues like the vaccination controversy. But ultimately the material feels rushed, superficial, and opinionated. Where you get deeper analysis, as in *Sentences*, there's still a kind of fascination with self that makes the writing seem pretentious, censored, or somehow manipulated for presentation.

These and similar projects raise the question of whether self-presentation online can really reveal who we are. Webcams are limited to visual information; blog-like diaries present a rush of text. On the other hand, the 'serious' blogs like *Arianna Online* and Wendy Seltzer's 'Legal Tags', while intellectually stimulating, don't really qualify as autobiography unless we are primarily interested in intellectual pursuits.

So, what kinds of self-portraits work well online? Secondary elaboration, that Freudian discovery of indirect artistic presentation, may be one approach. The following projects offer alternative perspectives. They all use Flash as a tool, but limit the aesthetic palette to stark black-and-white images and concise soundtracks. These 'moving self-portraits' evoke some of the mystery and complexity of both self and self-presentation in a way that straightforward revelation does not.

CØULD I BE DØING

SØMETHING ELSE BESIDES THIS?

LIKE SAVING MY SØUL?

ARTIST'S STATEMENTS
Young Hae Chang, *Heavy Industries*

Young Hae Chang's *Heavy Industries* are verbal narratives set to jazz. Unlike most online uses of Flash, Chang's work is minimalist and restrained. The projects are mostly capitalized black text on a white background, flashing a few words at a time across the screen with precise synchronization to a bebop or free-jazz accompaniment. One gets the sense that Young Hae Chang 'works' ideology by listening to the beat of the music and composing insights from it.

Samsung Means to Come, a fictional and erotic Web 'confession', begins with this passage, each line flashing one at a time:

A TRUE STORY
OF SEX,
MULTIPLE ORGASMS,

AND IS
THE WEB,

LIKE
HEAVEN,

ONE BIG
SPY

SATELLITE
ABOVE OUR
HEADS,

Above and below: *Artist Statement* No. 45, 730, 944: The Perfect Artistic Web Site.

AND MAKE
ME LONG
FOR WHAT?

AND SURPRISE,
MONEY.

The narrator sees an **LCD** ad, 'Samsung means to come', and becomes obsessed with getting Samsung to help her orgasm. In the process, she interrogates her inadequate husband and repressive mother-in-law, then settles on a fantasy of getting fucked from behind while washing dishes wearing pink elbow-length gloves. Is this a story of sexual liberation ('to come, again and again'), or is it a description of desire produced by the media ('How can Samsung make me come?')? Of course, the answer is an ironic one: the narrator finally comes while performing domestic duties in the presence of her mother-in-law. The piece provokes some obvious but disturbing questions about the construction of desire, critical to our sense of self. Is this 'Samsung Orgasm' really the liberation the narrator was hoping for? Will an orgasm produced by the multinational corporation that stimulated her desire free her? Or is corporate-constructed identity just the last reach of marketing?

Artist Statement, another project by Young Hae Chang, reveals the fascination of using the Web as a medium for self-expression, but if this is autobotography, it is also an interrogation of the link between self-publishing and multinationals, between desire and advertising, between self-absorption and connection to unknown neighbors. Once again, this digital self is split between the lure of self-expression and the threat of market-driven technologies. *Artist Statement* is an ironic portrait of the self as **ad banner**.

The work describes the artist's statement as 'the perfect Web site, I've been thinking about it for a few minutes now'. Two assumptions are challenged here in the space it takes to laugh: first, that a Web site constitutes creativity, and second, that it only takes a few moments to produce. 'The Web' flashes a few times on the screen, reminding us of our blind fascination with it. Next comes a reference to making something dumb: art. Then a series of questions about whether this 'creative practice' is really worthwhile: 'Isn't there something more important?' There are quick references to thinking about life and death, saving souls, reading a book, watching TV, to

the Internet as surveillance camera, making us worry about what we look like. For a moment, self-absorption seems to give way to a broader vision of how the self is embedded in society. Yet once *Artist Statement* has been uploaded, we get Narcissus in the mirror, trapped by the dazzle of the technology, lured away from human connection toward a technologically generated autism: 'you guessed it, that's me on the screen.' Here is the triumph of the capitalistic self, the *über*-consumer.

Not surprisingly, the narrator soon finds her pet project boring, like much of what passes for 'Web art', and starts using her imagination to try and figure out who her North Korean neighbors are: 'Should I use the Web to find out?' Immediately, we see that while it might be easy to use the Web to reveal the 'self', it might be more difficult to reveal our neighbors. Between the narrator, who is in South Korea, and her North Korean neighbors is a 'trap': a request for credit-card information. So, we find ourselves back with the surveillance satellites and with multinationals constantly mediating our experience. 'Planetary blackmail', the screen flashes, and you want to stop it for a moment to think, but it is moving too fast... 'buy, buy, buy online,' it says. As an artist's statement, this work touches on nearly every major issue confronting Web-production-as-art, all within a few minutes of rapid-fire narration. Most importantly, it interrogates the overly facile impulse to call what's online 'me'.

I'M NOT
SURE,

BUT
SOMETHING
THAT'S
MISSING

FLASH PORTRAITS

Han Hoogerbrugge, *Modern Living* and *Neurotica Series*

This page and opposite:
Modern Living and *NAILS*.

Han Hoogerbrugge's self-portraits began as cartoons, migrated to animated **GIF**s, then finally took shape as Flash animations. Each of the hundred black-and-white cartoonish shorts features the same white man in a black suit in various surreal performances or macabre acts. If these are self-portraits, the self being represented is mysterious, complex, more like a moving target than a consistent ego.

Modern Living is a kind of adult male's Wonderland, complete with a rabbit coming out of his crotch and a clock timing a stew made with his head. Though the portrait claims to be private and to capture inner workings, much of what we see deep within is from the external world: car brands in the brain, Disney in the air, consumer products chasing a boy on a tricycle and punishing him if he rejects them. There's clearly a sense of the internal traumatized, or at least threatened, by the external.

If there are depictions of unsurprising male violence, their cozy contexts make them seem strange. In once scene, four men eating at a table punch each other as you click on their backs, then return to eating their soup. The rhythm of consumption, then hair-trigger violence, back to consumption, is startling but familiar. The characters are so busy consuming that they don't notice the frequency or absurdity of their own acts of nastiness. Few of the pieces are predictable. All are a bit unnerving. Together they add up to a rethinking of what it means to be a male 'self'.

Hoogerbrugge's *Neurotica Series* comprises 'little stories of everyday life' representing a 'real-life person'. In the author's own words, '...the *Neurotica* series reflects my dreams, expectations, conflicts, experiences, hopes, defeats, fears, demons, questions, laughter, and lust. It's a self-portrait. It's a private thing.' In one scene, he's shooting an arrow at Donald Duck; in another he's in a casket beneath a sign that says he will live forever;

in yet another, he's pulling his face off like rubber only to reveal another beneath it. Because most animations loop, there's a sense of futility or inevitability in the actions. Some loops are nightmarish: he counts to thirty in front of an apocalyptic backdrop; a demon's face says yes or no with the opposite facial gestures; he fishes his own head out of a toilet; he's in infinite freefall until a click of the mouse inserts a sudden ground beneath him.

In order to make a discovery in any of these loops, the viewer has to rollover, or click the right part of the image to trigger it. Some loops are tricky to figure out. A number of the loops are games in which the object is to shoot or shock the man, with appropriate verbal or audio rewards. In nearly every animation, there's an urge to push the character into action. In the words of one viewer, 'It seems you cannot leave this person alone. You are poking, boiling, pushing, shocking, tripping, shooting, drowning, and forcing him to bow down to you, his culture.'[16]

Like Young Hae Chang's work, Hoogerbrugge's 'moving self-portraits' offer humorous, terse, and penetrating critiques of the kinds of subjectivities available to us as consumers of our culture and its technologies. The subjects are fragmented, compromised, co-opted by marketing multinationals, by product brands, by technologies that promise to free us right into the hands of credit-card commitments. And yet in both, there's a grin beneath this self-exposure, a sense that resistance is not entirely futile, and in fact might be quite playful.

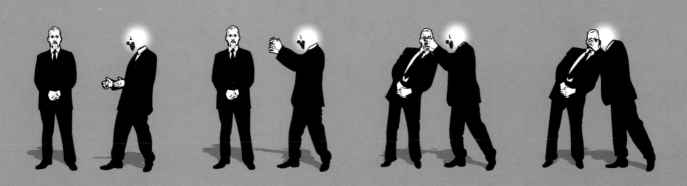

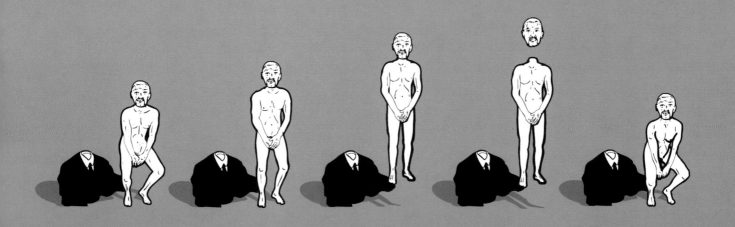

AUTOBIOGRAPHY AS MIRROR
Nobody Here

Nobody Here opens with a silhouette of a man seated before a computer typing. To his left, words appear on the screen as he types. To his right scrolls a list of key words, each of which alters the typed words if rolled over, or takes you directly to a related visual poem if clicked. Free of literary pretension, *Nobody Here* is among the more interesting self-portraits on the Web. What self is being portrayed remains a mystery, and that may offer the best kinds of revelation. Without the need to construct a conventional or coherent ego, what's left is elusive, mysterious, and yet strangely familiar.

The design is simple and uncluttered, a white background with minimal images and short, poetic text. Occasionally, the transition to the next screen is black with a simple phrase etched in white script: 'tired of complaining', 'focus', or a page full of 'write'. The feeling is of openness, pause, clarity. There is room to think in this space. To feel. To wonder. Between the concise and apt audio effects, there is silence. This site uses interactivity to lure viewers into self-discovery even as they may imagine they're trying to discover the self behind the text and images. What the viewer soon realizes is that, as the domain name reminds us, there's no 'body' in the work, that this is a virtual persona, and that as such it obeys slightly different laws of coherence than a typical autobiography. The full domain name, www.nobodyhere.com/just me, plays on this confusion of self and other, and also on the elusiveness of both in this interactive virtual space.

There are many allusions to the problematic nature of subjectivity. Every 'I' in the text is written in script (as opposed to type) and links back to the opening home page. One of the black transition screens links the self to suffering: 'Do I suffer enough?' Another leads to a three-way search for 'me' (via Yahoo), 'myself' (via Altavista) and 'I' (via excite). Another opens with four images which progressively turn to poetic text which ends with the phrase: 'The notion that I am me feels like a pebble in my shoe.' Another screen de-centers this subject: 'I wasn't the first one here' appears beneath an interactive image of wallpaper that can be ripped off layer by layer.

There are other gems of interactivity that reward persistence. One screen shows rows of pink Valentine candy hearts: if you click them, they crack; if you continue to click them, they turn into letters which eventually form the words: 'I break my heart as a precaution.' You won't see this if you are in too much of a hurry, if you just click long enough to break the hearts but not long enough to see the words emerge. There are also disturbing moments: a mouse that dissects itself, a note left for an interloper who turns out to be the self, teddy bears which tumble and keep trying to climb back up into the shape of a pyramid, a catalogue of chewed pieces of gum correlated to the women who might have chewed them, a message from the dead.

The 'bugs' section offers interesting responses from readers who register with a password and select a bug icon that accompanies their posts. One enthusiastic viewer left this interesting review, which begins with a quotation from the work:

'...and if he could describe it all, he would be an artist. but if he were an artist, there would be deeper wounds, which he could not describe.' after a week of returning repeatedly to this website, with delight and fascination and provoked thoughts, i realized that the only fitting description of it is 'Art'. I'd trotted forth many words to describe it: philosophy. diary. exuberant display of technical prowess. inspired auto-vivisection. poetry. Yes. All of these. Art.

Not all experiments in autobotography succeed in moving moments of self-revelation, of the author as well as of the viewer. *Nobody Here, Modern Living*, and *Heavy Industries'* Flash poetry are rare exceptions.

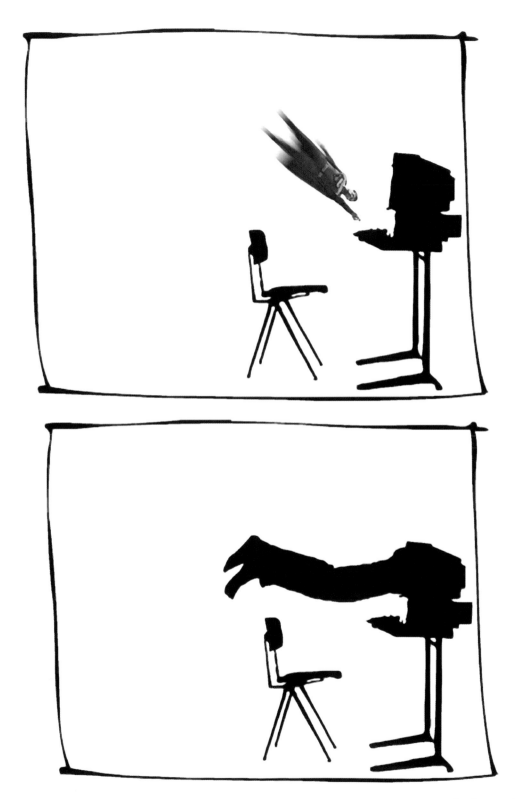

Becoming Post-Human

In many of the projects we've looked at so far, technology has been a tool to express, reflect, or represent a kind of self. But in many cases, that technology has also become part of that self. It's a small step from Stephen Mann's wearable cameras to Molly's surgically implanted razor nails and augmented eyes in William Gibson's novel *Neuromancer*. While blogging code does not necessarily induce birth, it does shape how even the blogging birth-mother experiences it. And while a video-streaming apparatus does not determine a young woman's life, it does give her some control over how that life is shaped by the media that surround her. We are all, already, shaped by the technologies that wire us to each other and to the rest of the world.

Donna Haraway sees utopian possibilities in these spaces, and gives us a description that works as well for Han Hoogerbrugge's moving images as for Mary Flanagan's technological unconscious: 'The cyborg is resolutely committed to partiality, irony, intimacy, and perversity. It is oppositional, utopian, and completely without innocence. No longer structured by the polarity of public and private...'[17] This interrogation of the ideological boundary between public and private resonates through Stephen Mann's and Jennifer Rigley's cameras, through blogged births and identitites, and through the revelations of hard drive that follow. Haraway claims that the 'ideologically charged question of what counts as daily activity, as experience, can be approached by exploiting the cyborg image ... and so means embracing the skilful task of reconstructing the boundaries of daily life, in partial connection with others, in communication with all of our parts.'[18]

Some of those parts are political, some deeply personal, but whether it's the return of a lost image on a hard drive, or the exploration of identities that are no longer there, these parts enter flows of information exchange made possible by plugging into wired technologies. As Katherine Hayles has argued, these new flows give rise to a 'post-human' embodiment. However, this 'post-human body' bears little resemblance to pop-culture stereotypes like Terminator or Tetsuo, as suggested by the cyborg self-portraits that follow.[19]

HARD DRIVE

0100101110101101.org, *Life Sharing*

For the art collective 0100101110101101.org information itself might be a kind of autobotography. *Life Sharing*, a project by this duo of Italian net provocateurs, argues that a person's life might best be represented by their computer hard drive. We spend hours with our computers, they point out, storing memories as photos or video, organizing our social circles via email, expressing our thoughts in text and our categorization schemes as desktop folders. Over time, the computer 'resembles more and more to its owner'. So sharing the contents of that computer with others becomes a way of sharing one's life.

While file-sharing enables users to swap selected files across vast networks, its anagram *Life Sharing* enables anyone with a Web browser to access an entire hard drive: private email, programs, ongoing projects, and archives. If this is a picture of a life, or at least a brain (or, more accurately, its prosthesis), then what kind of life or brain does it show? We see various art projects from the ripoff of the Vatican's Web site to hoax-reporting Nike's plan to take over a town square in Vienna. There are images of the projects and links to media coverage. There's a map of the Debian operating-system structure, as well as access to the authors' email for the five years the project ran live. While the material is fascinating, it is largely a record of a professional life rather than a personal one.

This of course may be a function of the medium. Exposing the entire hard drive of an artist to world-wide perusal might explain why this duo kept their personal names out of their projects and publicity. But this anonymity also manifests a rejection of the ego-genius model of art production promulgated by the traditional market-based art world.

Some have criticized *Life Sharing* for not being completely open — that is for 'hiding' security files that would allow others to hack the site. But good autobotography is less about complete revelation than it is about suggesting alternative constructions of subjectivity. And the questions we might ask of an analogy between life and hard drive are critical for the Internet age.

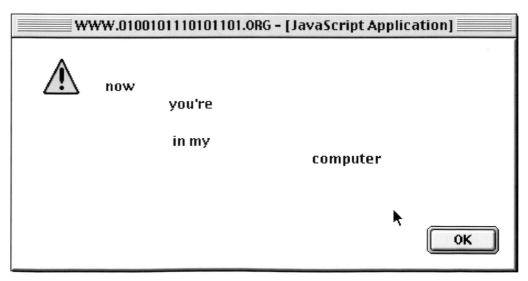

Life Sharing.

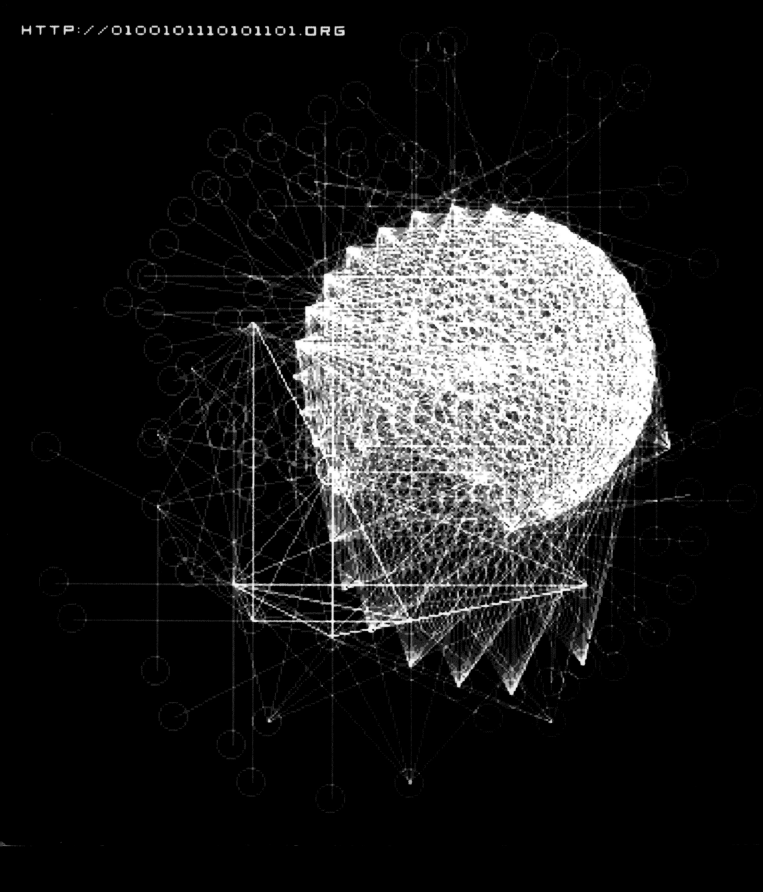

DIGITAL UNCONSCIOUS
Mary Flanagan, *[phage]* and *[collection]*

Like the artist group 0100101110101101.org, Mary Flanagan takes the computer hard drive as her starting point in her project *[phage]*. But rather than glossing over the surface data, she's interested in mining the depths.

Like such artist-made browsers as I/O/D's Web Stalker and Maciej Wisniewski's Netomat, Flanagan's *[phage]* is a data-mining application that offers an alternative visualization of electronic information – but instead of browsing the Internet, it browses your hard drive. A downloadable Director program that thinks it's a psychoanalyst, *[phage]* dredges up random images, texts, and sounds from the nooks and crannies on your C drive, then produces a 3D moving audio-visual image with the data. Flanagan reminds us that a hard drive is a dense layering of information, that any data saved to one may be recovered, even if previously erased, as long as no other data has been written in that particular block and sector. The hard drive is thus something more than a transparent medium; it is a 'place where the residues and actions of our lives are kept, partly recorded, erased'.[20] Not only can we find fragments of memory arranged in a chaotic and associative way, but we might find residues of the unconscious.

What is revealed in the process? In Flanagan's own words,

> *[phage]* creates a feminist map of the machine through its non-hierarchical organization and its divorce of creative control (and reproductive control) from the user to the machine. *[phage]* will allow the user to experience his or her computer memory as a palimpsest of his or her own life experiences rather than know the computer as simply a tool for daily use.

[collection] takes this project to the next level by networking the hard drives of many users together, thus producing a representation of a kind of 'collective unconscious' of a particular cluster of computers. Users download the *[collection]* software, which then dynamically combines the data on their hard drives into the familiar 3D representation of digitized memory. As information, this memory can be manipulated by the animation tools in Director and re-presented as a flow of audio-visual associations. It's tempting to claim that Flanagan's software lets us 'see' our memories – but more accurate to say that it gives images of the technologies by which we build prosthetic memories, both conscious and unconscious.

Life Sharing's file structure visualized via Web Stalker.

iCommerce: Self as Commodity

In a culture dominated by an ever-powerful and invasive market, where an individual's public identity is more likely to be described as 'consumer' than 'citizen', where freedom to buy goods seems more important than freedom over one's time and life choices, the self begins to look like a collection of possessions. When forest fires plagued the West Coast of the US around the turn of the millennium, the most common expression used by couples who had lost their homes and possessions was to say that they'd 'lost everything'. When so much of one's life is spent on accumulating possessions, it's easy to elide their loss with a loss of self. A few artists have taken this identification with one's possessions as a starting point for autobotography.

SELF-POSSESSED OR POSSESSED SELF?

Michael Mandiberg, *Shop Mandiberg*

Michael Mandiberg had such strong anxieties about selling out that he preferred to sell his possessions. *Shop Mandiberg*, an online e-commerce performance, advertised and sold all of the artist's possessions. The Web site supposedly contained everything he owned, including house keys, food, sex toys, favorite clothing, credit cards, passport, books, and drafting tools. This epitome of all yard sales was a reaction to the all-pervasive influence of malls, catalogues, and e-commerce. 'We select objects to own, wear, and consume,' Mandiberg explained.

> This collection of objects forms our "unique" visual identity. *Shop Mandiberg* aims to undo the process of shopping. By buying objects, you undo the work I did building my object-based identity. By buying my objects you can participate in the disintegration of my identity.

Mandiberg's deconstruction of the consumer-driven subjectivity that predominates in Western culture was frightening not because what he dismantled is so precious or valuable, but because he provided no alternative. If we stopped buying so much, and stopped working so much to afford things, what alternative uses might we have for our time and our lives? An economy built around consumption would find such a question either irrelevant or incendiary. But the movement for simple and sustainable living might find room in the space left by Mandiberg's emptying of the consumerist self: time for friends and family, time to enjoy the natural world, time to engage in creative or cultural work ... time to live.

Opposite and right: Shop Mandiberg.

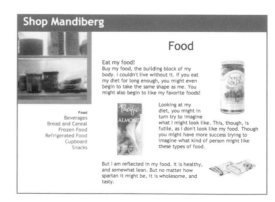

Shop Mandiberg

Consumer Products

Use my stuff!
The department store, the catalogue, and now the e-commerce site dominate our lives as individual consumers. We select objects to own, wear, and consume. This collection of objects forms our 'unique' visual identity.

Consumer Products
Art books
Literature books
General books
Computer books
Computer equipment
Camera equipment
Writing supplies
Drafting supplies
Toiletries
Medicine
Music
Miscellaneous

Shop Mandiberg aims to undo the process of shopping. By buying my objects, you undo the work I did in building my object based identity. By buying my objects you can participate in the disintegration of my identity.

Besides which, there are some very handy things I have. Check out the selection of precision cutting tools in the Drafting section, be sure not to miss my collections of art and computer books. They offer insights into my interests, (and skillsets...)

Shop Mandiberg

Clothes

Wear my identity!
Now is your chance to take away a piece of my identity. By buying my clothes, you not only have the opportunity to buy nice garments, you have the opportunity to become me.

Clothing
Underwear
Socks
Accessories
Pants
T-Shirts
Shirts
Short Sleeve Shirts
Coats
Bags
Shoes
Sweaters
Shorts
Sportswear
Suits

Imagine walking down the street, carrying my distinctive zebra print bag, or wearing one of my unforgettable coats. You can be me! Even more than being me, you can prevent me from having my own identity!

My friends know me for wearing these very singular clothes. They are shocked that I am willing to part with them, because their visual image of 'me' depends on these objects. If they were to see you wearing my clothes, might they not think it was me, if just for a moment...?

Shop Mandiberg

Personal Effects

Own my secrets!
Now you can own my own most private objects. Buy my wallet and become me before the eyes of bouncers and policemen everywhere.

Buy my checkbook or bankcard, and see if you can become me in the eyes of bank tellers and store merchants.

Personal Effects
Letters and Journals
Financial
Identification
Intimate
Art
Miscellaneous

Or buy my letters and journals and pretend that your mother sent you these cards, that your friends wrote you these postcards, and that you yourself wrote these words in the journal.

Shop Mandiberg

Home Furnishings

Make my home yours!
Furnish your home with the objects from mine! Now available from Shop Mandiberg are Michael Mandiberg's own selection of bedroom, study and kitchen furnishings. Featured in the Bedroom section are stylish, yet economical linens from Martha Stewart Living.

Home Furnishings
Bedroom
Study
Kitchen
Cleaning Supplies

In the study department, be sure to see the hi-tech ergonomic chair, with full height adjustment, front back seat tilt, and chair back tilt. It is certainly great for preventing lower back strain while working at a desk!

In the kitchen department be sure to see all of the very simple cooking utensils for the microwave chef! Are you an overworked urban wage slave? Do you eat too much microwaved canned soup? Than you need to check out the selection of pyrex containers, and ergonomic can openers available at Shop Mandiberg!

AUCTIONING RACE
Keith Obadike, *Blackness for Sale*

Michael Mandiberg's sale of his possessions suggests an attempt to reject market-based subjectivity, to reverse the actions of a lifetime of buying. For Keith Obadike, the market provided a way to sell a much more intractable kind of subjectivity, that based on race. *Blackness for Sale*, an eBay auction of Obadike's 'blackness', can be read as a rejection of an imposed and constructed identity, as well as a critique of the uses to which that identity has been put. eBay closed the auction after four days and twelve bids due to 'inappropriateness' but not before the value of Obadike's race peaked at $152.50. In *Blackness for Sale*, the market that once turned black bodies into commodities was appropriated to sell 'black experience'.

Obadike referred to his twenty-eight-year-old blackness as an 'heirloom' used primarily in the US; benefits included the ability to create black art, produce scholarship about other blacks, laugh at black humor, date other blacks, instill fear, and augment blackness in order to play 'blacker-than-thou' politics. The use of blackness for affirmative-action purposes came with a disclaimer: 'Limited time offer. May already be prohibited in some areas'. Warnings included subjecting the user to unemployment, legal discrimination, economic impotence, inability to vote, difficulty marketing art, and dismissal as an intellectual. In the tradition of the photographer Cindy Sherman, who turned the camera on herself and thus reclaimed the position of artist as subject, Obadike reclaimed a subject position *vis-à-vis* race. But this doesn't mean that he could escape being the object of racism the next time he walked down the street. *Blackness for Sale* reminds us of this dilemma by offering that experience to anyone willing to 'buy (into) it'.

BODY FOR SALE

Michael Daines; Cary Peppermint

'Exposure #8818'.

Two other artists have produced works which present the self as a commodity. Michael Daines, posing in T-shirt and jeans, face hidden, offered his body in an eBay auction: 'The body of a 16 year old male. Overall good condition with minor imperfections'. When interviewed by Eryk Salvaggio,[21] Daines admitted that the project might have been unsuccessful in getting him 'fame, fortune and sex' but that the 'internet seems to forgive my countless, countless mistakes'. He considered the action 'a very cheap pun' on prostitution and originally suggested that the proceeds would be donated to Amnesty International because 'in some part they benefit charities dealing with prostitution'.

Cary Peppermint takes this action a step farther in his eBay auction 'Use Cary Peppermint as Medium: Exposure #8818'. This work gives instructions as to how Peppermint's body can be used as an artistic medium:

> High bidder will email specific instructions/
> directions for Cary to perform then will receive
> a five– to fifteen-minute VHS tape of an 'art
> EXPOSURE via video'. Rights of reproduction
> and distribution go to the highest bidder as
> well as credit as 'director' of the art work.
> There are limits on the projects which are
> defined as anything approaching 'bodily harm'
> or anything that might 'reduce this project to a
> mono-channel of humor, irony or otherwise
> hackneyed form of entertainment'.

While these eBay auctions raise questions about the relationship of bodies to e-commerce and of both to Net art, we suspect that neither body is really for sale, and that neither is in any immediate physical danger from the markets they play in. Yet both works invite us to ponder the longer-term dangers caused by a commercial culture that defines the behavior, freedoms, and values of our biological bodies.

CONSUMER CAMOFLAGE
TraceNoizer

The previous examples treat aspects of self as commodity, as a kind of marketable, albeit private, property. But some people are more interested in taking themselves out of the market than putting themselves into it. In a world where every credit-card payment and login is registered in some corporation's databank to be bought and sold

Below: *TraceNoizer.*

with other personal data streams, it can be all too easy to **finger** a specific individual. Alternative press such as the *Utne Reader* occasionally profiles citizens interested in remaining as private as possible, some eschewing all credit cards, Social-Security numbers, bank credit, or any other public records of themselves. While it is difficult to cover your tracks online, there may be a way to hide your digital identity by the opposite strategy.

TraceNoizer automatically introduces alternative data about its users' credit cards, names, and so forth into the public space of the Web. It generates a number of fictitious home pages for a given person, each with different information, so that netizens can hide in the noise surrounding their own signal.

As with many online projects, the suggestiveness of the proposal outweighs the practical value of the application. Although the read_me jury found no evidence that *TraceNoizer*'s data clones made it into search-engine results at all, its algorithms are interesting for the fact that each new home page it produces is generated from the previous generation of data clone — analogous to a positive-feedback loop that amplifies errors anywhere in the translation. This game of telephone played with online identities reminded the read_me jury of the incestuousness of corporate search-engine queries such as Google's PageRank algorithm, which rewards sites that have attracted attention with more attention. As the jury put it, 'Given this fact, *TraceNoizer*'s system of having data reproduce by looking up its own ass seems an appropriate and entertaining response.' While much of the work described in this chapter is about revelation of some kind, it is interesting to see a project that attempts to conceal subjects rather than reveal them.

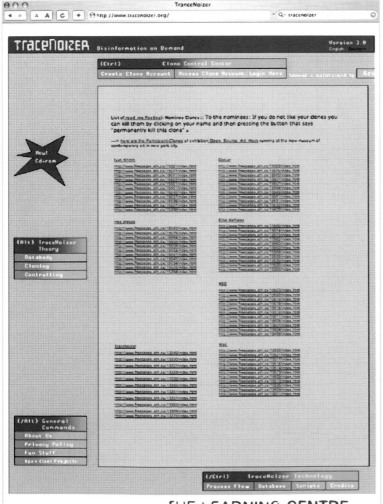

Invented Selves

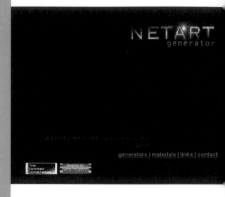

Email nicknames, **chat-room** handles, game characters, and other avatars allow us to create personae that inhabit virtual worlds. These personae allow us to play roles for which we have no real-world contexts, act out desires for which we have no names, and assume subjectivities for which we have no role models. The invention of these virtual selves has created a playful and perverse kind of autobiographical practice.

For example, plenty of contributors to online communities maintain multiple aliases. When someone refers to 'Netochka Nezvanova' on the Rhizome.org email list, for example, they are referring to a character who also goes by the designations /nn , antiorp, and integer. The voices and viewpoints of each of these identities may or may not sound like they emanate from a single person. Yet this kind of avatar schizophrenia is common online, since creating a new identity is as easy as signing up for a new email account. A related ruse is for a single artist to pretend to represent a much larger collective. Examples include Group Z and the Bureau of Inverse Technology, each of which is the vision and fruit of a single person but whose Web sites ape the look of an artists' collaborative and research think tank, respectively. More recently, the economies of some online games have grown to rival those of actual countries, and industry observers watching avatars bought and sold on eBay have begun to wonder who owns these digital personae and whether they might have rights of their own.[22]

To make matters more complex, the lives of some avatars spill outside the screen to affect real-life people with very real emotions. A male psychotherapist masquerading as a paraplegic named Julie gained considerable online reputation in the mid-1980s before he was unmasked by an admirer who tracked him down in his real-world apartment.[23] An avatar named Mr Bungle committed a well-documented 'rape' of another character in the LambdaMOO community by controlling that character's actions via a specially crafted programming trick and was later expelled from the community.[24] Similarly, when the online acquaintances of a pair of New York psychiatrists, Joan and Alex, learned they were the same person, Joan's intimate friends were bewildered and outraged – not so much because of the deception, but because Alex couldn't keep up with the demands of being two people and 'deleted' Joan. The grief was not for a real person but for an imagined but dear friend. When avatars are mistaken for 'real' persons in the 'real' world, social and political consequences may follow. Two works that deliberately trigger such responses are Cornelia Solfrank *et al.*'s *Female Extension* and 0100101110101101.org's *Darko Maver*.

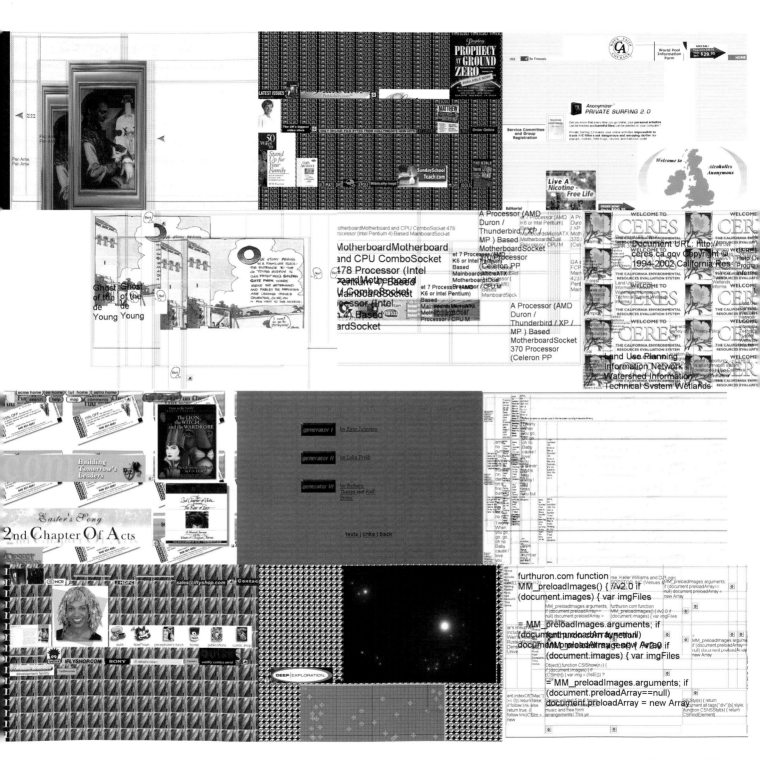

DIGITAL REPRODUCTION
Cornelia Solfrank, Barbara Thoens, Ralf Prehn,
et al., *Female Extension*

In 1997, the Hamburger Kunsthalle launched one of
the first museum-sponsored Net-art competitions,
'Extension'. At the time, the overwhelming majority
of online artists were men. Cornelia Solfrank and
a team of programmers created *Net Art Generator*
to right this imbalance by submitting 127 ersatz
Web works, each by a fictitious female artist, to the
exhibition jury for review. For example, 'Generator
III', contributed by Barbara Thoens and Ralf Prehn,
asked nothing more from a would-be Internet artist
than the artwork's title and creator's name. Once
these were input, clicking the 'create' button spit
out a Web page consisting of a hodgepodge of
images pulled from search-engine results based
on the title. For example, inputting the title 'Not
Again' in January 2003 produced a visual medley
featuring the World Trade Center burning, wreckage
of the Columbia Space Shuttle, and a Zimbabwean
journalist recently released from prison.

The pictorial mishmash produced by *Net
Art Generator* was convincing enough to fool
the exhibition organizers into writing a press
release touting '280 applications — Two thirds
are women.[25] On the day the Kunsthalle announced
the competition winners, Solfrank revealed her
ruse, *Female Extension*, in the process exposing the
fact that the jurors' high hopes for participation
by women artists were coupled with low aesthetic
expectations.

Solfrank's work took the Internet as both
material and object, as the competition instructions
specified. Yet none of the judges recognized this,
not simply because she was a woman, but because
they did not understand the nature of Internet art
sufficiently to imagine that an artist could write a
program that would create it.

Female Extension offered an unusual case of
invented selves. Each came complete with addresses,
phone numbers, and working email accounts on
different servers, as well as artworks entered in
international competition. Neither as complex as
typical avatars nor as abstract as unconscious
portraits of hard drives, these 'selves' might be
compared to a number of 'invented selves' produced
by artists: from Duchamp's Rrose Selavy to Rosanne
Allucquere Stone's transgendered identity to
Ray Kurzweil's Ramona.[26] All of these disrupt
conventional subject boundaries.

What made Solfranks's fabricated personae
unusual is that they were largely constructions
of computer code overlaid onto social code. Her
appropriation of a tool overwhelmingly relegated to
male users in order to engender a legion of female
artists was a clear misuse of code. Code is for
production, not reproduction. This frighteningly
fertile act of 'mothering' a legion of others,
recalling the she-monster of Ridley Scott's film
Aliens, so horrified and humiliated the Kunsthalle
exhibition's organizers that they cancelled all
future Internet art competitions there.

CRUEL RUSE

0100101110101101.org, *Darko Maver*

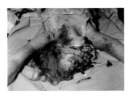

Darko Maver.

One of the more peculiar online autobotographies is that of Darko Maver. Darko Maver was a reclusive Serbo-Slovenian artist who roamed ex-Yugoslavia depositing gruesomely realistic puppets or models of murder victims in abandoned buildings and hotel rooms. The models were so realistic that they shocked and terrorized the local people who found them. Considered a politically incorrect artist because he exposed the brutality of war in the ravaged and plundered Balkans, Maver was arrested and jailed for unpatriotic activities, and there were reports of his death in the Potgorica penitentiary in April 1999. A victim of war, of censorship, of State brutality, and ultimately of the vampiric media that disseminated and sustained his mythic life, Maver exposed the violence of both the battlefield and the art gallery.

Soon after Mavor's death and a string of posthumous shows culminating in the forty-eighth Venice Biennale, a statement appeared on the Web site of 0100101110101101.org: 'I declare that I have invented the life and the works of art of the Serbian artist Darko Maver.' The documentary photos of this 'artwork' were revealed to be photographs of real-life atrocities perpetrated during the war in the Balkans, images taken from an online source. The art world sensationalized, then anesthetized, Maver's work and built his success on the bodies of the war's victims. In the disclaimer that appeared on 0100101110101101.org's Web site, we find the following explanation:

> His work, once properly homogenised and deprived of its expressive force, was ready to go through the canonical way which links galleries, exhibitions, the art market, and finally takes to the eternal peace of the museum, apex of an anaesthetic process, of disarmament and sterilization, a process which art has always suffered. The museum is a sheer temple where art is celebrated, faked and degraded, just as

prison degrades life making it unrecognizable. And the theorem, once more, proves to be exact: an artist (an identity), a style, the works ... and the system is ready to absorb everything and turn life into commodities.

At the core of this work is an examination of levels of violence. From the original murders, to the use of atrocity in artwork, to the commodification of bodily injury by critics and curators, *Darko Maver* reminds us that while artists are making 'shocking' artwork absorbed by the market, real violence is being perpetrated and ignored by a media-anesthetized world. This work challenges us with a critical life-or-death question: How can we connect art with life again? How can we recover from media-inspired numbness? The Internet is, of course, just one more medium. Will the new generation of artists use it as a conduit to enter the art establishment, or will they use it challenge the commodification of our lives and to bring art practice back to the communities that might benefit from a more engaged approach?

Given the effect of this work, we might ask ourselves if Darko Maver's life was any less 'real' than that of the many avatars we create to give expression to aspects of ourselves which find it difficult to inhabit the material world. A mythic figure, semiotically constructed in virtual and media spaces, *Darko Maver* may represent a revelation about our own dark unconscious. It would be easy to leave the blame for this disregard of human life in the lap of the art establishment and media. What is more difficult is recognizing our own culpability in the easy way we are seduced by technological wonders. Narcissus' crime was not just self-absorption but utter neglect of his fellow creatures. *Darko Maver* begs the question: Have we been so preoccupied with looking at ourselves in the media's dark mirrors that we can no longer see each other, even when we cry out in agony?

DESIGN ING POLIT ICS

Patrick Ball and Slobodan Milošević at the International Criminal Tribunal for the Former Yugoslavia.

Aware that small bits of code can undermine unwieldy systems, hackers of code and culture have breathed new life into political activism. 'Don't hate the media; become the media!' Jello Biafra advised a gathering of programmers.[1] 'Well, you may get an angry letter from your adopted organization,' advises the *Reamweaver* manual, 'but you can just say you were playing a funny surrealist game.'[2] These two positions span a range of activity, from creative forms of political expression to new virulent forms of art, from serious politics to irreverent play — from what might be called 'political design' to 'executable art.' The public discourse on Internet activism to date has blurred this distinction by referring to all online political activity with the generic term *hacktivism*, a portmanteau word suggesting a 'hacker-activist'. Armed with an arsenal of powerful new tools, hacktivists are disrupting World Trade Organization conferences and uploading biotech blueprints for home-grown tissue cultures. Yet while political designers and hacktivist artists work with the same tools and often produce similar results, it's critical to distinguish their long-term social functions. Politics attempts to change the world directly and with force; art seeks to question it, often with humor or irreverence. If politics seeks to destroy its enemies, art seeks to ridicule them. When Patrick Ball, the **open-source** programmer-*cum*-human-rights activist, presented database evidence at the war-crimes trial of ex-Yugoslavia's leader Slobodan Milošević, it was critical that his data be sound rather than surreal.[3] On the other hand, when *Reamweaver* activists used spurious GATT (General Agreement on Tariffs and Trade) invitations to champion commerce blatantly over democracy, it was equally critical that their masquerade be hyperbolic enough to raise eyebrows.

While this distinction between hacktivist design and hacktivist art is fundamental, it is not always obvious, either to the current generation of hackers or to the institutions and operating systems they hack. If *Reamweaver*'s tactics are only part of a funny surrealist game, then why would the WTO try to shut it down? Apparently, some kinds of playful hacking can have serious, if indirect, consequences. This is because hacktivism wields a kind of power largely unavailable to artists before the advent of digital culture: it can be executed.

While *execute* is a term often used to describe the workings of computer programs, the same term also describes a biological antecedent in the immune system. When so-called helper T-cells, alerted to the presence of foreign agents, proliferate madly, disperse throughout the bloodstream, trigger the massive reproduction of so-called B-cells, and change the entire body environment in order to defend it against invasion, they are also executing code, albeit of a biological kind. 'To execute', in the world of code, means to turn the potential power of instructions into the actual power of behavior. 'To execute' means to enact the code. But there are many codes at play in both the immunological and social bodies. The immune system executes its code when it recognizes invasion of the body by foreign code (e.g. a virus); digital art executes its code when it recognizes invasion of the social body by codes that appear foreign or harmful, whether they are cultural, legal, or social. < >

HACKING THE COURTROOM
David Touretzky,
Gallery of CSS Descramblers

Executable culture can be found in some of the most unlikely places. David Touretzky, a computer scientist at Carnegie-Mellon University in Pittsburgh, assembled one of the most influential examples on a Web site, which he called a 'gallery', even though it will probably never be mentioned in *ARTnews*. Touretzky's *Gallery of CSS Descramblers* aimed to debunk a particular myth about computers and, in the process, influence a legal judgment that, he believed, was about to abrogate the Constitutional right to free speech.

The judgment in question, Universal v. Reimerdes, challenged the right of online magazines and Web-site operators to publish or link to a computer program claimed by the plaintiffs to be 'illegal' according to the Digital Millennium Copyright Act. This program, known as DeCSS, had been designed neither by Luddites intent on destroying hard drives nor by hackers bent on spreading viruses. It was a software utility written by three programmers, of whom the best known, Jon Johansen, was a sixteen-year-old Norwegian kid who'd realized that the 'Content Scrambling System' software that prevents DVDs from being pirated also prevented him from viewing *Star Wars* and *Gone with the Wind* on his GNU/Linux operating system. Their utility decrypted his DVDs so he could watch them. Sound harmless enough? The Motion Picture Association of America didn't think so, and neither did District Judge Lewis Kaplan, who ordered the code and links expunged from the Web.

Against the defendent's argument that censoring DeCSS software was akin to stifling free speech, Judge Kaplan contended that computer code was unlike speech because it was executable. As a practicing programmer, however, Touretzky believed that there was a continuum between software and speech, one that could not easily be divided and legislated, and he set out to prove it.

DeCSS code on a tie.

His call for variations on 'illegal' DeCSS code generated a vast array of responses along the spectrum between executable and expression. Some of the variations suggest utter geekhood: professional programmers translated DeCSS into numerous computer languages (C source code, Perl code, Standard ML); a more academically inclined contributor wrote an abstract mathematical description of the algorithm. Those of a more 'artistic' bent embedded the code in familiar media such as a **GIF** image, a movie, a T-shirt, a Yahoo greeting card, and a song; the song attracted enough attention to be banned from the popular music-distribution site MP3.com. Several contributors created 'how-to' manuals in plain English, or as explained by JavaScript agents, or even in haiku:

> How to decrypt a DVD
> ...
>
> Arrays' elements
> start with zero and count up
> from there, don't forget!
>
> Integers are four
> bytes long, or thirty-two bits,
> which is the same thing.
>
> To decode these discs,
> you need a master key, as
> hardware vendors get ...

While many of these examples were clearly created in the spirit of fun, they also raised profound questions about the philosophical and legal status of various forms of expression. One contribution was written in a theoretical software language that has never run on any machine. Assuming this ineffectual code is legal now, would it become illegal once someone created a compiler for it? In which case who would be liable for infringing the law, the author of the fictional program or the creator of the compiler? Should distribution of mathematical formulae by their creators be outlawed? Consider a particularly clever artwork from the gallery, created by embedding the illegal code directly into the official DVD logo. For

HACKING CAPITALISM

®™ark, *rtmark.com*

Touretzky's *Gallery of CSS Descramblers* is clearly revelatory, perverse, and executable. Yet despite its invocation of a 'gallery', precious few dealers or curators from the offline art world have ever heard of it. In ironic contrast, one of the most successful examples of hacktivist art, by ®™ark — an entry in the Biennial of the Whitney Museum of American Art — eschews the term *gallery* altogether in favor of the phrase 'activist clearinghouse'.

®™ark channels money and resources to people who dream up clever ways to subvert multinational capitalism. It has sponsored hacks of gender-biased computer games, posted bogus Web sites that pretend to represent American presidential candidates, and sent ersatz representatives of the WTO to spout imperialist ideas at international conferences. Subterfuges like these are more carefully targeted than pranks but less solemn than political campaigns or underground movements. Yet they are not exactly political art in the tradition of Géricault or Picasso either, since — rather than representing issues in an art context — ®™ark actually intervenes in the real world, prompting interviews by CNN and cease-and-desist letters from the WTO.

One of the earliest and best-known 'cultural hacks' supported by ®™ark was to switch the voice-boxes of three hundred Barbie and G.I. Joe dolls in 1993, so that unsuspecting girls bought Barbies that barked 'Commence firing' instead of cooing 'Let's go shopping.' Of course, it is rare that someone who

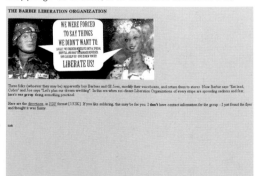

gets the idea to switch the voice-boxes of gender-stereotyped dolls actually works in a toy factory. What ®™ark does is to channel such ideas to people in a position to accomplish them — in this case, the 'Barbie Liberation Organization'. Ideally, ®™ark

Left and below: The 'Barbie Liberation Organization'.

also channels financial backing to such causes, though in practice the amounts 'pledged' are usually measured in the hundreds of dollars.

If ®™ark's strategy is to use the tools of capital to subvert it, the structure of *rtmark.com* apes the model of the mutual-fund portfolio. Funds such as OBIT ('Add Afghan dead to S-11 obituaries') and GOLF ('Replace golf greens with edible greens') are listed by the four-letter-abbreviation scheme familiar from the New York Stock Exchange. Most of ®™ark's calls to action go unfulfilled, but there are notable exceptions. In 1996, ®™ark channeled $5,000 contributed by a New York shopkeeper to a Silicon Valley programmer who inserted unauthorized code into his company's popular *Simcopter* shoot-'em-up game. In place of the usual reward for blowing up targets — a date with a buxom babe — the modified version of the game offered scantily clad boys kissing, thus sneaking homoerotic content into a gaming culture defined by extreme machismo.

When ®™ark was accepted into the 2000 Whitney Biennial — the first such exhibition to include works of Internet art — this seemed to cement its status as 'art' despite the fact that the site's pseudonymous authors never use the term *art* to describe their work. As its contribution, ®™ark simply submitted their home page, to be projected

Touretzky, this image offered a 'hard case' with which to thwart a meretricious line of judicial reasoning. There is a subtle and important difference between protesting a court decision and furnishing a legal conundrum that calls that decision into question. A button with a red cancellation mark over the letters 'CSS' raises consciousness. The altered DVD logo, by contrast, executes both computer code (via optical character recognition) and legal code (by undermining a court decision).

This project and the rest of Touretsky's gallery highlighted the arbitrary nature of Judge Kaplan's decision to draw the line somewhere amid this unruly assortment of variations so that executables lay on one side and expressions on the other. The logos and haikus grouped in Touretzky's gallery create a social impact not usually associated with art. Géricault's *The Raft of the Medusa* and Picasso's *Guernica* represent politics; DeCSS art, on the other hand, *executes* politics. An early version of Touretzky's gallery was cited in legal argument when the case was appealed, and the decision was upheld. The appeals court ruled that DeCSS was 'dangerous' speech – analogous to shouting 'Fire!' in a crowded theater – and therefore wasn't as protected as ordinary speech. Touretsky's victory

was in making sure that DeCSS was evaluated as speech and thus establishing a precedent that in the future code would be subject to the same protection as speech.

Below: DeCSS code embedded in the DVD logo.

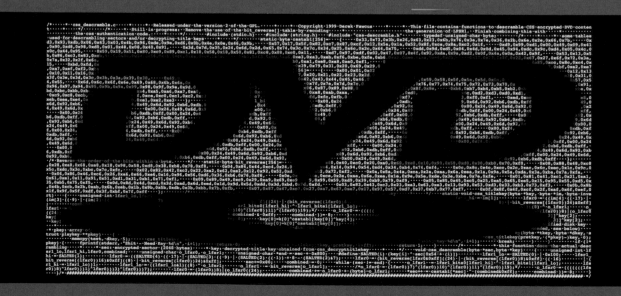

on a wall and interacted with via a keyboard. Unbeknownst to the museum's curatorial staff, however, ®™ark had offered to 'lend' its space on the wall to other artists during the run of the show. Visitors who accessed *rtmark.com* from the Whitney were automatically redirected to urls submitted by other visitors. (®™ark even created an email address, show@rtmark.com, especially for this purpose.) Even when honored as art-world insiders, ®™ark produced a crack in the Duchampian frame, a fissure leading to the space beyond the art world's confines, very much as a killer T-cell produces a gap in an attacking virus to disable it.

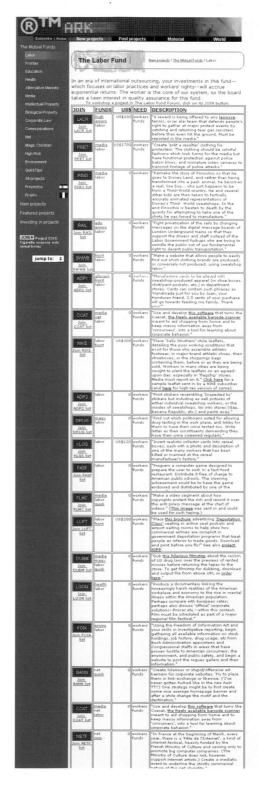

Right: ®™ark mutual funds.

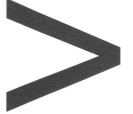

Tim Scott, DeCSS code
embedded in a photograph
of Motion Picture
Association of America
President Jack Valenti.

Executability has given hacktivists not only an arsenal of new tools but a much wider arena in which to exercise these new powers. Because computers are now linked via a global network, code that affects a single operating system can be redirected to execute on computers around the world. No longer confined to the sanctuaries of gallery and museum, digital work has been executed in government-agency databases, in corporate Web ad banners, and on the hard drives of private citizens. Although the Internet is its primary means of dispersal, hacktivism's effects are felt far beyond Web pages and e-mail lists. You're more likely to learn about it while sitting in a courtroom than in a museum. As ®™ark's 'Ray Thomas' has explained: 'If you're trying to be an activist, don't bother spending any time in the traditional art scene. It doesn't have any significant effect on the real world. No politicians look to the art world to see what to do. Artists who want to be activists should be spending their time on the world.'[4]

Hackers vs. Hacktivists; Political Design vs. Executable Art

Hacktivists like David Touretzky and ®™ark share many qualities with ordinary hackers. Impatient with the bureaucratic bottlenecks and squabbling that plague legislative decision-making, both groups eschew politics by the book in favor of unofficial movements and underground actions. Both groups also engage in **glocal** politics, as when a geographically dispersed network of hackers supported the 'Free Kevin Mitnick' campaign to help the first famous hacker ever to be put in jail. Both groups also accept – or cultivate – a public image of being outside the mainstream. Hackers and hacktivists are also both known for a playful form of politics – such as overloading a repressive regime's Web site by repeatedly asking if 'democracy.html' is on its server.

But most hackers are not hacktivists. Hackers aim for work that is executable in technological contexts but not legal ones. While there are hackers with strong **author function**s – Phiber Optik or jaromil, for example – many are content simply to poke around unnoticed in the bowels of some government's **UNIX** directories and leave the site without a trace. Indeed, the ability to evade the attention of anyone besides their peers is a skill highly prized by these trespassers on immaterial real estate – and that gives them the opposite goal to ®™ark and Touretzky. In contrast with the hacker ideal of an elusive 'crypto-anarchy',[5] hacktivists are hackers with a cause. In this aspect, they are more like terrorists than hackers; they value attention more than votes, but they seek that attention from the world at large rather than just from their peers. With this wider range of powers and venues comes an increased responsibility to the social body in which hacktivism operates.

Within hacktivism, we can distinguish a spectrum of practices depending on the degree of social responsibility of the work, from political design to executable art. While the goal of the immune system is to destroy foreign agents, artists are a bit more cautious. Code, of the immune or even the legal variety, can kill. Do digital artists want to wield the same power? Or would this undermine the very condition that makes art valuable: the preservation of a safe arena for experimentation and play? Politics without imagination often leads to violence and war. And while a 'toy war' between etoy.com and eToys.com may help us to imagine a better society, a real war between these parties would destroy the social body that art is committed to keeping healthy. To the extent that a work operates in the field of power, trying to destroy its enemy, it veers toward political design; to the extent that a work operates in the field of play, pointing at the emperor's nakedness rather than plotting his assassination, it veers toward executable art.

Political Design

As we saw earlier, every software architecture has political implications, whether deliberate (as in Microsoft's monopolistic integration of its Explorer browser into its

Below: *The File Room* and Wendy Seltzer's home page.

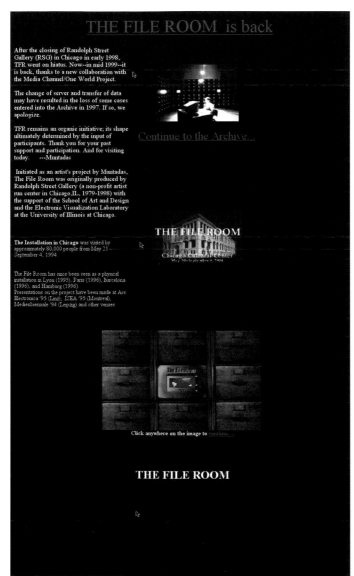

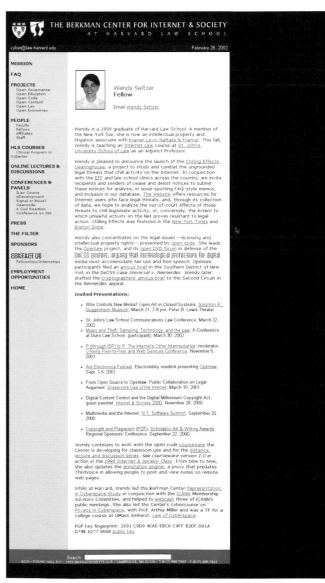

The Trojan Cow Project

The Trojan Cow email server is unavailable. The Meme Factory's FTP site is down until 2002. Please come back for downloads then.

Welcome,

If you wish to submit a comment to the Copyright Office regarding the Digital Millennium Copyright Act, you've come to a good place

Warning, before submitting a comment through the Trojancow service, you should read this page with care so you know what you're getting in to

What Cow?

You should note that appended to your comment will be one of two original art works, of a cow This is possible because the Copyright Office wishes to place all comments on their web site, and they find it easier to do this if the comments are in PDF format And, of course, images can be included in PDF files

Wadda mean Trojan?

Well, it turns out that if you were to have _both_ original art works, both cows, and you knew what to do with them, you would find that there is copyrighted material cleverly, and effectively, protected by technological means from those who would illegally, according to the Digital Millennium Copyright Act, obtain access to this material It also happens that a portion of the technologically protected material is the DVD-CAA v. 521 - Reply Declaration of John J. Hoy, Exhibit B This is a public US court document containing the text of the DVD decryption code that got that poor 16 year old in Norway arrested

I've heard that the DVD decryption code attracts lawyers. Can I get in trouble for using or setting up the Trojancow service?

I'm no lawyer, but I wouldn't think so You see, any one Trojancow artwork contains only a portion of the information necessary to _construct_ the DVD decryption code Here's the analogy supposing you didn't want to get caught with a latte (you know, the stuff made with expresso coffee and milk.) Well, if you have only the milk, or only the coffee, there's no latte You need both the milk and the coffee, and an expresso machine to make latte One cow artwork corresponds to the milk, the other to the coffee The expresso machine corresponds to the program an evil copyright violator would have to write to obtain the DVD decryption code (See next section.)

Prove that there's hidden DVD decryption code.

I'm not going to, you'll just have to take my word for it You see, right now I value the license to view the protected material at about 10 million dollars I figure that's probably enough to keep me rolling in lawyers for a while, should I need to go there Anyone, the Motion Picture Association, for instance, who wishes to check on the "content" of the Trojancow artwork will have to come up with the money I'm torn, because I very much would like to release the code (written in guile) that protects my copyrighted material so others can benefit from it However, at this time it's not happening

Ok, so how do I send a cow to the Copyright Office for inclusion on their web site?

1) Have a look at their request for comment and come up with something good to say You may also wish to see their extension of the deadline in which they expanded the data formats they accept to include mime attachment encoded plain ASCII text

Remember, this is _public_ comment You don't want to make the crew your hanging with look like hostile malcontents, even if they are

I wish I could provide a good example, but I'm pressed for time

2) Write an e-mail to one of the Trojancow servers listed below Our recommendation is to use the following format

The copyright office requires the following information with your submission

```
name
title
organization
mailing address
telephone number
fax number
e-mail address
```

Please begin your e-mail with this information, with no leading blank lines Please follow this information with at least one blank line

Note You could, of course, claim to be anybody Before you abrogate your identity, please remember that freedom isn't free If nobody takes a stand, they'll be nobody to stand up for what's right

You will receive an e-mail back suitable for re-sending to the copyright office If you have followed our formatting guidelines, the textual information will be the your contact information as shown above, and a PDF attachment containing the contents of your original e-mail and a cow artwork

You may wish the PDF to differ slightly from the e-mail sent to the Trojancow server For example, you plan to Cc. the President of the United States when you send your message to the copyright office You'd like the PDF to show this Cc. header so that the folks at the copyright office will know that you're going straight to the top with your comments But you don't want to Cc. the President until you send the real message, he shouldn't see your experiments with the Trojancow service So, you want the Trojancow service to put an e-mail header (Cc.) into the PDF, a header that's not in the message you send to the service For other reasons, you may want to change the appearance of an e-mail header that you _have_ included in your message to the service To do these things, you'll need an e-mail program that allows you to add additional e-mail headers. Traditional programs like elm, pine, mail, or emacs allow you to do this, but I don't think that the fancy GUI ones like Eudora or Outlook allow it (Although I haven't looked at Eudora Pro.) See the documentation that comes with your e-mail program

Here's how to use the feature, for those of you willing and able to diddle with your e-mail headers The writer may add a X-Trojancow-* headers to the e-mail sent to the Trojancow service In the generated PDF, the 'X-Trojancow-' part is removed and the resulting headers become part of the PDF Any existing headers with conflicting names are replaced To get back to our Cc. example, add the extra header

```
X-Trojancow-Cc: president@whitehouse.gov
```

in your mail to the Trojancow service This produces a PDF that shows the 'email header'

```
Cc: president@whitehouse.gov
```

along with the rest of the headers

By default, you'll get a

```
To: 1201@loc.gov (Office of the General Counsel, Copyright
    Office, Library of Congress)
```

in the PDF instead of the To: [trojancowservice] of the e-mail sent to the server This address this is where your comments should be mailed

3) When you get a satisfactory e-mail back, send it on to the Copyright Office at

```
To: '1201@loc.gov (Office of the General Counsel, Copyright
     Office, Library of Congress)'
```

The available Trojancow e-mail addresses are

Whoops, we're moving our systems around and have broken the trojancow e-mail service You can write to me, kop@meme.com, to ask about the service

(Please don't mail to these unless you have a comment for the Copyright Office Thanks.)

- trojancow_a@meme.com
- trojancow_b@meme.com

Why hasn't The Meme Factory set up a Trojancow e-mail service?

We now have, but this is why we hadn't previously

(This gives the trojancow program permissions to be run by sendmail.)

```
ln -s /usr/local/bin/trojancow /etc/smrsh/
```

Add one of these these aliases to enable the program

```
trojancow_A      : "| /etc/smrsh/trojancow /usr/share/trojancow/letter_A.tex"
trojancow_B      : "| /etc/smrsh/trojancow /usr/share/trojancow/letter_B.tex"
```

And then run

```
newaliases
```

to make the aliases active

Try sending trojancow_A@yourdomain.com an e-mail and see if it works!

When you get it working, please e-mail whoever's maintaining the master list of trojancow servers

If you have troubles, you might check this, although I may have all the paths hardcoded by now

Be sure that /usr/local/bin is in $PATH If not, edit /usr/local/bin/trojancow to explicitly reference /usr/local/bin/trojancow.pl

Security considerations

There shouldn't be any No backticking is done and no user submitted material is ever evaluated Anyhow, that's what I think Youse pays no money and youse takes yer chances

Potential bugs

I can't get perl to exec metasend when long e-mail headers are folded, long subjects for example And it looks like metasend doesn't fold either This could be a problem, depending on the mail transport agents on either end

Thank you for your participation in the Trojancow Project
(Have a cow, man!)

Regards,

Karl O. Pinc kop@meme.com
President, The Meme Factory, Inc.

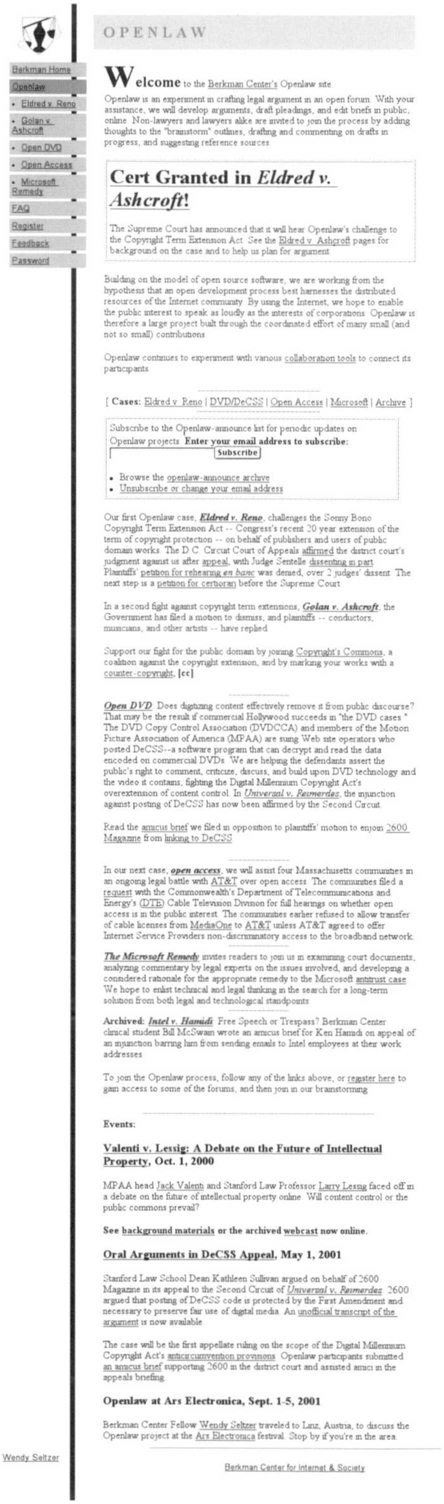

OPENLAW

Berkman Home
Openlaw
- Eldred v. Reno
- Golan v. Ashcroft
- Open DVD
- Open Access
- Microsoft Remedy

FAQ
Register
Feedback
Password

Welcome to the Berkman Center's Openlaw site

Openlaw is an experiment in crafting legal argument in an open forum With your assistance, we will develop arguments, draft pleadings, and edit briefs in public, online Non-lawyers and lawyers alike are invited to join the process by adding thoughts to the "brainstorm" outlines, drafting and commenting on drafts in progress, and suggesting reference sources

Cert Granted in *Eldred v. Ashcroft*!

The Supreme Court has announced that it will hear Openlaw's challenge to the Copyright Term Extension Act See the Eldred v. Ashcroft pages for background on the case and to help us plan for argument

Building on the model of open source software, we are working from the hypothesis that an open development process best harnesses the distributed resources of the Internet community By using the Internet, we hope to enable the public interest to speak as loudly as the interests of corporations Openlaw is therefore a large project built through the coordinated effort of many small (and not so small) contributions

Openlaw continues to experiment with various collaboration tools to connect its participants

[**Cases:** Eldred v. Reno | DVD/DeCSS | Open Access | Microsoft | Archive]

Subscribe to the Openlaw-announce list for periodic updates on Openlaw projects **Enter your email address to subscribe:**
Subscribe

- Browse the openlaw-announce archive
- Unsubscribe or change your email address

Our first Openlaw case, ***Eldred v. Reno***, challenges the Sonny Bono Copyright Term Extension Act -- Congress's recent 20 year extension of the term of copyright protection -- on behalf of publishers and users of public domain works The D.C. Circuit Court of Appeals affirmed the district court's judgment against us after appeal, with Judge Sentelle dissenting in part Plaintiffs' petition for rehearing *en banc* was denied, over 2 judges' dissent The next step is a petition for certiorari before the Supreme Court

In a second fight against copyright term extensions, ***Golan v. Ashcroft***, the Government has filed a motion to dismiss, and plaintiffs -- conductors, musicians, and other artists -- have replied

Support our fight for the public domain by joining Copyright's Commons, a coalition against the copyright extension, and by marking your works with a counter-copyright, **[cc]**

Open DVD Does digitizing content effectively remove it from public discourse? That may be the result if commercial Hollywood succeeds in "the DVD cases." The DVD Copy Control Association (DVDCCA) and members of the Motion Picture Association of America (MPAA) are suing Web site operators who posted DeCSS--a software program that can decrypt and read the data encoded on commercial DVDs We are helping the defendants assert the public's right to comment, criticize, discuss, and build upon DVD technology and the video it contains, fighting the Digital Millennium Copyright Act's overextension of content control In *Universal v. Reimerdes*, the injunction against posting of DeCSS has now been affirmed by the Second Circuit

Read the amicus brief we filed in opposition to plaintiffs' motion to enjoin 2600 Magazine from linking to DeCSS

In our next case, ***open access***, we will assist four Massachusetts communities in an ongoing legal battle with AT&T over open access The communities filed a request with the Commonwealth's Department of Telecommunications and Energy's (DTE) Cable Television Division for full hearings on whether open access is in the public interest The communities earlier refused to allow transfer of cable licenses from MediaOne to AT&T unless AT&T agreed to offer Internet Service Providers non-discriminatory access to the broadband network

The Microsoft Remedy invites readers to join us in examining court documents, analyzing commentary by legal experts on the issues involved, and developing a considered rationale for the appropriate remedy to the Microsoft antitrust case We hope to enlist technical and legal thinking in the search for a long-term solution from both legal and technological standpoints

Archived: *Intel v. Hamidi* Free Speech or Trespass? Berkman Center clinical student Bill McSwain wrote an amicus brief for Ken Hamidi on appeal of an injunction barring him from sending emails to Intel employees at their work addresses

To join the Openlaw process, follow any of the links above, or register here to gain access to some of the forums, and then join in our brainstorming

Events:

Valenti v. Lessig: A Debate on the Future of Intellectual Property, Oct. 1, 2000

MPAA head Jack Valenti and Stanford Law Professor Larry Lessig faced off in a debate on the future of intellectual property online Will content control or the public commons prevail?

See background materials or the archived webcast now online.

Oral Arguments in DeCSS Appeal, May 1, 2001

Stanford Law School Dean Kathleen Sullivan argued on behalf of 2600 Magazine in its appeal to the Second Circuit of *Universal v. Reimerdes*. 2600 argued that posting of DeCSS code is protected by the First Amendment and necessary to preserve fair use of digital media An unofficial transcript of the argument is now available

The case will be the first appellate ruling on the scope of the Digital Millennium Copyright Act's anticircumvention provisions Openlaw participants submitted an amicus brief supporting 2600 in the district court and assisted amici in the appeals briefing

Openlaw at Ars Electronica, Sept. 1-5, 2001

Berkman Center Fellow Wendy Seltzer traveled to Linz, Austria, to discuss the Openlaw project at the Ars Electronica festival Stop by if you're in the area

Wendy Seltzer

Berkman Center for Internet & Society

Windows operating system) or unintended (as in AOL Instant Messenger's potential for trading pirated music). Unlike software companies with implicit agendas, however, political designers wear their politics on their sleeves. Most political designers espouse an open society, and they view their work as an antidote to corporate or governmental attempts to close it. What distinguishes individual political designers is less their ends than their means – less the parties they belong to than the protocols they wield.[6]

The digital weaponry used by political designers ranges from databases to peer-to-peer networks to open code or open-content repositories. The computer scientist Patrick Ball builds databases to track tortured dissidents in Sri Lanka and Guatamala. In Ball's hands, Perl scripts and **JOIN statement**s may be able to accomplish what the grenades and assault rifles of indigenous guerrillas never could: bring the plight of an oppressed people to the attention of the World Court. Antoni Muntada's *File Room* is the online extension of a roomful of metal file cabinets containing paper records of censorship cases. Although it has been included in exhibitions of online art, *File Room* fits more easily alongside Ball's work as an instance of political design. Comparable parallels exist for other protocols. The Guerrilla Girls' letter repository *BroadBand* recalls Wendy Seltzer's *OpenLaw* and *Chilling Effects* Web sites of the same year, even though the former came from artists and the latter from a legal activist. **Peer-to-peer application**s such as the music-trading service *Napster* have been repurposed by Christian Ryan and others for new, albeit parallel uses.

Even the original *Napster* qualifies as a good example of this speculative species of political design. Intentionally or not, *Napster* created the expectation that music (and, by extension, other manifestations of digital culture) should be free. In a scant six months, a little program coded by a handful of teenagers gave an entire generation a taste of open access to music. Now that this expectation exists, it will be very difficult to take away. Even as Napster (or its clones) are co-opted by corporations, those companies run the risk of alienating their consumer base if they fail to fulfill the same expectations as the original software. Indeed, 70 per cent of Americans surveyed by Jupiter Media Metrix in 2002 said they couldn't see paying for *any* kind of online content. It is inconceivable to imagine so many minds swayed by street protests or *New York Times* editorials.

All of these are excellent examples of why the World Wide Web was created in the first place: to empower a broader community of people through the sharing of information. In that sense, *BroadBand* is indeed the logical extension of the posters that the Guerrilla Girls used to paste in the streets of SoHo in Manhattan; there's no reason for modern-day Levelers to be content with seventeenth-century technologies for circulating information outside established institutions. It does not necessarily follow, however, that these instances of political design are art.

Executable Art
At issue is not whether art can tackle political subjects but how it tackles them. The Barbie voice-box switch, the *Simcopter* hack, the Biennial redirect, and even the 'mutual funds' on ®™ark's Web site could all be considered executable culture, since they consist of instructions to be carried out by people or machines. At its best, executable art combines the social reach of political design with the perverse playfulness of hacking. Like political designers, hacktivist artists often piggyback their messages onto the global telecommunication system, with the result that their reach is as broad as their subject. It's easy to underestimate what an innovation this is for political art;

Napster logo.

Opposite: The *Trojan Cow Project* and *OpenLaw*.

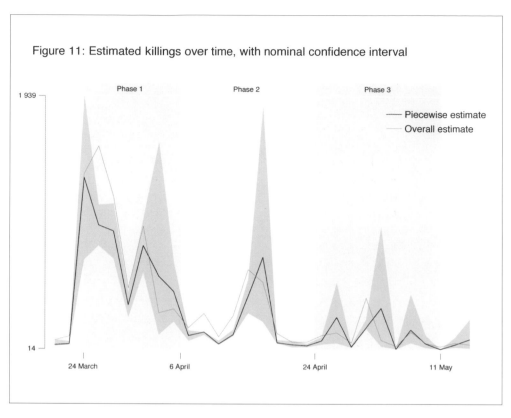

Figure 11: Estimated killings over time, with nominal confidence interval

Phase 1   Phase 2   Phase 3

1 939

—— Piecewise estimate
—— Overall estimate

14

24 March   6 April   24 April   11 May

Right: Patrick Ball's graphic evidence of Serbian atrocities.

it's as though Picasso had stenciled *Guernica* onto the bombs loaded by *Luftwaffe* pilots.

It's tempting to ascribe the awesome power of Patrick Ball's testimony and *Napster*'s reach to executable art – tempting but misguided. Simply put, it is counterproductive to give artists this kind of power. A political designer with bad politics can wreak havoc on the world. But artists must be free to explore unconventional, untested, even dangerous values with impunity. This is true for pre-digital political art as well. No-one minded when Hitler acted out his frustrations in the arena of oil painting, but when he invaded Poland he subjected others involuntarily to his speculative fantasies. Leni Riefenstahl's film *The Triumph of the Will* was a masterpiece of theater, but it was also a political weapon glorifying the Third Reich. In recent times, the most egregious example of confusing art and politics was the scandal provoked by the alleged reaction of the German avant-garde composer Karlheinz Stockhausen to al Qaeda's attack on the World Trade Center: 'That characters can bring about in one act what we in music cannot dream of, that people practice madly for 10 years, completely, fanatically, for a concert and then die. That is the greatest work of art for the whole cosmos. I could not do that. Against that, we, composers, are nothing.'[7] Whether or not the quote was misattributed, the horrific inappropriateness of evaluating the act of murdering three thousand people as art brought the difference between direct political intervention and artistic expression into stark relief.

Which is ultimately why Touretzky's *Gallery of CSS Descramblers*, together with the artifacts it contains, is art, while Ball's testimony is not. The executable weaponry wielded by Ball was based on interviews, government records, and testimony by

Albanian border guards. His statistics proved that killings and refugee flows in Kosovo were independent of military activity by NATO or the Kosovo Liberation Army but tied directly to Serb attacks. This work helped indict Slobodan Milošević—a direct political effect. Like Ball's databases, Touretzky's work has influenced the course of legal history. Where Touretzky departs from Ball is that his success lay not in indicting a defendant but in clearing one. Touretzky's gallery wasn't meant to prove a case but to challenge a way of thinking.

Art arms its audience with neither evidence nor explosives but with a protected arena in which to challenge the status quo without confronting it head-on. Because art sidesteps the direct political power exercised by Patrick Ball or Mohammed Atta, it encourages its audience to join in the play, ultimately freeing them of political and cultural dichotomies that pit right against wrong, left against right. Like the children in a fenced-in playground who roam further toward the edges than in a fenceless one, the constraints of art liberate the spirit of play. And play is the creative energy with which humans make and remake the world.

Below: net.flag.

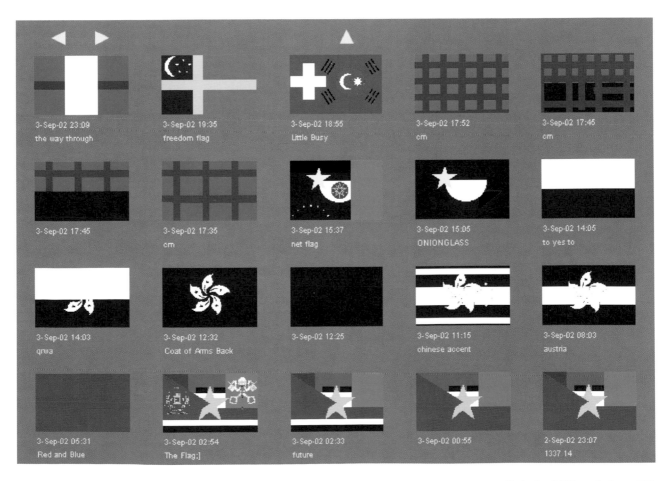

EDGE STUDIES

Perverse Geography

Domain names like Microsoft.com or Hell.com are the human-readable addresses of the Internet. Some companies spend exorbitant sums purchasing such names or defending their trademarks over them – for in an attention economy like the Web, the right domain name can mean the difference between a dot-com's success and its failure. This commercialization of ordinary words has not gone unnoticed by hacktivist artists, whose responses have ranged from consciousness-raising to paradigm-shifting.

is on a mission But don't asking him to define what it is His CV bored teen and home computer hacker in 80s Stevenage   and
in Bristol   organiser and
digital culture activist or his phrase artivist in London is replete with the necessary qualifications for a 90s sub-culture citizen but what s interesting about is that if you want to describe to someone what he actually does there s simply no handy category that you can slot him into

If you had to classify him you could do worse than call him an organiser of art events Some of these take place online some of them in RL most of them have something to do with technology though not all One early event that hit the headlines was his 1994   when distributed the numbers of the telephone kiosks around Kings Cross station using the Internet and asked whoever found them to choose one call it at a specific time and chat with whoever picked up the phone The incident was a resounding success at 6 pm one August afternoon the are was transformed into a massive techno crowd dancing to the sound of ringing telephones according to

More recently in collaboration with his   an ex-Greenham activist and bus driver he set up a
which mimicked the real one and asked employees to send in their pets for vivisection and experimentation Glaxo were alarmed enough to issue a public statement and have the offending site removed

But why has this one-time graffiti artist and stained glass window apprentice embraced the net When I was on the street I was always looking for new tools and I was always looking to do battle with the front-end though I hesitate to say the front end of what exactly For me the real excitement of the net was that it exposed many different types of people Also the new medium gave someone like   who had little or no resources - the chance to engage head on with large-scale organisations I've always attacked big things When I was a kid I always used to pick fights with people that were bigger than me I suppose I've carried on doing

This year is the one in which   has really begun to get recognition by the burgeoning European digital arts scene that conference hops its way around the continent from one year's end to the next This is the year he says that net art is going to be absorbed into electronic art in a big way But although his travel schedule is beginning to look completely insane   has been doing a bit of conference organising of his own Last year pissed off with gatherings like Digital Dreams which cost thousands of pounds to stage and gave no one access to any of the big names he put together the Netmare conference (TK) were there was no distinction between audience and speaker at the moment he is organising a series of informal lecture meetings called   at the   in Winchester Wharf Already though   sees the possibilities for staging really challenging events on the net decreasing All those things which the Net initially exposed are now being covered over The real form of control is not police confiscating servers but financial dictates The potential for different possibilities is being diminished by money For example a lot of people who used to do challenging work are business people in their own right now and this is effectively a form of self-censorship Also and this is only a suspicion but a strong one search engines are beginning to deliberately ignore certain kinds of content The sites of   to take one case were refused by Yahoo because they were meaningless by Yahoos standards

With this in mind   is dreaming up ways to sabotage other technologies like   and   But he is not going to go around smashing cameras that's not his style by smashing cameras you only reinforced the system You need to get people to begin to doubt the system That's what I do - I   The idea is to introduce bad data into such systems using techniques of illusion so that they cease to become trustworthy - optical illusions for cameras inconsistencies and false identities for the databases Will it work Judge for yourself   is demonstrating his new techniques in Lancaster in June for details see his website

James Flint

ATTENTION ECONOMY

Heath Bunting, _readme.html (Own, Be Owned, or Remain Invisible)

Right: And.com and The.com.

One of the earliest instigators of hacktivist art, British 'net.artist' Heath Bunting drew attention to the politics of domain names well before the trademark disputes over 'etoy' and 'Leonardo'. In characteristic low-tech style, he transformed a paragraph of autobiographical description into a demonstration of the power of names just by making every word on the page clickable. In the opening sentence 'Heath Bunting is on a mission,' he linked 'is' to 'is.com', 'on' to 'on.com', and so on. The work's subtitle — *Own, Be Owned, or Remain Invisible* — speaks volumes about the power of names in an attention economy. To click on this deadpan concatenation of urls is to realize immediately the extent to which words are increasingly owned by corporations. As executable technologies go, Bunting's weaponry is Stone-Age — the ordinary hyperlink — but he gets a lot of bang for his buck.

ICANN.SUCKS

Paul Garrin, *Name.space*

A former video editor for Nam June Paik and an installation artist in his own right, Paul Garrin has spent the better part of a decade developing a quasi-commercial alternative to the conventional Domain Name System established by the founders of the Internet. Like the official naming service administered by the Internet Corporation for Assigned Names and Numbers (ICANN), Garrin's *Name.space* project maps names to individual Web servers; the trick is that his system is a completely different naming convention. Change the proxy setting in your browser preferences to a machine on Garrin's network, and the world changes too: suddenly, MyTerribleDomainName.com becomes MyTerrificDomainName.artist or .activism (or even .sucks, as in AOL.sucks). The effect is as though you could put on a pair of glasses that reconfigured the streets of your town according to a new address system, one as navigable (if not more so) than the existing one.

Garrin's proposed shuffling of Web addresses has sparked volumes of online debate over its political merit. Ted Byfield, moderator of the influential online forum nettime, has expressed concern that as a business model *Name.space* won't be immune from the same political pressures as ICANN. To the extent that it survives as a business by kowtowing to trademark law and closed-door decision-making, *Name.space* will not be a work of art. Nevertheless, in its present embryonic form, it provides an excellent example of how to piggyback onto the existing system so as to open people's minds to new possibilities.

Right: Name.space.
Opposite: _readme.html.

Perverse Information

Information is power, as the examples of *OpenLaw* and *BroadBand* demonstrate, and the Web allows hacktivists to reveal information which established interests would rather keep hidden. Numerous examples of political design exploit this aspect of the Internet, including *Adbusters*, *Autonomedia, Disinformation, Indy Media Center, Interactivist Info Exchange, Mediachannel, Subvertise,* and *Surveillance Camera Players.* Alongside these important projects are information services that are just too quirky to be taken seriously – even if they masquerade as bona-fide corporations. Some of them have an obvious use. *iSee,* a project of the Institute for Applied Autonomy and the New York Surveillance Camera Project, offers maps of Manhattan which highlight routes with the fewest surveillance cameras. Another mapping project targeted at New Yorkers, *WhereDoYouWantToGoToday.com,* charts the location of publicly accessible toilets in midtown. (You can be sure that Microsoft's attorneys were none too happy about the pun on the Microsoft Network's advertising slogan.)

Right: Media Channel and Interactivist Info Exchange.

BASEMENT BIOTECH

Heath Bunting and Natalie Jeremijenko,
Biotech Hobbyist

In some cases, a site's nuts-and-bolts details are only a springboard to more profound questions about social structures its visitors may take for granted. Heath Bunting and Natalie Jeremijenko's *BioTech Hobbyist* site instructs untrained visitors on how to grow spare skin and other tissue cultures in their basements. While the site mimics the 'do-it-yourself' spirit of an 'Amateur Scientist' column in *Scientific American* magazine, the underlying effect is to demystify biotechnology and perhaps make its ethical dilemmas more concrete in the minds of lay citizens. (They are already concrete in the lives of biotech artists such as Steve Kurtz, whose block was cordoned off in 2004 when the FBI discovered Petri dishes in his studio.) *Biotech Hobbyist* reminds us that the reaches of this technological revolution span not just copper wires and ethernet cables but neurons, capillaries, and the criminal-justice system.

Right: *Subvertise.*

OUTING THE OLD BOYS NETWORK
Josh On, *They Rule*

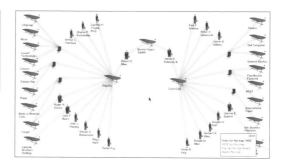

One of the best examples of an artwork that uses Internet technology to make the hidden structures of social power visible, *They Rule* is an expandable diagram showing the board members of the most influential American corporations. Unlike organizational charts and annual reports, which only indicate the members of any given board, *They Rule* traces the hidden connections among corporate power brokers. Using this interface, for example, it's possible to discover that members of the boards of the so-called competitors Coke and Pepsi actually sit together on the board of a third corporation, Bristol-Myers Squibb. *They Rule* occupies the intersection of political design and hacktivism. Although it derives from publicly available information rather than private testimony, the database underlying the scripted interface exploits the same principle as Patrick Ball's: once you get enough information in one place, you can draw connections you might not otherwise apprehend. *They Rule* also demonstrates how an artist — someone experienced in making the obscure visible — can render information in a legible, and hence instructive, form. When we can see the agendas shared by managers of education investment funds, insurance companies, pharmaceuticals, and big oil, we can finally visualize the hidden economic interests that determine local and national policy decisions. Josh On's project reveals the influence of CEO's in a supposed representative democracy: in the US, They Rule.

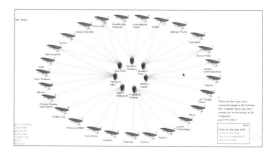

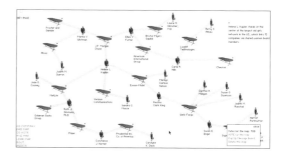

These pages: Four of *They Rule*'s maps.

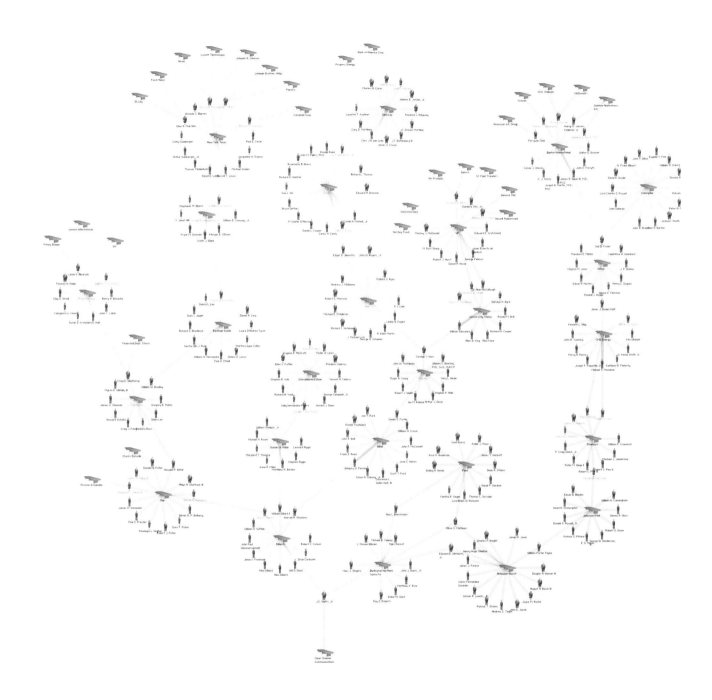

Perverse Politics

The Internet has yet to deliver on the electronic republic pundits promised in the 1990s. The 'Athenian Age' of enhanced democracy once predicted by Al Gore was much shorter-lived than the original, if indeed it drew breath at all, and with the election fiascos and terrorist attacks following the turn of the century, the Bush administration easily drowned out pleas for online town meetings and voting with clamor for roving wiretaps and encryption controls. All of which just turned the clock back a decade, to a time when the task of exploring new forms of electronic democracy fell to activists and artists. The creators of the following sites may wield fancier tools now than were available ten years ago, but their spirit echoes the days when the Internet was democracy's new frontier.

[157]   [Migration to NYC

NON-GEOGRAPHIC NATION

Ingo Gunther, *Refugee Republic*

The Web realization of this project by media artist Ingo Gunther proposes to create a non-geographic nation composed of the world's refugees, arguing that they represent an untapped resource comprising a 'comprehensive spectrum of cultures, civilizations, and religions'. Compared to non geographic nationalities like *Nova Roma*,[8] an online collective of self-described 'direct spiritual successors to the Roman Empire', Refugee Republic is a sobering reality check – for it is a homeland made up of all the people who currently don't have

Below and opposite: Refugee Republic.

one. Aside from the downloadable passport cover, the site is less a practical experiment in deterritorialized government than a conceptual gesture aimed at raising consciousness about the plight of refugees. Gunther's vision of a demographic outside conventional political boundaries echoes John Moore's description of the political potential of the globally connected populist movement, the 'Second Superpower'. This emerging power is not a nation but a 'new form of international player, constituted by the 'will of the people' in a global social movement.[9]

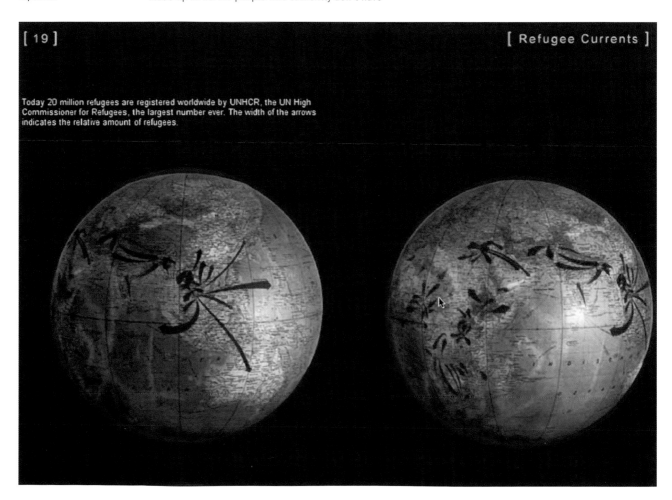

[19]   [Refugee Currents]

Today 20 million refugees are registered worldwide by UNHCR, the UN High Commissioner for Refugees, the largest number ever. The width of the arrows indicates the relative amount of refugees.

A FLAG FOR NO-MANS-LAND
Mark Napier, *net.flag*

What happens to an emblem of solitary statehood when that state's internal affairs become entangled with geopolitical commitments? How can the notion of a flag reflect global politics rather than pining for a nostalgic nationalism that no longer exists? Mark Napier's *net.flag* is one answer to these questions.

net.flag is an emblem for the Internet as a new territory, more fluid and flexible than the political boundaries of nations, yet composed of fiercely or playfully loyal people from various geographical regions and ideologies. Its design changes constantly, manipulated by users who make selections from menus of familiar flag motifs: stars, fields of color, bold patterns, insignia, and stripes. As *net.flag*'s viewers add their contributions to the palimpsest, the cumulative identity of the flag changes as one country's insignia or symbols temporarily overlap those of another. Since each element of a flag generally represents a symbol chosen by that country's founders, *net.flag* also includes a 'browse history' feature that permits access to the evolution of its symbolic value — that is, the percentage of signs indicating 'peace', 'valor', or 'blood' present in the flag at a given moment.

As one proof of the passion netizens feel about their communities, this symbolism has become the playground for some mock — and some rather serious — international competition. One viewer doggedly added a glut of white crosses from the Greek flag, ensuring that the Greek cross would topple the American stars and stripes as the most popular symbol on the chart.[10] *net.flag* reminds us that Greek nationalism is not necessarily confined to 'Greek soil' – but, conversely, that communities may also be driven by principles rather than geography, as in flags consisting only of symbols for valor or peace. National boundaries are arbitrary and do not always represent our true communities of interest.

net.flag.

DO-IT-YOURSELF SPYWARE
RSG (Radical Software Group), *Carnivore*

Carnivore client by area3.

Based on the FBI wiretapping software of the same name, *Carnivore* uses 'packet-sniffing' — a technology that eavesdrops on telecommunications at the most basic level — to create vivid depictions of raw data. *Carnivore* consists of two parts. First, the actual box ties into a local area network (the community of users in an office, say) and serves the resulting data stream via the Internet; second, users can download and run a variety of artist-made interfaces to visualize those data streams. So far, *Carnivore* has only been let loose in fenced-in pastures — at participating galleries, for example — but with a new downloadable version called *Carnivore PE*, RSG's project of demystifying FBI technology can now reach the masses. To date, a handful of founder Alex Galloway's fellow artists, among them Joshua Davis, Entropy8Zuper!, and Scott Snibbe, have contributed to these *Carnivore* 'clients'; their interfaces interpret network data variously as billowing circles, expanding supernovae, and even a **VRML** update on the Monopoly board game.

EXECUTABLE LITERATURE

Metamute Meets ECHELON –

A Literary Competition

Kilderkin

Her eyes **eavesdropping** on him in the garden, his chosen **zone** of play, she sloughed off her skins of fret that she was just one of his **watchers**. Whatever **mindwar** this **utopia** bred in her, he was **safe**, lent this **freedom** to wander from the **basement** below her into the sunken **shelter** of the **iris** beds, the petal **rain** of **cornflower** dew-stuck she saw **smuggle** summer sky-blue over his **sneakers** each time he returned. And these **zen** blues must, she nagged, clear his **force** of that **dictionary** of **spookwords** such an **argus** of **psycho** eyes had until now with such **mania** bound him. The garden could be for today the **hope** of a heaven on earth where she would **forecast** with the confidence of a **monarchist** a tomorrow the same.

A boy in his garden, not a **target** for **hitwords** or fetish for burning flesh with any **enigma** or **sweeping package** of diagnoses that were but **viruses** in disguise. She was **debugging** him as he toyed among the daisies, but her **mindwar** spun her like a tossed **dice** in her own house until she could laugh at her own attention deficit disorders, her random access memory.

He was at his **Firewall**. The day blazing. Here he need never say anything. But in his mind these crumbling stones were given a name, his **Firewall**. As it was once on fire. And his task was to gather the ash in his hands and **blow** it to the winds. The finest **dust** in an endless supply. Overhead the clouds harvested his hands, sulphureous, **burned** with his unrelenting **replay**, reaping the hot yellow like there would be no tomorrow. His vision saw the **Mayfly** mutate into the **Firefly** and the poplars wands of **bronze** cast in the heat. Only this time it would work, this new born child dropped into oblivion in the box of this **asylum**. She called him her **Sundevil**, how he would keep her waiting, beyond hope of his turning from the **secure shell** of his **Flame** he must keep alive, even if it was but **dust**...

ECHELON, the worldwide intelligence network run by the US and its English-speaking allies, automatically monitors telephone calls, faxes, and emails by comparing them against a list of suspicious keywords like *mailbomb*, *rebels*, or *Enemy of the State*. To raise awareness of government surveillance, hacktivists previously tried to flood email systems with messages including these keywords, but ECHELON is purportedly too smart to be fooled by lists of words out of context. In response, journalists at *Mute* magazine invited authors to craft works of fiction that employ the maximum number of keywords in a literary narrative. For example, one passage incorporated the trigger words *eavesdropping*, *zone*, *play*, *watchers*, *mindwar*, *utopia*, and *safe*: 'Her eyes eavesdropping on him in the garden, his chosen zone of play ... she was just one of his watchers. Whatever mindwar this utopia bred in her, he was safe.' The winners, archived in the magazine's online publication *Metamute*, may not merit a Pulitzer Prize, but the contest is proof that Tom Clancy doesn't have a lock on spook-inspired literature. More importantly, these projects demonstrate that a monkeywrench as simple as electronic poetry can subvert and expose the most sophisticated forms of technological control.

Above: A story from the 'Metamute Meets ECHELON' contest, with trigger words highlighted.

Perverse Tools

If domain names furnish the addresses of Web sites, search engines like Google are the maps by which they are found – and they are no less a target for subversion by hacktivists with attitude.

CYBER-SQUATTING ON A CORPORATE DOMAIN

etoy, *Digital Hijack*; Heath Bunting, *Realty*

Above: *Digital Hijack.*

Online services provided by corporations are just as vulnerable to being hijacked by hacktivists as protocols developed by governments. In fact, a 'digital hijack' of search engines was one of the first online artworks to gain widespread attention, nabbing a Golden Nica at the Ars Electronica festival in 1996. For this project, the etoy.com artist collective wrote software which analyzed the way search engines rank Web pages — for example, by looking for key words in HTML meta-tags — and then used that information to redirect traffic away from corporate sites. Unsuspecting viewers who clicked on, say, the top-ranked link in an Infoseek query about Porsche were transported to an etoy page informing them that they had just been 'hijacked'. As a mere demonstration of technical prowess, *Digital Hijack* would have been hacking rather than hacktivism. But at a time when consumer watchdog groups were beginning to accuse search engines of selling rankings to the highest bidder,[11] it exposed a hidden corruptibility in a supposedly objective research tool.

In his perversion of search engines, Heath Bunting dealt an even more underhanded blow to the growing commercialization of the Web in the late 1990s. Like etoy, he created Web pages that 'hijacked' searches on mainstays of consumer culture, but his pages contained simple scripted redirects which bounced the visitor to a competitor's Web site. When a click on a high-ranking url in a search on 'Nike' brings visitors to the Adidas Web site, the millions spent by corporate giants on branding and advertising are undercut by a few lines of computer code written by a single consumer.

Opposite: *Images from Google Adwords Happening.*

Prices of some words

Traffic Estimator *			
Keyword	Clicks / Day	Average Cost-Per-Click	Cost / Day
anal	390.0	$0.83	$319.90
art	800.0	$0.52	$409.67
bin laden	250.0	$0.10	$24.37
britney spears	490.0	$0.30	$144.20
capitalism	30.0	$0.10	$2.74
communism	2.1	$0.16	$0.33
death	92.0	$0.47	$42.66
dream	390.0	$0.17	$63.07
free	5700.0	$1.33	$7,569.23
freedom	5.1	$0.37	$1.88
gay	2200.0	$1.02	$2,239.56
hemorroid	0.5	$0.16	$0.08
language	650.0	$0.37	$237.30
lesbian	740.0	$0.80	$584.62
love	730.0	$1.74	$1,264.72
mankind	8.0	$0.59	$4.70
money	350.0	$0.81	$281.46
net art	0.9	$0.05	$0.05
self	80.0	$0.85	$67.72
sex	7500.0	$0.52	$3,836.79
suicide	18.0	$0.27	$4.72
symptom	23.0	$0.30	$6.83
Overall	**20449.6**	$0.84	$17,106.49

Like most online ventures, the popular search engine Google relies on advertising revenue instead of charging users for its service. Google intended its Adwords campaign to allow companies to position context-specific promotions adjacent to its search results, so that companies like Honda could buy the keyword *car* and place the phrase 'Click here for great deals on Accords' next to Google search results that incorporated that word. The artist Christophe Bruno realized that he could piggyback a 'targeted poetic happening' onto this automated advertising protocol. Having bought the word *dream*, for example, he submitted the following 'advertisement':

mary !!!
I love you
come back
john

Speech is supposed to be free, but Bruno's intervention brought to light the economic value of words as determined by the frequency of search requests. As of April 2002, the word *free* was worth $7,569, the word *sex* was worth $3,837, the word *art* $410, and the phrase 'net art' only $0.05. Bruno paid his money like everyone else — so why did Google's managers terminate his ads once they got wind of them? Like etoy and Bunting, Bruno gave online consumers pause — a reason to reflect rather than simply obey the conditioned impulse to shop. For Google and its advertisers, this detour on the information superhighway threatened to shake their advertisers' faith in e-commerce by undermining the predictable electronic pathways on which it depended.

Words aren't free anymore
bicornuate-bicervical uterus
one-eyed hemi-vagina
www.unbehagen.com

Perverse Property

Many surfers are unaware that every Web page they visit is temporarily downloaded to a directory on their hard drive called the 'cache'. A select few use their cache as a political weapon, a brute-force means to duplicate – and hence render access to – closed culture.

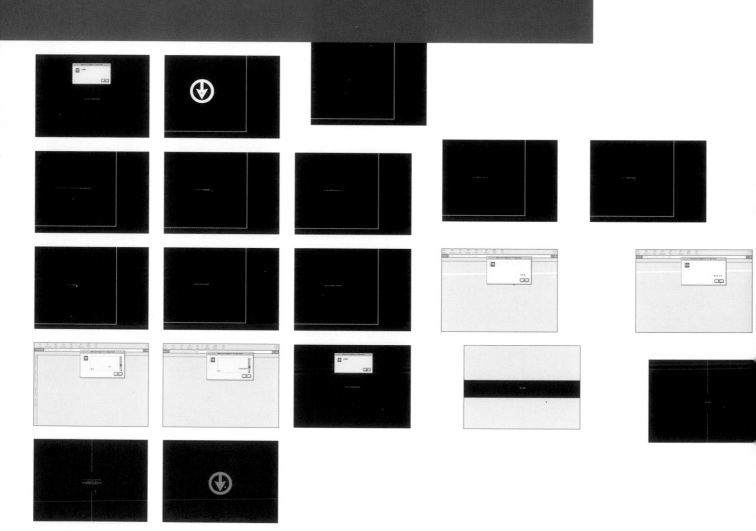

Hell.com.

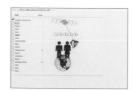

FREEING THE ART MARKET
Vuk Cosic, *Documenta Done*

Catherine David, curator of the 1997 international exhibition Documenta X, invited the Dutch media activists Geert Lovink and Pit Schultz, together with the Swiss Web designer and artist Simon Lamuniere, to create a Web site that would incorporate the many lectures and projects presented on the occasion of the exhibition and its 'Hybrid Workspace' media component. Given

the project's emphasis on encouraging the dissemination of information and perspectives, news of David's plans to close the Web site at exhibition's end and re-issue the material on a CD-ROM to be sold in the trade came as a surprise to many netizens. Before the show closed, Vuk Cosic, a Slovenian artist active in defining the movement that called itself net.art, took matters into his own hands and cloned most of the site onto his own server. He then opened his site to the public — to the consternation of Documenta's organizers.

PUBLICIZING THE PRIVATE WEB
www.0100101110101101.org, *Hell.com*

Below and above: *Documenta Done.*

Caching allows artists not only to re-create projects but also to modify them. With the help of caching, 0100101110101101.org, the elusive programmers of the *Life Sharing* project mentioned earlier, created a perfect example of how the duplicability of digital files, when combined with the Internet's easy access, conspire to defeat any attempt at cultural exclusion. In 1995, an organization began to host online exhibitions of Web-based artworks at the domain Hell.com. Unlike the numerous online exhibitions that preceded it, from ada·web to 'Beyond Interface', Hell.com was a private site. Visitors to its home page were greeted with a series of all-black screens marked only by enigmatic questions in minuscule white text. Even the answers to the questions were off-putting rather than revealing: 'What is Hell.com? Hell.com is a private, parallel Web.' 'How can I get in? You can't.' 'How can I be a guest? You can't.' True to its words, Hell.com was an experiment in replicating online the exclusivity of the offline art world — a world in which success is measured by invitations to private cocktail parties and museum openings. Hell's gatekeepers periodically emailed a

selection of guests passwords for temporary access or invitations to private openings where they could see works on terminals and meet the artists.

But Hell.com made a mistake. It offered access for a predetermined forty-eight-hour period to members of the Rhizome email list. The protagonists of 0100101110101101.org seized the opportunity to download most of the Hell.com site onto their own server, where the gates of Hell were thrown open for all viewers. Hell's art projects were preserved more or less intact, but the answers to the questions on the infernal front page acquired a decidedly more egalitarian tone in the process: 'What is Hell.com? Hell.com is a free parallel web.' 'How can I get in? Access is granted to everybody.' 'How can I be a guest? Please understand: you don't need any fuckin' permission!' In a matter of hours, the artists of 0100101110101101.org had turned private art into public art, from exclusive property into common culture. Given the ease with which digital files can be cloned, technology was on their side.[12] The law, of course, was on Hell.com's side – but, given that only a handful of people knew who the elusive 0100101110101101.org artists were, the cease-and-desist letters to their representatives had little effect.

CREATIVE CLONING

The Yes Men, Plagiarist.org, and Detritus.net, *Reamweaver*

A pun on Macromedia's popular Dreamweaver Web-design software, *Reamweaver* automates the process of caching other sites to create alternative versions. Following in the tradition of ®™ark's misappropriation of domain names like GWBush.com, a group of hacktivists known as The Yes Men nabbed the domain name Gatt.org and posted what appeared to be the World Trade Organization's official site dedicated to the controversial GATT trade legislation. When an unsuspecting association of international lawyers invited a spokesman from Gatt.org to speak at their conference, that spokesman declared that commerce had superceded democracy and voting was obsolete — an extremist agenda but one that was nevertheless an extrapolation of the WTO's own policies. This masquerade was politically executable, in the sense that a simple domain registration created a believable, if illegitimate, pretext for a degree of public attention normally only accorded to government officials.

Reamweaver, meanwhile, is the digital equivalent of The Yes Men's executable performance. As the 'manual' for the application explains: '*Reamweaver* lets you automatically "funhouse-mirror" anyone's website — an ability you can use to obtain speaking opportunities on behalf of your adopted organization.' When an unsuspecting user visits a page on your ersatz organization's site, *Reamweaver* gets the page from the target domain, changes the words as you specify, and displays the altered text together with the original images and layout. Although these 'funhouse-mirror' versions can be ridiculous in the extreme, it's easy to imagine the havoc a *Reamweaver* user could wreak by replacing the word *minority* with *underclass* or *terrorists* with *freedom fighters* to create an alternative reading of an organization's Web site. While ®™ark and its associates generally steer away

from calling themselves artists, when required to defend their actions humor becomes a convenient pretext. Under a 'Legal Risk?' rubric, the *Reamweaver* manual reads:

Well, you may get an angry letter from your adopted organization, but you can always ignore it or, if you like, adopt another organization instead by changing one line in reamweaver.conf [the configuration file that stores information about the site and its authors].

These pages: Ersatz brochures, Web sites, and bumper stickers from The Yes Men.

Perverse Warfare

Hactivist artists who join ranks can wield power normally reserved for well-organized activists. Yet the accountability of executable art is different from the accountability of political designers and other cultural guerrillas, as demonstrated by one of executable art's signature victories: *Toywar*.

CORPORATE TAKEOVER

®™ark, etoy, *et al.*, *Toywar*

Unlike political activists, artists march to the beats of their own drummers. But for three months during the turn of the millennium, a virtual army of artists marched together with a common mission: to repel a corporation's attempt to commandeer an artistic Web domain.

In November 1999, the online toy retailer eToys.com managed to shut down the Web site of the venerable artist collective etoy.com — the same artists responsible for misusing search engines to create *Digital Hijack*. Although the artists had registered their domain name two years before the trinket salesmen registered theirs, the corporation happened to register their trademark first. Ignoring the fact that US trademarks don't have automatic jurisdiction over an international territory like cyberspace, a California judge granted a temporary injunction blocking public access to the artists' domain. The timing of this action, a few months before the Christmas that many predicted would be the first real moneymaking season for e-commerce, seemed to confirm that corporate giants would soon overpower grass-roots collectives by hijacking the democratic protocols that had spurred the early Internet.

Domain names are one of those protocols. Unlike physical addresses like Fifth Avenue or Broadway, Web addresses like etoy.com or eToys.com are available on a first-come, first-served basis and are not priced competitively; the first time they were registered, CocaCola.com and MyWebSiteSucks.com both cost about $20 a year. Once you register a domain name, it's yours to keep as long as you shell out the annual fee. Because of this, the toy seller's attempt to muscle in on territory the artists had already claimed was particularly offensive to many netizens. eToys Inc. may have paid out of their own coffers to trumpet their brand name on subways and TV spots, but US taxpayers underwrote the technology that makes eToys.com go somewhere when you type it into your browser.

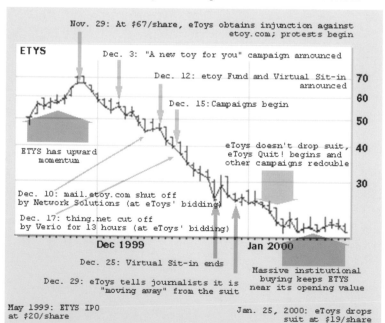

Nov. 29: At $67/share, eToys obtains injunction against etoy.com; protests begin

ETYS

Dec. 3: "A new toy for you" campaign announced

Dec. 12: etoy Fund and Virtual Sit-in announced

Dec. 15: Campaigns begin

ETYS has upward momentum

eToys doesn't drop suit, eToys Quit! begins and other campaigns redouble

Dec. 10: mail.etoy.com shut off by Network Solutions (at eToys' bidding)

Dec. 17: thing.net cut off by Verio for 13 hours (at eToys' bidding)

Dec 1999   Jan 2000

70
60
50
40
30

Dec. 25: Virtual Sit-in ends

Dec. 29: eToys tells journalists it is "moving away" from the suit

Massive institutional buying keeps ETYS near its opening value

May 1999: ETYS IPO at $20/share

Jan. 25, 2000: eToys drops suit at $19/share

Responding to a call for a campaign against the toy giant orchestrated by ®™ark and etoy 'agent' Reinhold Grether, online artists and hackers emailed journalists, posted exhortations to disinvest on electronic bulletin boards frequented by eToys stockholders, and used virtual sit-in software to tie up the toy purveyor's server with random subscribers and counterfeit shopping carts. None of these 'etoy soldiers' were compensated for their services, though ®™ark put up $200 for any hacker who could post a protest directly on eToys' own home page (no-one did). But the spurious visitors automatically generated by the Floodnet-style software cast into doubt eToys' hit counts, which happen to be one of the benchmarks by which investors value their stock. That stock tumbled 70 per cent off its original value over the course of ®™ark's 'toywar', and eToys.com formally withdrew their suit in January 2000.

Despite this seemingly 'all out' attack, *Toywar's* generals knew that constraints are essential to play. According to Reinhold Grether, etoy's soldiers considered but rejected a 'killer bullet' that would have shut down the eToys.com Web site altogether. As one participant wrote, 'I'm not ready to trade the distributed, swarming community of activists model for a single tactical nuke.'[13] etoy artists understood the difference between executing code and executing people. As etoy AGENT.ZAI put it:

> ...what we knew was that if we just set up a nice (&boring) list where people can put their names and express their bad feelings about capitalism etc. a lot of people will probably do it ... but it

will not help at all ... instead we decided to involve people into a very special process. not in the traditional way but in an entertaining story. it worked because people loved to be part of the 'war' that was not really terrible (no killings ... the only thing that could be lost was a domain name and lots of money). it was not by chance that we called it 'TOY-war' ... we tried to play with the irony of the situation ... but hit many peoples deep feelings.[14]

To say that art must play within constraints doesn't cripple its long-term political power. On the contrary, art's peculiar position grants it a twisted kind of protection. When asked if the weapons of *Toywar* weren't potentially dangerous in the wrong hands, ®™ark's 'Ray Thomas' replied that Floodnet software inherently favored the little guy over the bigwig. In response to the question 'What if someone used it against your own Web site?' he replied, 'Then it would just give us more publicity.'[15] ®™ark, like all hacktivist art, is provocative rather than prescriptive. Hacktivist art's power comes less from answers than from questions, less from effectiveness than from play. And in this fundamental way, though it may share the immune system's goals and functions in the ways that it executes code to protect the body, it differs from the immune system.

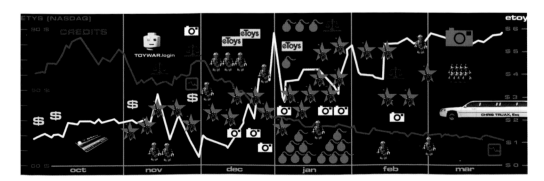

Toywar timelines.

REVIEWING
YOUR
COMMU
NITY

The functions of art discussed in previous chapters – perversity, arrest, revelation, and, to some extent, even executability – are primarily functions of an artwork itself, requiring only the presence of a single creator and a single viewer to spark the collective unconscious. Yet no matter how successfully a work may function as art for this pair of agents, it can never perform a meaningful role in society unless its recognition expands beyond this private circle. While the function examined in this chapter, recognition, is not a characteristic of a work but of the context in which it is embedded, it is nevertheless essential to art. This is obvious for the executable works of political design examined in the preceding chapter, but it is also true for **hypernovel**s and game environments that aim to stretch imaginations one viewer at a time. For art to wield power, it must function within a community that recognizes it.

A lymphocyte whose antibody matches a foreign agent sounds a chemical alarm to the immune system. That signal must travel throughout the entire bloodstream, triggering a cascading set of responses from summoning macrophages to attracting other lymphocytes, in order for the invader to be effectively neutralized and incorporated. That mechanism of recognition has a parallel in the social body. When an artwork latches onto a technological meme, that work's influence can be measured by how thoroughly it alerts mechanisms of cultural and social recognition – and, as we'll see in this chapter, the Internet can be just as effective as the bloodstream for spreading such influence.

Nevertheless, in a biological body, the optimum consequence of recognition is assimilation: not only is the virus disabled, but millions of antibodies bearing templates of its shape – effectively neutralized copies of the original – float around the bloodstream as ammunition against future infection. While art aims for recognition, however, it loses its power if it is similarly assimilated. Unlike its immunological equivalent, the best art never fails to ignite a fever of some kind; the recognition it seeks from the social body is not assimilation but re-cognition: the re-examination of tacit beliefs or conventional perceptions. To remain effective, art must balance on this razor's edge, inviting attention, encouraging new understanding, but resisting full co-optation, lest it lest its 'neutralized copies' turn into cultural clichés or diluted banalities. **< >**

A DIAGRAM OF DIALOGUE
Warren Sack, *Conversation Map*

Conversation Map is a browser for Usenet newsgroups and email lists that visualizes large-scale conversations as networks of branching lines. Its graphical interface allows users to 'see' both social and semantic relationships that have emerged during the discussion. A user can tell the substance from the spam without having to peruse the actual threads of a newsgroup; for example, a message on sci.environment promoting 'aquafuel' leaves a lone dot on the screen, while a message on consumer demand for electric cars forks into a tangle of replies and counter-replies. Separate panels of the interface offer diagrams of related social and semantic networks; these indicate that the electric-car conversation included 'malcolm.scott' and 'wmbjk' talking about themes of 'energy' and 'get-up-and-go'.

Sack didn't create a community; he revealed one. He is not a founder of Usenet or even a participant in the discussions charted by his software; indeed, he intends *Conversation Map* to be applied to any form of 'large scale conversation', whether the participants are discussing Balkan politics or Britney Spears. His map is a recognition network: an application that reveals focused communities of affinity and meaning.

For its part, *Conversation Map* has itself become recognized in corners of both the artistic and scientific worlds, though each community gave it la different reception. While a computer scientist studying at MIT's Media Lab, Sack initially publicized his work in artificial-intelligence journals and at anthropology conferences. 'I wasn't really thinking about it as an art project,' he says.

I went away for three years and did this in the closet, and wasn't sure who'd be interested in it at all. When I started showing it, it turned out there were a lot of people in the art world who understood what I was doing. I think of it as an art project because some of my best collaborators and people I'm in dialogue with are in the art world. And they [the artists] were the first.[1]

Does the fact that Sack has been recognized in a few art contexts — the work has been featured in *Cabinet*, a magazine of art and culture, and in the Walker Art Center's virtual 'Gallery 9' — make him an artist, even though the community his work represents has nothing to do with art? Or was it recognized because it was inherently revelatory and arresting? If there is still debate about whether *Conversation Map* is at the center of digital-art practice, there is no doubt that it is expanding the edges. A look at a recognition network built by an artist for artists will help to elucidate this question.

Left: *Conversation Map.*

FULL DISCLOSURE AND ARTISTIC PROCESS

Olia Lialina *et al.*, *Last Real Net Art Museum*

If artworks are born in communities, what would the 'extended family' of such work look like? In her *Last Real Net Art Museum*, the veteran Internet artist Olia Lialina challenges her viewers to expand their image of a collection of artworks beyond a museum's dusty warehouse to accommodate the **asynchronous**, **distributed**, and multi-authored production typical of today's electronic networks.

At first glance, there appears to be only one artwork in this 'museum': Lialina's own 'My Boyfriend Came Back from the War', a hypertext story originally created in black-and-white images and text within an HTML page that bifurcates into new frames with every click. A closer inspection reveals that the staff of *Last Real Net Art Museum* don't exactly treat this work with white gloves. Instead, Lialina's collaborators devour, chew apart, and spit back new versions of 'My Boyfriend', each in a different medium. The results of her invitation to remake her project range from an elaborate Flash animation of the story by online collaborators Entropy8Zuper! to a text-only translation by Roman Leibov. Winning the award for the most succinct distillation of the project is Mike Konstantinov's banner ad, an animated **GIF** that blinks out:

> My boyfriend
>   came back!
> FROM THE WAR
> After
> DINNER (the **real** taste!) (open every day)
> They left us
> ALONE

To complement these artistic spin-offs, Lialina has compiled a meticulous log of all the real-life people who played a part in the original production of the work. These 'associates' range from film distributor Pip Chodorov, who corrected the English in the first version, to net artist Vuk Cosic, who first linked to 'My Boyfriend' from another Web site, to critic Lev Manovich, who first wrote a review of the work.

Last Real Net Art Museum highlights the differences between an emblematic work of Internet art like 'My Boyfriend' and a conventional painting or sculpture. 'My Boyfriend' challenges the notion of originality; it is easily appropriated and 'remixed'; it thrives in a supportive community; it creates its own museum space; it blurs the boundary between artwork and community, drawing attention to the interdependence of the two; it encourages play and humor. Yet *Last Real Net Art Museum* also makes a compelling argument that artworks in any medium are the products of communities rather than individuals. Lialina's title suggests that the traditional trajectory of artistic success, from intimate community to élite market, de-fangs the artwork by uprooting it from the ecology of semantically and socially networked agents that produced it. Perhaps the community represented in *Museum* are also mourners, grieving not only for the story's war-torn lovers but also for the impending loss of these small creative communities as the museum and gallery world begins to appropriate Internet art.[2]

By fostering connection rather than detachment, *Last Real Net Art Museum* resembles *Conversation Map* more than traditional recognition mechanisms such as brick-and-mortar museums. However, Lialina's project differs from Sack's message board interface in that it represents an improvised community rather than an established one. Members of a Usenet group like sci.environment knew they were part of a community before *Conversation Map* came along, but the entrepreneurs, programmers, and critics associated with 'My Boyfriend' were not part of a recognizable community before *Last Real Net Art Museum* exposed it.

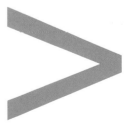

Above: 'My Boyfriend Came Back from the War', as interpreted by Mike Konstantinov; Entropy8Zuper! (Auriea Harvey and Michael Samyn); and Stephanie Tonn, Ulrike Roth, and Junling Niu.

The Limits of Identity-based Recognition

In the traditional art world, recognition has been equated with the name of the artist. A painting is 'a Picasso'; a collector purchases 'a Nauman'. But as long as curators and gallery visitors rely on the name of the artist to establish the genius, style, and credibility of the artwork, they will miss out on a large share of the creativity bursting forth on the Internet. The art world's bias toward the single-artist model of genius, and its time-honored techniques for 'branding' such geniuses, fail to accommodate artists who work in collaboratives or don't stick to a signature medium and style.[3] Online creativity offers a confounding set of obstacles for the single artist model. Digital artists have abandoned, deconstructed, parodied, and reconfigured identity, taking the artist's name as the very site of a new and perverse activity. The play of avatars is one way in which such artists have resisted co-optation and kept alive the invitation to 're-cognize'.

Models of Community-based Recognition

If the Internet has provided digital artists with new ways to escape a fixed identity, it also enables new methods for identifying, tracking, and otherwise recognizing community-based creativity. For, as we shall see, rather than being a product of a solitary ego, creativity in fact emerges in distinct and supportive communities. The play of avatars can't happen in vacuum. Putting on a mask while you're alone in the woods is no disguise.

Even when historians do acknowledge the role of communities in artistic practice, they often treat them as unbending monoliths that artists either unconsciously uphold or struggle to overturn. Whether a Marxist critic is slamming artists for rehearsing capitalist ideology or lauding those who deconstruct it, neither picture reflects the ways in which creators and their communities respond to and shape each other. What we see in digital practice is much more complex: artists disperse into their communities, splintering into collectives, pseudonyms, and bot-writers, and these new entities both define and are defined by the messageboards and chat rooms they inhabit. The Internet may be a global medium, but it has produced innumerable local cultures.

This is not to say that audiences and communities are always supportive or encouraging. At minimum these communities simply need to pay attention to their artists, whether that attention consists of wonder, critique, bewilderment, fear, rejection, or approbation. This attention is different from the political effect produced by the executable art discussed earlier. Like political design, the innovations studied here may reveal hidden flows of power, but that power is discursive rather than executable. It is an authority much revered in the art world: the power to confer recognition. Unlike revelation, which can strike an individual artist or viewer, recognition is a social phenomenon. It suggests the ability to see, label, discuss, and spread opinions about works of art. Recognition is the social buzz produced by creative acts – an appreciation no longer limited to curators or collectors but including anyone with a modem who stumbles onto these communities and shares their judgments with others.

Ambiguity and Accountability

The fact that many of the works in this book are hard to recognize as art is not accidental. Artists on the Internet sometimes manipulate recognizability the way Cézanne measured out paint in his late landscapes, dabbing on just enough to pique his viewers' interest without completing the picture for them.

While art online has become increasingly fluid, transitory, and difficult to recognize, Internet-powered recognition networks have meanwhile become a ripe field for innovation in and of themselves. Community builders have experimented with a variety of competing trust metrics that have appeared in the last decade, spurred on by the same advances in digital technology that enable online artists to elude recognition. Each of the communities we will examine in this chapter relies on a different trust metric, from 'invitation only' (a curated show) to 'free for all' (an unmoderated messageboard), from 'call and response' (an open-code project) to 'police thyself' (a peer-filtered blog). First, we'll tackle the general question of whether and how a recognition network might qualify as a work of art. Then, we'll examine the interplay of different kinds of recognition. And finally, our edge studies will look at each of the four trust metrics in turn, asking which forms of creativity are captured by each recognition network, and which slip through the cracks.

Can a Recognition Network be Art?

The notion that a project dedicated to recognizing artworks might itself qualify as one sounds like a category error, akin to confusing a museum with a painting it contains. Yet the situation is not as cut and dried as that, since tech-savvy artists like Olia Lialina can build recognition networks on the Internet that rival the 'virtual museums' of some brick-and-mortar institutions. If we are to test the possibilities of meta-recognition – to recognize the recognition networks themselves as art – we must think outside our usual preconceptions.

First, it's important to realize that online art is too multi-layered to judge by superficial appearances alone. One recognition network we will examine, *StarryNight*, resembles in title and imagery a painting by Van Gogh. But these textual and visual puns don't automatically make *StarryNight* art, any more than *Conversation Map*'s lack of resemblance to a painting hanging at MoMA in New York disqualifies it from being art. These projects should endure as art because they fulfill art-like functions – not because they present art-like façades.[4]

Second, we must resist the temptation to categorize a recognition network as art if and only if it was made by an 'artist'. As this book has tried to argue, some of the most important advances in art of the Internet age have been made by innovators who didn't consort with or call themselves artists. This puts Olia Lialina on the same level as MIT Media Lab scientist Warren Sack; it's not where creators come from but what they do that counts.[5]

Similarly, we must not judge artworks by the company they keep. The connections that *Last Real Net Art Museum* draws are between artists and about art, while the connections that *Conversation Map* traces range in subject from Bosnia to biofuel. Nevertheless, if we fall into the trap of assuming that only the shapers of *art* communities can be artists, then we are caught in the same circular reasoning demonstrated by Duchamp's readymades: trying to define art by its proximity to itself. Picasso's painting of a woman ironing is no less art than his portrait of Georges Braque.

For many works discussed in this chapter, defining art by association is a tempting but misguided approach. The open-access radio station *Radioqualia* is unquestionably an innovative model for an egalitarian community; its users' contributions are restricted only by the time-slot divisions coded into its Frequency Clock interface. But is *Radioqualia* art? New-media curator Steve Dietz has argued that it is, because it 'reveals how the architecture of cyberspace determines what we can and can't do'.[6] But then why wouldn't Napster be art? Only because Napster's founder, Sean Fanning, doesn't rub shoulders with new-media artists at Ars Electronica like *Radioqualia*'s founders do? While *Radioqualia* is certainly revelatory, it is not nearly as perverse as comparable community networks such as *Desktop IS* or *DeskSwap*. Indeed, there is no reason for it to be, because it depends on a transparent interface and purpose to achieve its political goal. Like *Napster*, *Radioqualia* is more political design than art.

One last pitfall is to categorize art by medium. It is true that *Conversation Map* is written in the same medium, Java, as many online art projects. Medium-based art definitions may have worked in the age of ink-on-paper reviews of oil-on-canvas art, but they won't work now – unless we want to declare every Java-based e-commerce portal and chat client an artwork. As we saw earlier, not every software program qualifies as a work of art. Our definition of art shouldn't rely on a work's appearance, provenance, subject matter, or medium but on its function. How do this chapter's prompt and counterprompt measure up against the art-like behaviors we have identified in previous chapters?

Art-like Functions of Recognition Networks

Whether a recognition network is art depends less on the cultural artifacts it purports to recognize than on the intensity of the other art-like functions it exhibits. *Conversation Map* and *Last Real Net Art Museum* are arresting in that they represents the quotidia of online conversation or interpersonal relationships in a form that invites contemplation. Both projects also reveal a discursive community to itself, drawing a global map that was hitherto buried in local transactions. Both are executable – at least in the weak sense that they are Java applets or HTML pages that run on the user's computer. Although it is built with the most humdrum code, *Last Real Net Art Museum* is perhaps the more executable of the two, since its gallery of 'My Boyfriend' re-creations can be read as an implicit instruction for others to remix the work as well.

The function in which the two projects differ most is perversity. *Last Real Net Art Museum* offers the most wrongheaded approach to recognition, for it documents Lialina's aesthetic material in fulsome detail only to give it away for other artists to cannibalize or caricature. *Conversation Map*'s forthright approach doesn't disqualify it from being art, but its apparent lack of perversity does place more weight on its capacity for arrest, revelation, or execution. Finally, of course, both interfaces have also garnered recognition among creative communities, which, as this chapter has argued, is another essential requirement for art to function socially.

To function socially may require recognition, but to function socially as art requires the right kind of recognition. Works from popular and mass culture regularly achieve the status of household names, and occasionally even a work born in an avant-garde milieu joins the pervasive cultural vernacular of Christmas carols and Marvel superheroes. But the optimum recognition for an artwork is not simply mind-share. By resisting co-optation by commercial interests and other forms of facile recognition, a challenging work may retain the ability to trigger moments of re-cognition. Creators who aim to satisfy this more demanding measure of success, however, face a trade-off in local versus global recognition.

As this chapter's survey of global villages suggests, recognition networks vary by community. Founders of such communities have devised a diversity of methods – visual prominence in an interface, inclusion in filtered 'digests' of email discussions, virtual real estate, teleported gestures, **karma, XP** – by which to recognize the contributions of their members. These new recognition networks can help some art from the edge gain recognition from the lay public, but the most innovative and unstable forms of authorship will only be recognized within the communities shaped by these tools.

This ephemeral, local manifestation may be a necessary condition of certain kinds of creativity. Because digital technologies proliferate with such speed, it is difficult for the entire culture to keep abreast of the latest Web plug-ins and mobile-phone features – much less the latest artistic efforts created with these platforms. However, loosely knit groups of creators can experiment with the new tools and ideas, and present their discoveries to specialized communities. Experts in those niche communities can guide the progress of these innovators and track the memes local to their area of expertise. The discursiveness of these experiments makes them important as art research[7] even if they have not matured to the point of becoming a genre – that is, become codified or preserved in a form others outside the community can readily experience. Nor should the value of these discoveries be diminished because they have not yet achieved a form accessible to the lay public. There's no point in dumbing down artistic research to serve a larger audience if its potency is diluted as a result.

Artists who resist being incorporated into the mainstream view themselves as the real deal, as do critics who inhabit the subcultures that support such challenging work. Sliding from margin to mainstream may be more acceptable – and more common – online than off,[8] but the transition has both benefits and costs. The more attenuated the art, the easier it will be to appropriate and disseminate, but at the cost of a weak or easily co-opted signal. Yet art that depends too closely on inbred references or inside jokes may end up obscure or meaningless when the niche that birthed it dissolves or is colonized by a new constituency.

Trade across Boundaries

This book's introduction argues that the most vigorous protection from hazardous agents, biological or technological, may come from immunological pools that are only loosely connected. Most digital artists emerge within small like-minded communities, the equivalents of such pools. These communities propose their own 'antibodies' to the technological memes invading the larger societies from which they hail. Each is more or less successful in its local encounters with viral memes; what ensures the survivability of the global community is a connected diversity of varied strategies. But who provides those connections?

There is no central stock exchange for recognition currencies where brokers can trade *Slashdot* karma for *Everything2* Experience Points. But as the historian of science Peter Galison has noted, the interface between two economies need not take the form of a universally accepted exchange rate or translation matrix. Instead, Galison has described the boundaries between subcultures as dispersed trading zones, 'intermediate domain[s] in which procedures could be coordinated locally even where broader meanings clashed': 'Subcultures trade. Anthropologists have extensively studied how ... two dissimilar groups can find common ground. They can exchange fish for baskets, enforcing subtle equations of correspondence between quantity, quality, and type, and yet utterly disagree on the broader (global) significance of the items exchanged.'[9]

The items thus exchanged may lose meaning or become altered in the process, but what's important is that the boundary between subcultures is porous rather than impermeable. In the new-media world, well-connected bloggers and email addicts route daily cultural updates from one community to another, just as their silicon equivalents route emails, urls, and instant messages back and forth through the Internet's electronic gateways at the speed of light. Provided they resist the temptations to reduce works to academic sound bites or art-historical niches, such 'human routers' can extend the value of a local innovation outside the subculture that birthed it.

Of course, porting art research can be a dicey proposition compared to porting scientific research, since art is notoriously dependent on medium and context. Art transmitted via paraphrase or documentation can never be experienced the way its original creator and beholders knew it. However, even if the look and feel may change, art's value as *research* may survive sufficiently across communal boundaries[10] to leave behind a few cultural threads in the technological maze that we can use to weave disparate communities together.

Opposite: Marcos Weskamp, *Synapsis*, a network visualization tool based on *Carnivore*.

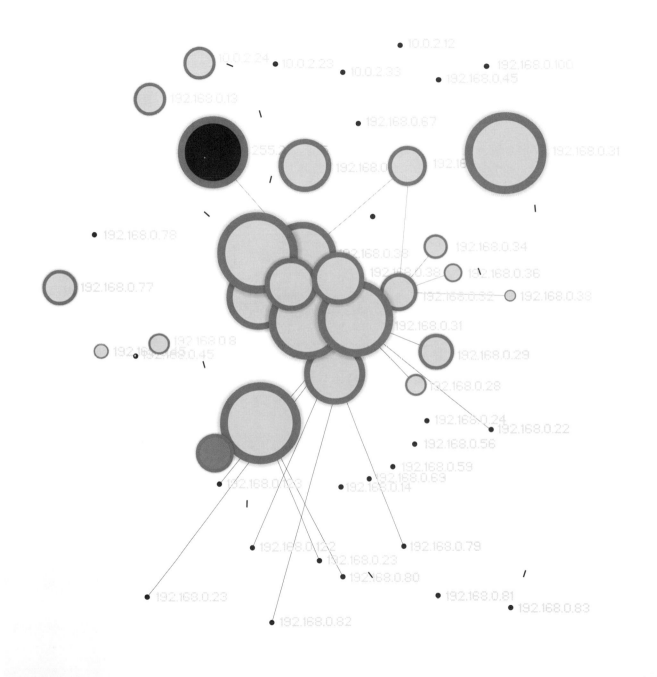

10.0.2.24
10.0.2.23
10.0.2.33
10.0.2.12
192.168.0.100
192.168.0.45
192.168.0.13
192.168.0.67
255.2
192.168.0
192.168.0.31
192.168.0.78
192.168.0.33
192.168.0.34
192.168.0.36
192.168.0.38
192.168.0.77
192.168.0.32
192.168.0.38
192.168.0.31
192.168.0.8
192.168.0.29
192.168.0.45
192.168.0.28
192.168.0.24
192.168.0.22
192.168.0.56
192.168.0.59
192.168.0.33
192.168.0.69
192.168.0.14
192.168.0.122
192.168.0.79
192.168.0.23
192.168.0.80
192.168.0.81
192.168.0.23
192.168.0.83
192.168.0.82

EDGE STUDIES

By Invitation Only: Recognition by Gatekeeper

Some online communities follow the time-tested model of the art world's offline recognition mechanisms, where a single person or jury decides who's in and who's out. Even Web sites controlled by a gatekeeper, however, can range from strictly controlled to fairly egalitarian. The artists featured in online exhibitions like 'Beyond Interface' or 'CODeDOC' represent a curator's rolodex more than an entire community; by contrast, moderated email lists like *nettime* keep their caretakers busy censoring spam or digesting **flame wars**, yet permit a diverse-enough range of opinions to qualify as an open community.

A GLOBAL WORLD REVEALED
MadMundo

Above: *Madmundo*.

MadMundo, an alternative online news source, borrows the invitation-only model of conventional journalism, complete with a stable of reporters, expert commentators, and a centralized news outlet. What makes *MadMundo* more of a community than the *New York Times* or CNN is the global approach it takes to investigating a question that originates in the mind of a single citizen, from an unemployed auto worker in Brazil who wants to know why he lost his job, to the widow of a 9/11 pilot who wants to know what the world's nations are doing to stop airline hijacking.

MadMundo offers a welcome antidote to the typical TV news report, which focuses so much on a particular location — picture the proverbial reporter standing in front of the White House — that it misses more important stories which require the piecing together of events or trends in separate corners of the world. *MadMundo*, by contrast, distributes both its solicitation of stories and its reportage: the editorial policy is lateral rather than hierarchical, responding to connections uncovered by its reporters. And although most of the work is done by professionals, the *MadMundo* Web site invites viewers to submit story ideas or comment on them.

One such story focused on Christophe, the thirty-three-year-old founder of a technology firm in Berlin, who wondered why there were so few workers skilled in information technologies for him to choose from. *MadMundo* reporters in New Delhi and Bulgaria profiled IT workers in each city, learning in the process the economic difficulties these workers faced in supporting their families, as well as the obstacles placed in the way of immigration by developed countries. Having covered these stories, *MadMundo* then reported on the status of a controversial bill about foreign visas back in Germany, thus bringing their coverage of the issue full circle. By weaving together compiled video and text from various locales to represent these points of view, *MadMundo* charts the political and demographic undercurrents that increasingly determine the everyday reality of our globalized economy.

A COMMUNITY WITH CONFLICT
Janet Cohen, Keith Frank, and Jon Ippolito,
Agree To Disagree Online

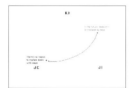

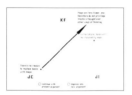

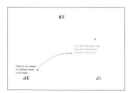

It is a commonplace assumption that communities, online and otherwise, arise out of mutual interest, as is the case with a Usenet group devoted to breast-cancer survivors or Grateful Dead fans. But this assumption underplays one of the Internet's greatest strengths, which is accommodating people of different geographies and ideologies. The adversarial collaborations at three.org are devoted to foregrounding, rather than concealing, the conflicts between different points of view.

Agree To Disagree Online, for example, maps a community whose members violently disagree. In this case, the argument begins when someone throws out the statement 'In the future, books will be replaced by maps.' As the three participants reply in turn, each of their statements is plotted according to how much agreement it garners from the other two: inflammatory statements remain on the periphery, while the center represents consensus. Visitors to the Web site can control the pace and level of detail of the argument, as well as choose to follow digressions made to different topics, from the Watergate political scandal of the 1970s to how buffalos roam. *Agree To Disagree Online* gives visual form to the flame wars and communications breakdowns that so characterize Internet culture.

The participants in *Agree To Disagree Online* may not have trusted each other's judgment about the future of books, but they do have faith in the ground rules they collaboratively set for their discourse. These ground rules include a rotating order of discussion, which guarantees that everyone has equal opportunity to speak. The rules also specify a mechanism for achieving consensus as a community, in this case by mutual agreement. And they specify the mathematics behind the map, which renders back-and-forth polemics as a bipolar stitch and consensus building as a spiraling toward the center. Unlike communities shaped by editors or

moderators, recognition in the *Agree To Disagree Online* drawing is not determined from the top down but from a code crafted 'by the community for the community'.

Of course, this contentious community is 'by invitation only', a prescription the adversarial collaborators justify by claiming that arguments among strangers can never be as frank as arguments among people who know each other well. In the collaborators' eyes, a good argument requires good rapport; otherwise it will devolve into polite conversation or fisticuffs.

Below: *Agree To Disagree Online.*

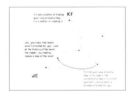

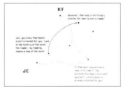

ON THE NET WITHOUT A NET
Antoinette LaFarge, et al., The Plaintext Players

While *Agree To Disagree Online*'s social code is fixed, The Plaintext Players follow a more fluid set of codes: the guidelines of improvisational theater. Since 1994, they have improvised dramas based on loosely prepared scenarios in text-based online environments such as **MOO**s. For each series, founder Antoinette LaFarge or a guest director finds and casts the performers and directs the performances in real time.

The transcripts archived from these online improvisations are ripe with varieties of authorship-bending; some recall the explorations of Modernist playwrights such as Luigi Pirandello or Tom Stoppard, whose actors self-consciously meditate on their role as actors; others have little or no precedent in offline theater, as when actors pick up each other's characters interchangeably, a form of spoofing encouraged by the fact that some chat environments don't block a user from signing in with someone else's 'handle'.[11] This fluid and fragmentary polylogue is conveyed by a transcript from a 1997 Plaintext Players performance called *Orpheus*:

> Digital.Director says, 'And now, without further or future ado: Today we are telling the story of Orpheus, the musician who went to hell to get his wife back after she was bitten by a snake.' Zeus drinks another cup of coffee.
> Digital.Director says, 'Only the details are being changed to protect the innocent. There will be no snake today. In place of the snake ...'
> Orpheus says, 'No snake? What do you mean, no snake?'
> Digital.Director says, 'What I said, no snake.'
> Orpheus exclaims, 'Come on — I wanted to play the snake! Why do I always have to play the dork? The complete idiot? The sucker?'

In a reversal of the conventions of modern stage drama, an official Plaintext Players script is often compiled *from* rather than *for* a series of performances. For example, 'The Roman Forum', a series of linked online improvisations and stage events coinciding with the 2000 Democratic National Convention, explored the roots of the American political spectacle through a live improvisation each day of the convention, in which five virtual Roman personages responded to the events of that week as they unfolded. The players quickly edited the text generated during this improvisation into a script, which became the basis for a stage event at Side Street Live in downtown Los Angeles, and the resulting text and video were archived on the Plaintext Player Web site. Here's an excerpt:

> QUINTUS
> Can't say I do. I have heard that actors were not very well respected.
> PETRONIUS
> Well, not surprising since you started out a slave profession. From the first century on pantomimes became popular — much more popular than plays. Became popular, as in new art form.
> QUINTUS
> And it does seem like much of it was comedic in the lowest meaning of that word.

Archived scripts such as this end up more consistent in quality — if also more conventional in flavor — than the meandering MOO improvisations. The Plaintext Players Web site nevertheless champions the experimental value of the more improvisatory form of online authorship:

> Online performance exploits a number of the most idiosyncratic aspects of the Internet: the sense of being immersed in a virtual world; the ability of people anywhere in the real world to be virtually present in the same time-space; the collective preference for pseudonymous interaction; and the beauty of lag as a disrupter of normal communications.[12]

The Plaintext Players give us an example of an invited community operating on fluid but fairly egalitarian codes. While the group does have a director, her role is not so much to control the players as to help elicit a rich set of improvisational gestures and techniques. At their best, this community reminds us of the ways that 'playing

with identity' is not just a quirk of our virtual
worlds but a feature of both our political landscape
and our traditional media experience. For most
of us, that means consuming stories scripted in
advance, recited by actors or pop stars, and fixed in
CDs, sitcoms, and celluloid. Unless, of course, we log
into a MOO and reclaim a space to act out our own
dreams.

Excerpt from 'The Roman
Forum'.

PETRONIUS
Quintus, you know anything much about your profession?

QUINTUS
Can't say I do. I have heard that actors were not very well respected.

PETRONIUS
Well, not surprising since you started out a slave profession. From the first century
on pantomimes became popular‹much more popular than plays. Became popular, as
in new art form.

QUINTUS
And it does seem like much of it was comedic in the lowest meaning of that word.
Actors wore fabulous masks. Fart jokes were BIG.
(he mimes a tiny fart...poof)
Evidently it degenerated into vulgar and tasteless spectacles.

PETRONIUS
Clearly a rising profession.

Free for All: Recognition by Interface

To many, the Internet may represent the last hope for a truly democratic society, but – to paraphrase Oscar Wilde – democracy is rarely pure and never simple. The designers of egalitarian communities have it worse than Ben Franklin and Tom Jefferson, who never had to worry about schizoid avatars, crypto-anarchists, or viruses in email attachments. One of the biggest challenges is the fact that the more popular an open community, the less secure and reliable the level of discourse. As Clay Shirky has noted,[13] virtual communities that grow too large tend to be doomed by their own success. In the worst-case scenario, their increased visibility attracts cranks, spammers, and 'trolls'— people who seed a discussion board with inflammatory messages just to incite a flame war. Even in the best-case scenario, large communities may turn from many-to-many to one-to-many when the sheer volume of contributions intimidates new members into lurking silently rather than participating actively.

This degradation is perhaps most evident in email, which began as an extremely efficient tool used by a few. In the Internet's early days, before swelling online populations created the signal-to-noise problem that exists now, email discussion lists were the mainstay of cultural discourse. Early list servers that were popular with artists and critics disenchanted with the profit-driven brick-and-mortar art world included The Thing, Echo, and nettime. Founded by Wolfgang Staehle in 1991, The Thing began in New York as a threaded messageboard but later expanded to include connections in Vienna and Berlin. The Thing's network actually predated the Internet; its technicians routed email among these global connections via dedicated dial-up lines.[14] Echo and nettime were initially more focused in their geographic constituencies, the former biased toward New York artists and cultural critics and the later toward European media criticism.

Even as unstructured a tool as person-to-person email can create informal, if transient, communities. Jokes and rumors spread faster via email than via chain-mail letters or cocktail-party banter, and odd bits of digital folk art can quickly become household names in the global village. The meteoric popularity of quirky parodies like Wazzup, Oddtodd, and All Your Base Are Belong to Us[15] can catch even veteran online observers off guard.[16] Sometimes this humor has a political bent; soon after the September 11 terrorist attacks, jpegs of Lady Liberty with a baby and a gun and anti-Osama bin Laden Flash animations swarmed through American email in- and outboxes.

Yet the same egalitarian access that brings electronic folk art to a netizen's in-box also brings the Melissa virus, ads for penis enlargement, and Nigerian bank-deposit scams. The digital dreck clogging the average email account has risen to such flood levels that savvy netizens are beginning to rotate through accounts as fast as once a year. But disposable email addresses are hardly the glue one expects to hold an accountable society together, so the shapers of some communities have set out to explore innovative ways to separate the wheat from the chaff.

In communities with thousands of members, where it is harder for every participant to know, and hence trust, every other participant, collaboration in building the community tends to be more asymmetric: the founders wield more control than the other participants, because the founders set the ground rules. Departing from the paradigm of the email list – and straining the very notion of community – many designers of egalitarian communities abandon the goal of fostering communication among the participants, and focus instead on enabling members to post digital files or other artifacts to share and re-mix. Some critics insist verbal communication is essential to virtual community and scoff at the notion that a site like Last Real Net Art Museum might represent a bona-fide social body. Nevertheless, the popularity of these communal workspaces suggests that the Internet has forced an expansion in the definition of community, as it has in the definition of art.

Whether they offer culture or chitchat, all free-for-all communities live in constant danger of degenerating into anarchy. The longest-lived tend to avail themselves of a subtle means of controlling the signal-to-noise ratio: an interface that restricts the form expression takes in a given community.[17] Most of the sites we look at in this chapter rely on an interface to police their communities.

A DEDICATED WALL FOR ELECTRONIC GRAFFITI
Alex Galloway et al., *Keiko.Suzuki.slogan.cgi*

Rhizome.org takes its name from the botanical term for the underground stems that connect plants into living networks, a metaphor for grassroots community and non-hierarchical structure championed by the philosophers Gilles Deleuze and Felix Guattari. Since its founding in 1996, Rhizome.org has become one of the world's leading online resources for new-media artists. It claims over 17,000 members in more than 118 countries, three-quarters of whom consider themselves to be artists, and its Web site attracts ten million hits per month. Rhizome's staple offerings include a variety of email lists and an archive of online artworks.

To help its community visualize and use these resources, Rhizome has also invited a number of its member-artists to step back and look at the Big Picture by creating a series of alternative interfaces to its email archive.

If *Conversation Map* is a lens for revealing meaning in mayhem, some interfaces built for Rhizome perversely encourage its users to make *more* mayhem. Although Rhizome depends on the names cited in user logins and email headers, it has also implemented some of the very devices by which posters to ordinary newsgroups evade the clear recognition of their online identities. In response to a glut of emails on the Rhizome list purporting to be from pop star Britney Spears, for example, Rhizome's then technical director Alex Galloway set up an 'anonymizer' called *Spears Spoofer*, a Web form that allows any user to post to Rhizome using this pseudonym.

Another device Galloway programmed into the Rhizome interface is *Keiko.Suzuki.slogan.cgi*, an online form that allows any Rhizome member to modify the default 'signature', or last line, of every user's email. Rhizome's members responded by treating this communal signature interface exactly as a graffiti artist would treat a boxcar: as a medium for broadcasting their own messages under other member's noses.[18] At the bottom of every Rhizome email, alongside the usual line about terms of service or subscription details, appeared a slogan that rotated periodically as Rhizomers used Galloway's interface to program a new series of signatures:[19]

> Approximately 47.48201% of this page is net.art.
> Preaching to the choir since 1996.
> sex, libyan, PLO, taliban, that should get the filters poppin
> The quickest way to a man's heart is through his ribcage.
> + you use the word 'antichrist' like it's a bad thing ...
> +you spoof, i'll toss rocks

Eryk Salvaggio submitted a series of signature lines consisting only of the word *yes* separated by seemingly arbitrary spaces. Only the original Web interface to change signature lines revealed the pattern behind these random typographical addenda: clicking on the 'history' menu to see previous signature lines revealed a hidden message buried in the sequence of separate lines:

YESYES	YES	YESYESYESYESYES		
YES YES	YES	YES		YES
YES YES	YES	YES		YES
YES YES YES	YES			YES
YES	YESYES	YESYESYESYESYES		

Because Rhizome's 'terms of service' were automatically listed at the bottom of each email, one electronic wag used Galloway's interface to add the line 'Subscribers to Rhizome Raw are not subject to the terms', which rendered Rhizome's legal notice null and void. Such anti-establishment gestures are an occupational hazard for the founders of free-for-all communities.

The perversity of the anonymous signature lines generated by Galloway's Rhizome form lends credence to *Keiko.Suzuki.slogan.cgi*'s status as art. But who is *Keiko.Suzuki.slogan.cgi*'s artist: the signature-line changer or Galloway himself? This chapter's introduction argued that shapers of recognition networks can be artists, but this assumes that the system they put in place successfully encourages creative misuse. If Galloway's form had solicited nothing more than banal attempts at sincere Rhizome slogans – 'Rhizome: The Online Art Resource' or 'Join Rhizome today!' – then *Keiko.Suzuki.slogan.cgi* might not ever have qualified as art. In this case, however, both coder – Alex Galloway – and community – the creative agents who took advantage of his mischievous interface – might qualify as 'artists' in this collaborative effort. Traditional aesthetics admits oil paintings and bronze sculptures as art regardless of how their audience uses them. Yet the dependency on audience exhibited by *Keiko.Suzuki.slogan.cgi* is less a vulnerability peculiar to community-driven artworks than a consequence of the functional definition this book proposes for art of all kinds. A canvas that is plastered into a wall as construction material – something that is reputed to have happened to Van Gogh paintings he sold to pay off debts — is not art, no matter what its creator intended.

Keiko.Suzuki.slogan.cgi

This form allows you to change the signature file that appears at the bottom of each posting to the Rhizome email list.

Current Rhizome Raw signature file:

```
+ Under the paving stones, the beach.
-> Rhizome.org
-> post: list@rhizome.org
-> questions: info@rhizome.org
-> subscribe/unsubscribe: http://rhizome.org/subscribe.rhiz
-> give: http://rhizome.org/support

Subscribers to Rhizome Raw are subject to the terms set out in the
Member Agreement available online at http://rhizome.org/info/29.php3
```

Or, the signature file of your dreams ...

```
+  I love you!
-> Rhizome.org
-> post: list@rhizome.org
-> questions: info@rhizome.org
-> subscribe/unsubscribe: http://rhizome.org/subscribe.rhiz
-> give: http://rhizome.org/support
+
Subscribers to Rhizome Raw are subject to the terms set out in the
```

STARS OF THE CYBER-FIRMAMENT
Alex Galloway, Mark Tribe, and Martin Wattenberg, *StarryNight*

A more graphic interface for Rhizome, *StarryNight*, represents each text as a star in the night sky.[20] If *Keiko.Suzuki.slogan.cgi* and *Spears Spoofer* are closer in spirit to Lialina's perverse *Last Real Net Art Museum*, *StarryNight* recalls Sack's evocative yet ultimately utilitarian *Conversation Map*. The brightness of each star is a measure of how many times online visitors have clicked on it — as though the dustcovers of library books got shinier as successive borrowers left their fingerprints on them, *StarryNight* also features a dynamic method for visualizing data: viewers who select a theme such as 'gender' or 'virtual reality' see a constellation linking all the stars representing texts with that theme. *StarryNight* is a cartography of cyberspace that literally connects the dots of online culture.

Below: Detail of StarryNight.

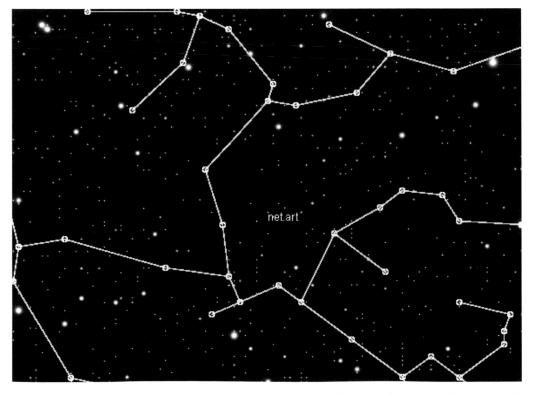

NET.ARTISTS ON THE LOOSE
7-11

Many of the identity-bending techniques that Rhizome.org incorporated into its interface were consciously based on novelties introduced in the 7-11 list server, an online forum that broached many issues regarding communication as performance. As early discussion lists like *nettime* grew, many of their more mainstream participants became less patient with creative experimentation with emails, which were frequently indistinguishable from error messages or spam.[21] In response, some artists broke ranks to create list servers specifically for artistic exploration. *7-11* was one of those breakaway communities, created as a virtual playground for the first wave of Internet artists.

An online laboratory for pioneer Internet artists such as Heath Bunting, Vuk Cosic, jodi, and Alexei Shulgin, *7-11* introduced many netizens to other forms of online performance. Galloway first saw ASCII art on *7-11*, while online artist Fredric Madre credits *7-11* for birthing 'spam art'.[22] In one of the best-known perversions performed on the list, Bunting got hold of a homework assignment that Natalie Bookchin had assigned her class, 'Intro to Computing in the Arts', and posted it to *7-11*. A dozen veteran net artists interpreted the assignment and emailed it to Bookchin for grading.[23]

Galloway has confirmed[24] that the signature-line form he built into Rhizome.org was an explicit homage to a similar *7-11* invention. In fact, he named *Keiko.Suzuki.slogan.cgi* after the mysterious Japanese moderator and 'hostess' of the *7-11* list,[25] whose identity was spoofed so often that her name became an all-purpose pseudonym.[26]

Despite the obvious influence it wielded on individual net artists and new-media platforms like Rhizome.org, *7-11* is impossible for present-day artists or viewers to experience in any meaningful way. Once activity on the list died out, so did a living context for understanding its mercurial avatars and inside jokes. While *7-11* functioned as an important recognition network during its heyday, it was too fluid and self-referential for its meaning to be contained by a static text archive. And *7-11*'s interface, the majordomo email software, is too generic to consider as art by itself.

Some argue that the designers of communities like *7-11* should build them to be sustainable; others say that museums should take a more active interest in documenting or preserving them; still others claim that such communities are ephemeral in nature and should be allowed to die a natural death. In any case, it's important to bear in mind the short lifespan of most cutting-edge recognition networks as we examine more instances of egalitarian communities.

A PEER-TO-PEER EXHIBITION
Alexei Shulgin *et al.*, *Refresh*

While the artists of *7-11* perverted email into a performative medium, Alexei Shulgin's *Refresh* perverted the client–server architecture of the Web to produce an impromptu community that anticipated later egalitarian architectures such as **wiki**s and peer-to-peer networks. (Shulgin admits that his ideas emerged from discussions on lists such as *7–11*.)[27] Shulgin created a community knit together only by a single HTML feature called the 'refresh' tag, which can be set to jump automatically from one Web page to another after, say, ten seconds. On the *Refresh* Web site, he instructed participants to choose where they wanted to insert a page among the list of existing ones. The new participant then emailed the previous page's owner to change the link to the new page, and added a refresh tag to his or her own Web page pointed toward the next page in the sequence.

In its open call for participation, *Refresh* recalled the egalitarian 'assemblings' of Vittorio Baroni or Ken Friedman from the 1970s, photocopied periodicals amassed by the editors and then mailed via the postal system. *Refresh* was an egalitarian recognition network, but — like its mail-art predecessors — it depended on other recognition networks for its audience. Only artists already reading a list server such as *7-11* would have known they could contribute to *Refresh*, just as only artists already on a mailing list such as Friedman's hefty rolodex would have known they could contribute to an assembling.

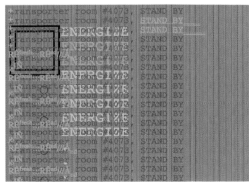

Clockwise from upper left: *Refresh* pages by jodi, The Thing, Absurd.org, and V2.

THE SECRET LIFE OF DESKTOPS
Alexei Shulgin *et al.*, *Desktop IS*

In another of Shulgin's early interface-inspired communities, the artist invited netizens to submit screenshots of their computer desktops, which he re-posted on his Web site. He received sixty-odd desktops over the course of the six months during which he ran the project.

If, as we intimated previously, a hard drive contains a life story, then the computer desktop is its table of contents. Shulgin's 'instant' community promises this sort of revelation, but in fact the hundred or so desktop images offer less a peek into users' personal lives than deliberate attempts to treat the desktop as a canvas for creative expression. Rachel Baker's Macintosh desktop, for example, clusters specially named folders near ordinary applications to pun on their names ('bakerssexuality/protectedby/Virex DropScan').

If Baker makes meaning by legibility, fellow netizen Michael Samyn tantalizes by obscurity; he loads so many applications into his Windows taskbar that it swells to conceal the offending half of a pornographic image he has set as his desktop background. By revealing the secret life of desktops, Shulgin again connects identity and performance.

Right, clockwise from upper left: *Desktops* by Amit Brakin, Steve Scott, Vesna Manojlovic, and Buk Head.

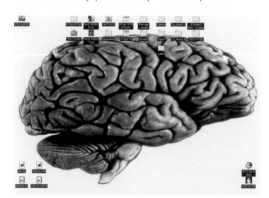

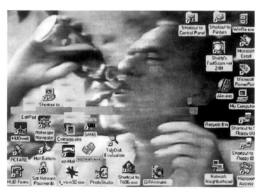

I'LL SHOW YOU MINE IF YOU SHOW ME YOURS

Mark Daggett, *DeskSwap*

DeskSwap is a multi-user screensaver — an update of Shulgin's *Desktop IS* which exploits the peer-to-peer architecture that powers file-sharing tools like *Napster* and *Gnutella*, described earlier. When a *DeskSwap* user stops using the computer, the application swaps a snapshot of the user's screen with that of another user currently on the *DeskSwap* network. This leads to an intentional, if unpredictable, breach of privacy, as a personal email or Quicken account pops up on the computer screen of a stranger halfway around the world — or worse, in the next cubicle over.

Like other egalitarian recognition networks, *DeskSwap* is unlikely to promote the recognition of particular artworks. It may, however, promote the recognition of an unusual canvas for art-making —

the computer desktop — as well as a new community — the people willing to suffer this peculiar invasion of privacy in exchange for an aesthetic experience. Because *DeskSwap* runs live, from users' current screens, they have less control over the contents. Its invitation to glimpse the computer files of a random person is potentially more revealing than any actual striptease.

This project foregrounds a paradox peculiar to online communities, which is that the partial or complete anonymity of its users often triggers exercises in intimacy. And even more interesting is the frequent link between these kinds of intimacy and creative expression. Do intimate communities inspire creativity, or is it only by dint of creative effort that intimate communities can be built on an increasingly impersonal Internet?

Right: *DeskSwap.*

SPREADING THE SPECTRUM
Honor Hargar and Adam Hyde, *Radioqualia*

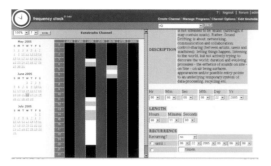

As the art historian Dieter Daniels has pointed out,[28] radio was originally a two-way medium; every receiver was inherently a transmitter, permitting every radio owner to broadcast as well as listen. A map of the radio network proposed by the American Independent Relay League in 1916 looks strikingly similar to one of the electronic backbones of the Internet circa 1990. After the First World War, however, the US government decided that the strategic importance of radio was too great to let individual citizens clog the airwaves with conversations about Aunt Millie's health and the weather in Saint Paul, and restricted 'ham operators' to the short-wave band. Commercial lobbies soon pried the longer wavelengths out of the government's hands, and in the subsequent decades what had been a many-to-many medium became one of the most monopolized outlets for mass media.

Or did it? Recent innovations of the digital revolution, from **pirate radio** to **spread spectrum**, have opened up new networks outside the gates of commercial broadcasting. One of the more interesting of these interventions is the online collaboration *Radioqualia*, founded in 1998 with the goal of shifting radio from the most exclusive to the most inclusive of media:

> In the hierarchy of media, radio reigns. There are more computers than modems, more phones than computers, and more radios than phones. Radio is the closest we have to an egalitarian method of information distribution.[29]

Radioqualia's founders created a Web site called Frequency Clock in which any surfer can establish her own radio channel, scheduling predetermined sound and even video programs or leaving these slots open for others to fill.

HISTORY FROM THE SOURCE
Martin Wattenberg, *Idealine*

What *Radioqualia* is to radio, Martin Wattenberg's *Idealine* is to history — Internet art history, that is. For this project commissioned by the Whitney Museum of American Art, Wattenberg posted a request for help on several Internet art-related email lists. Almost a hundred artists responded by visiting the *Idealine* site and adding to his database information about Internet art they had created or felt was important. The result is an open repository for the brief but vibrant history of online art.

Wattenberg was not content to leave these historical tidbits pigeonholed in a humdrum database table. Instead, he built a fan of luminous threads which map the dominant themes and technologies that emerged in online art from 1995 to the present. As the user moves a mouse over the threads, these part to reveal titles of artworks; clicking on these titles can launch the work or reveal more about its context.

Idealine underscores how critical an egalitarian community's interface is to its success. In this case, Wattenberg chose an apt metaphor and rendered it in a consistent and compelling form: 'From the beginning, net art has travelled multiple paths ... Each individual artist picks up these threads and weaves them in novel combinations.'

A LAND GRAB IN CYBERSPACE

Casqueiro Atlantico Laboratorio Cultural (teresa alonso novo, omi, looks brunner, malex spiegel) in collaboration with Johannes Gees, and the help of Roger Luechinger, Gino Esposito and Silke Sporn, *Communimage*

Communimage is an egalitarian community whose interface accepts static images rather than texts or sound. This interface is an enormous grid of square 'patches' contributed by the public; since its launch in 1999, approximately twenty thousand patches have been uploaded by seventeen hundred visitors from sixty-five countries. Even more than in email lists, the interface of Communimage obscures the authorship of its patches; in places it looks more like a seamless visual fabric than a grid of distinct images.

In some ways, Communimage's vast electronic collage resembles traditional quilting circles, community projects to which members would bring pieces of fabric, time, labor, and stories. Because contributors can 'stitch' their images onto any edge of Communimage's grid, however, the result is more tattered rag than tidy bedspread. Reflecting the anarchic ethic of the community, this emergent overall shape is in many ways more interesting than the Photoshopped clowns and psychedelic abstractions contributed by individual *Communimage* users.

Left: *Communimage.*

COLLABORATION IN HYPERSPACE
Ed Stastny with Jon Van Oast, *Sito*

The original inspiration for *Communimage* came from *Sito*, a venerable grid-based community active since December 1995. Over the many years of its evolution, *Sito*'s creators pushed the grid that underlay its collaborative interface into an increasingly non-Euclidean shape where what's far enough in front of you may be behind you. Because the space of *Sito*'s virtual grid is simply a visualization of the database that keeps track of its image locations, that space can depart from the geometry of everyday life to explore surprising possibilities.

Hygrid, for example, is a *Sito* interface in which the sides of image patches are connected by more than just the simple adjacency of flat space. In Hygrid's twisted topology, the same square might be linked to a column of squares at the top of a given

Right: *Sito*.
Below: *Apartment*.

patch *and* to a row of squares leading from the left edge of a given patch — like a quilt bent back upon itself. Advanced users can set up 'wurmhoels' that bridge distant portions of the Hygrid.

Gridcosm, another of *Sito*'s non-Euclidean interfaces, consists of a series of three-by-three grids of images. Once all nine squares are occupied, the entire grid shrinks down to replace the central square and eight new blank squares surround it to create a new three-by-three grid, at which point the process begins again. Gridcosm also includes a viewer that allows users to plumb the depths of this communal 'tunnel vision'.

VERBAL URBANISM
Marek Walczak and Martin Wattenberg with Jonathan Feinberg, *Apartment*

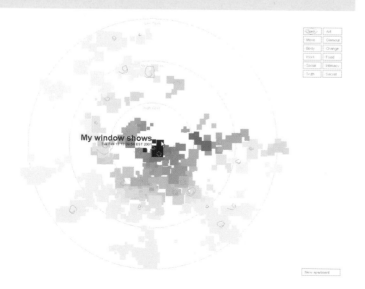

If the 'city plans' of *Communimage* and *Sito* are pieced together from images, the city plan of *Apartment* is pieced together from words. When viewers type a sentence into a text box on the site, *Apartment* translates this sentiment from a linguistic space into an architectural one: the words float onto the blueprint of a virtual dwelling whose layout and proportions are determined by their connotations. The sentence 'I love to eat pretzels while I'm typing', for example, might build a bedroom ('love'), an office ('typing') and a double-sized kitchen ('eat' and 'pretzels').

Apartment's poetic architecture can be navigated on the scale of an entire community or of an individual household. Users can save their apartments and view them in the context of apartments built by other visitors. Unlike most city plans, *Apartment*'s virtual geography can be customized by its users, who can select a word like *love* and watch the city re-organize itself, as love-related apartments converge on the city center while unrelated ones disperse to outlying suburbs.

COMMUNITY OR CON GAME?
Kenneth Goldberg, *Telegarden*

Visitors to Ken Goldberg's venerable *Telegarden* Web site contribute neither images nor words but effort: the work of tending a real-world garden. Although most of *Telegarden*'s virtual gardeners are thousands of miles away from the seeds and soil under their care, the interface allows them to control a robot arm equipped with a view camera, a pneumatic trowel for planting seeds, and a watering can. By sowing virtual seeds and trickling synthetic rain, so the site suggests, visitors trigger the release of real seeds and rain, thus participating on a global scale in the cultivation of a local ecosystem.

Yet the response by online viewers and critics to Goldberg's purported virtual community has been less environmentalist and more epistemological. How do we know, after all, that there is such a garden as the one depicted on his site? Perhaps the images of

seedlings are an elaborate hoax. Rather than bristle at this suspicion, Goldberg has reveled in it, creating parallel works that, for example, invite viewers to deface an American dollar bill (a Federal crime) or control a ouija board. He has even coined a term for this investigation: 'telepistemology' — how we know what we know online.[30]

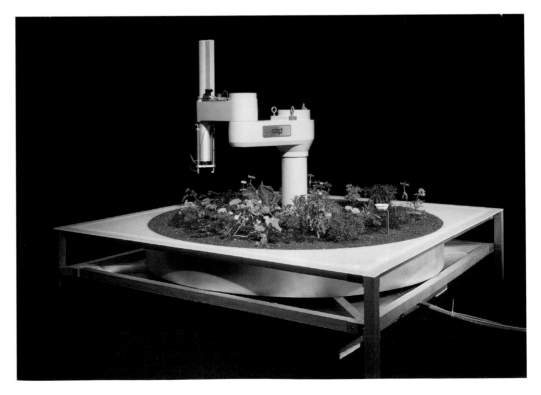

Right: *Telegarden*.

PUBLIC HOUSING IN CYBERSPACE
Mr. Wong's Soup'artments

Mr. Wong's Soup'artments give users a chance to create a visual and virtual community, but on an urban rather than a national scale. Billed as 'The World's Tallest Virtual Building', this droll interface is a cartoonish skyscraper in which each floor is an image contributed by a different participant. Mr. Wong's remarkable edifice includes floors consisting of architecturally correct penthouses with pixilated graffiti, heliports, soccer stadiums, cemeteries, fish tanks, and even a set of enormous teeth.

Mr. Wong enforces a few more rules of participation than some free-for-all communities, but they are simple enough to be listed in a text box hovering near the building's apex: no **anti-aliased image**s, no ads, no plagiarism, no animation, no politics, and no porn. These rules haven't deterred three hundred contributors from taking up residency, making Mr. Wong's skyscraper three times taller in virtual space than the Empire State Building is in real space.

These pages and following spread: *Mr. Wong's Soup'artments.*

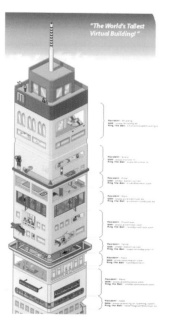

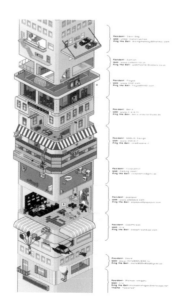

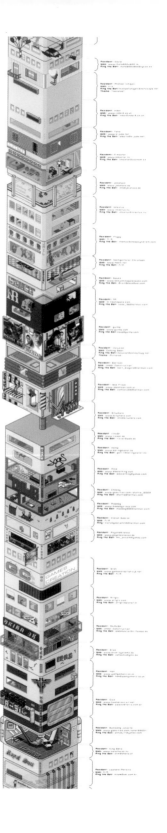

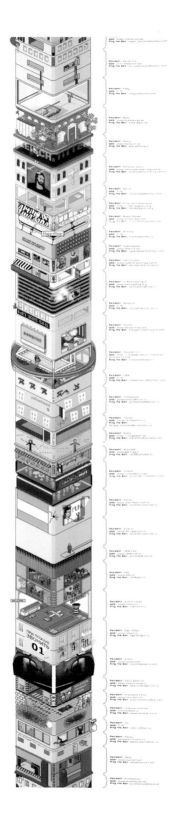

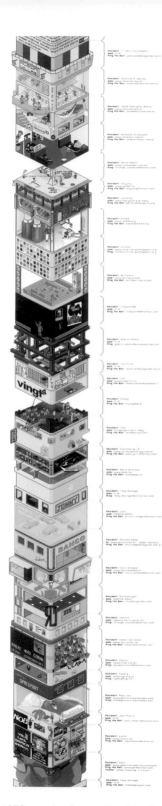

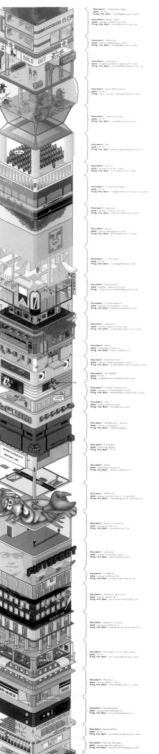

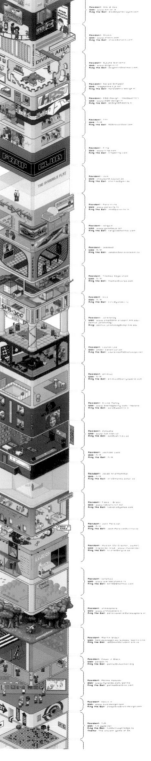

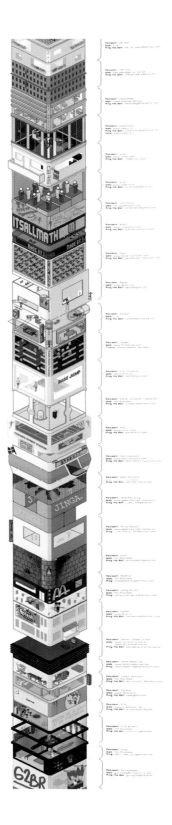

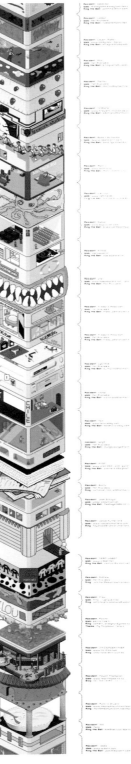

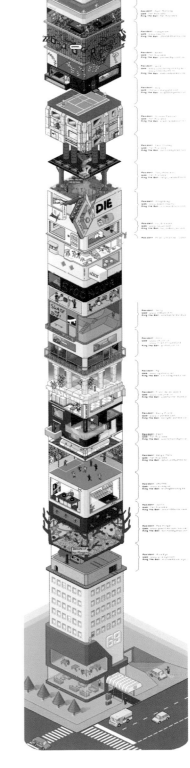

Call and Response: Recognition by Common Agenda

Egalitarian politics are fine, some artists and critics claim, but not everyone can be an artist. The assumption here, driven by the genius-artist paradigm, is that artists must dedicate years of training, study, and studio time to be able to produce art – and that the average citizen has neither the training nor the skills nor the inclination to do this well. Of course, this begs the question of what might happen if we gave more people tools and the time to create. Nevertheless, even many egalitarian-minded community organizers believe that people need more than an interface to point them in the right direction.

Paradigms for these hybrid structures of control and freedom can be found in very different realms. Augusto Boal's experiments in 'Theater of the Oppressed' suggest some ways in which performance can be structured to eliminate the player/audience divide. Other community models focus on a more explicit agenda rather than a social or aesthetic focus. These agenda-driven communities populate much Web real estate, from bungie-jumping blogs to women's-health Web rings, from literary indexes like WebDelSol to political-action networks like MoveOn.org. Common interests do not always produce community, but when they do, well-designed social architectures can inspire a loyalty that makes their members more likely to tolerate some degree of structural inequality.

The open-code model of the operating system GNU/Linux,[31] for example, follows a tree structure in which more control is granted to developers closer to the core. GNU/Linux's coordinator, Linus Torvalds, presides over a group of senior developers who manage the kernal – the 'trunk' of the tree. This group nominates individuals to manage modules of GNU/Linux that can be developed in relative isolation – the 'branches' forking off the trunk. Finally, these individuals invite users anywhere to check out offshoots of these modules – 'leaves' dangling from the branches. Although anyone can check out a leaf, only users who extend features or squash bugs in a way approved by that module's moderators will be allowed to replace the existing leaf with their revised one. This ensures that every user has the opportunity to write some of the software, with increased responsibility as a reward for substantial contribution.

Stricter agenda-driven communities include the '@home' projects in distributed computing. The first and most famous, SETI@home, is an application users can download and run in place of a screensaver. SETI@home does productive work with the unused cycles of thousands of ordinary PCs, commandeering them when their owners are asleep or not at their desks, cranking through data gathered from telescopes aimed at space in search of signs of extraterrestrial intelligence. Like an ordinary screensaver, SETI@home obediently surrenders the computer to its user when it's time to get back to work on that spreadsheet or email to Mom. Several other challenges in distributed computing, from modelling the folding structure of proteins to finding a cure for AIDS, have tried to emulate the phenomenal popularity of SETI@home. All promise to let ordinary citizens contribute to cutting-edge scientific research, even if, as the artist and writer Natalie Jeremijenko has pointed out, the actual processing – and hence the detailed agendas of these projects – is obscured from users.[32] Nevertheless, a few online communities have dared to explore more balanced author/reader hybrids.

Below: {Fray}.

My happy memories of my brother are, I suspect, not really my memories at all. My mom has great, silly stories about my brother and me as kids, but I don't remember them. I suspect I've been lied to.

The only happy memory I'm certain of is the two of us running up the stairs to the second-floor landing and dropping the cat over the side to see if he would land on his feet.

The toss.

The spinning drop.

The over-the-shoulder.

We giggled like mad as we tortured the poor cat. I was in preschool then, so my brother must have been around eleven years old. Old enough to know better.

RÉPONDEZ S'IL VOUS PLÂIT
Derek Powazek, {Fray}

Derek Powazek's {Fray} has been publishing short non-fiction stories at a rate of about one per month since 1996. Each story features a catchy opener followed by the rest of the text laid out in a visually arresting landscape or design, a final question, and an opening for readers to post similar stories. Powazek's own piece, 'Playing with Fire', tells the story of a young wannabe fireman who accidentally set his own garage alight and just barely managed to put the blaze out. The story ends with {Fray}'s trademark question to readers — in this case,

'What did you want to be as a kid?' 'Toothbrush Envy', a story by Don Burns of lovers leaving toothbrushes in his bathroom to mark territory, ends with the question: 'Do you have issues?'

Each seed story becomes a conceptual hub for a web of other stories and responses posted by readers. What is remarkable about all this 'amateur' writing is its power. Literary agents may not find the next Flannery O'Connor or Zora Neal Hurston on {Fray}, but they will find stories whose raw energy is surprising and fresh. Mostly simple epiphanies without much back-story, they are terse, focused, and minimal, and most feel like authentic revelations.

Below: *SETI@home.*

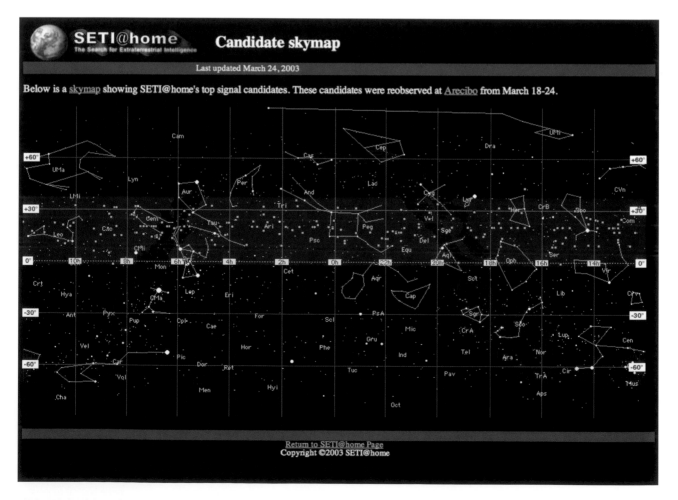

WHAT EVENT CHANGED YOUR LIFE?
Margot Lovejoy with Hal Eagar, Marek Walczak, Jon Legere, and Charles Bae, *Turns*

The opening screen of *Turns* is completely black except for phrases that slowly come into focus: 'My son was conceived out of teenage love.' 'I have in fact made some enemies.' 'The smarter choice would be to give him up.' 'I fell in instant lust.' 'I bled for 16 days straight. I poured blood.' 'I felt I could neither continue nor leave.' Then, one word at a time, the central question appears: 'What event changed your life?' This question unites an eclectic and unusual collection of real-life stories interlinked by keyword via a database. The interface to *Turns* is an organic-looking[33] Flash Web site that allows users to filter through stories of life-changing experiences. The central image is a translucent womblike circle set in a blood-colored background; small knots of yellow scatter over its surface, arranged according to topics such as intimacy, immigration, war, identity, career, and family. Clicking on a yellow knot opens a window to that story. After reading a story, users can post their own story or response. Like *{Fray}*, *Turns* is an experiment in social memory. Because its interlinked stories can be explored through the back-end database, each person who contributes a story can relate it to the stories of others.

Because the entries to *Turns* are unedited, and because there is no selection process (other than rejection for inappropriate entries), the writing is immediate, rough, and raw. Entries are composed on the fly, in a window of the Flash interface, without the possibility of correction or change. But amid the ubiquitous typographical and grammatical errors, we see writers describe child abuse, the loss of children to hostile spouses, the humiliations of immigration. While *{Fray}* provides a bridge between the single-author model and the community one, and thus offers better guidance for those eager to become authors, *Turns* steps right into the cultural abyss. With Boalian trust in the abilities of the untutored to tell their stories in a profound and moving way, *Turns* relies almost entirely on the interface and database to produce a community of writers.

Right: *Turns.*

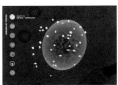

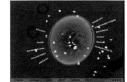

Police Thyself: Recognition by the Community

Egalitarian and call-and-response interfaces grant a voice to more members of a community than curated sites, but to achieve a truly democratic community requires more than anarchy or agenda. The voices of its citizens must count, in a quite literal sense: democracies function by election, referendum, or some other calculation of the community's net priorities. Unlike the cumbersome process of voting in real-world elections, online rating schemes can be automated by code operating behind the scenes on a Web server; this enables adventurous community founders to invent rules that enable the community to police itself – and even to adjust and update these trust metrics over time. Trust metrics can measure the quality or relevance of contributions, or even the reliability of particular individuals. Since they depend on ratings from the community, however, they can reward the loyalty of the most committed members while allowing newcomers to earn their place within the community. Some of these communities rely on the labor of their members, others rely on structures built into the code, and still others use both methods.

Login
Why Login?
Why Subscribe?

Sections
Main
Apache
Apple
AskSlashdot
7 more
Books
BSD
Developers
1 more
Games
7 more
Interviews
IT
Linux
4 more
Politics
Science
2 more
YRO

Help
FAQ
Bugs

Stories
Old Stories
Old Polls
Topics
Hall of Fame
Submit Story

About
Supporters
Code
Awards

Services
Broadband
PriceGrabber
Product Guide
Special Offers

Ask Slashdot: Limitations in Current Breed of Palm Handhelds?

Posted by Cliff on Sunday December 12, @03:00PM
from the search-for-improved-functionality dept.

JabrTheHut asks: "*Having been a Palm user for over two years now, I've upgraded to a Tungsten T3. While the features I'm used to using have not changed, I have become increasingly frustrated by what I see as a lack of progress. It doesn't seem to want to deal with text files (there is no import feature for the Palm Desktop notepad or memo pad, for example). Also there seems to be no way to copy arbitrary files to the Palm - all files must be "owned" by an application. With a 256MB SD card I expected to use it to copy files between work and home. Has anyone else noticed these or other shortcomings and have figured out ways around them?*"

(**Read More...** | 21 of 31 comments | ask.slashdot.org)

Science: More Antennas, Faster Wireless

Posted by timothy on Sunday December 12, @02:07PM
from the aim-high dept.

rouge86 writes "*The New Scientist has a story on how researchers broke the network speed record using a wireless network and multiple antennas. They plan to use the demonstration to show how powerful multiple antennas can be. Applications include power saving on mobile phones and reducing interference.*"

(**Read More...** | 21 of 40 comments | science.slashdot.org)

Science: The Year In Ideas

Posted by timothy on Sunday December 12, @01:13PM
from the what'dja-think? dept.

No_Weak_Heart writes "*The New York Times Magazine (registration required) presents its annual compendium of ideas. The list ranges from acoustic keyboard eavesdropping to land-mine-detecting plants to water that isn't wet. What catches your fancy? And what do you think is missing?*"

(**Read More...** | 73 of 115 comments | science.slashdot.org)

Science: Geminid Meteor Shower

Posted by CmdrTaco on Sunday December 12, @11:56AM
from the break-out-your-hard-hat dept.

An anonymous reader writes "*physorg.com is carrying a story on the upcoming Geminid meteor shower, which will peak on December 13th. This is usually a high-rate meteor shower, and this year will be no different. The early morning hours are the best time to see them. Space.com is also reporting on the shower. This shower was also covered by Slashdot in 2003, 2002, and 2001.*"

(**Read More...** | 62 of 82 comments | science.slashdot.org)

Apple: The Tablet Mac Becomes Reality

Interviews
· Ask Wil Wheaton
Anything (Part Deux)
· Tycho and Gabe Res
to Your Questions
· Richard Garriott on R
Garriott
· Jack Emmert Respon
Your Questions
· Trekkies Director Ro
Nygard Answers
· Ask Gabe and Tycho
Penny Arcade
· Ask Director of 'Trek
Roger Nygard
· Ask City of Heroes I
Designer Jack Emmert
· Ask Ubuntu Founde
Astronaut) Mark
Shuttleworth
· Neal Stephenson Res
With Wit and Humor

Slashdot Login
Nickname:

Password:

☐ Public Terminal
Log in

[Create a new accou

Slashdot Poll
Video game world I v
to live in:
○ Final Fantasy
○ Doom 3
○ Grand Theft Auto:
○ Pitfall
○ City of Heros
○ World of Warcraft
○ The Sims
○ E.T. the Extra-Terre
Vote | Results | Po

REVENGE OF THE NERDS
Rob Malda, *Slashdot*

Although they never had the digital tools to perfect their vision, the Fluxus artists of the 1960s understood the potential of what the art historian Craig Saper called 'intimate bureaucracies'. The German artist Josef Beuys, for example, founded the German Green Party and the Free International University with the goal of exploring the 'possibility of decentralized self-administration'.[34] The self-policing communities envisioned by Fluxus artists rarely persevered in a stable form — but now digital democracies can harness the power of computers to realize what previously could be dismissed as utopian fantasies. In the best-known example of a contemporary community renowned for its network codes, programmer Rob Malda started a Web site in Michigan in 1997 so that a handful of friends could post and discuss news about emerging technologies. To Malda's delight, *Slashdot* soon became popular outside his small circle, but to his dismay, as the number of posts climbed into the thousands, the signal began to get lost in the noise. At first, he and his buddies tried to moderate the discussion themselves, but the task quickly outstripped their time and abilities. As programmers, though, the *Slashdot* team were able to code their way out of the problem by building forms to let moderators rate other posts and filter the discussions accordingly ('I only want to see posts on this topic rated 4 or better').

Over time, Malda and his community have periodically refined their 'slashcode' — in effect re-chiseling the Ten Commandments that rule their community. Some refinements have given increased power to its netizens: to relieve the founding fathers from doing all the rating, slashcode now rotates moderators periodically across *Slashdot*'s registered users in a sort of electronic jury duty. Slashcode also calculates a karma for each user based on the cumulative ratings their posts have garnered; users with high karma wield more power in rating posts than users with low karma. To counterbalance this distributed power, Malda has also enabled senior Slashdotters to meta-moderate the moderators, with the goal of keeping the original vision of the community from falling prey to a capricious herd mentality.

Although its Byzantine rules are a constant and heated topic of debate, *Slashdot*'s popularity hasn't suffered as a result. With fifty million pageviews per month, *Slashdot* has given rise to an eponymous term: to be 'slashdotted' is to have someone link to your Web site in a *Slashdot* post only to have the resultant tsumani of curious Slashdotters crash your server as they arrive at your virtual doorstep.

Malda minored in art but believes Slashdot 'is no more art than yesterday's newspaper'.[35] Yet even if *Slashdot* may not be art per se, it suggests a more democratic and efficient means of recognizing new developments than the coterie of curators and critics who guarded the art world's gates in the twentieth century.

EVERY WRITER IS A CRITIC
Nathan Oostendorp, *Everything2*

Based on the same slashcode as *Slashdot*, *Everything2* offers writers the chance to submit short texts and to score each other's remarks. Users whose submissions are 'cooled', or posted to the front page, acquire Experience Points, or XP. Writers who acquire more XP can rise to higher levels where they have more control over the rankings of others.

The result is an exceptionally quirky but highly readable open-source encyclopedia. Unlike purely egalitarian precedents such as Wikipedia, where any visitor can edit an entry and all entries are at the same level, *Everything2*'s attention economy encourages eccentric or provocative subjects. Entries range from things like 'transuranic element' to personalities like 'Hinduist deity Kubera' to ideas like 'Judging people by their intelligence is no different from judging them by their looks'. While *Slashdot*'s writing is conversational, *Everything2*'s is crafted; while *Slashdot* links to outside news, *Everything2* stories usually link to other *Everything2* stories, encouraging a focused, if inbred, community.

SPAWNING ONLINE CREATIVITY
Joline Blais, Jon Ippolito, John Bell, Matt James, Justin Russell, Owen Smith, and Mike Scott, *The Pool*

Tanya is looking for an audio track to incorporate into her video. Eric wants feedback on his concept for a hypertext novel. Juanita wants to find a collaborator who's interested in cyberfeminism and knows Flash. Peer-filtered communities require a 'pool' of ideas, prototypes, and resources that allow users to build on each other's work. That aqueous metaphor underlies the interface for *The Pool*, a shared resource for online art, code, and texts originally assembled by and for students of new media.

Part online archive, part version-tracking software, *The Pool* emphasizes distributed learning and authorship. When surfers access artworks and texts, they automatically gather factual and evaluative information about them for use by future surfers. Contributors can float a concept for others to implement, or take the bait offered by others to explore, debug, or remix existing works. In place of the single-artist, single-artwork paradigm favored by the overwhelming majority of documentation systems, *The Pool* documents — and stimulates — collaboration in a variety of forms, including multi-user, asynchronous, and cross-medium projects.

One example of *The Pool*'s emphasis on distributed authorship is its distinction between the initial conception of an artwork and its subsequent versions. *The Pool*'s structure is designed to make it easy to track the 'wake' left by a contributor's idea as it gets picked up by new artists or rendered in new media, or is accessed by different users with different technologies over subsequent years.

Opposite: The Art Pool and Theme Pool.

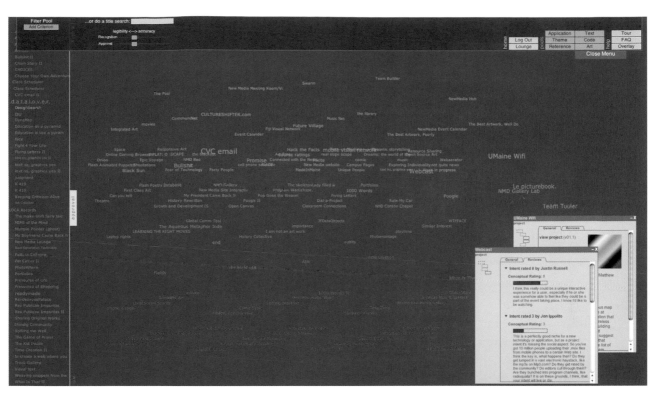

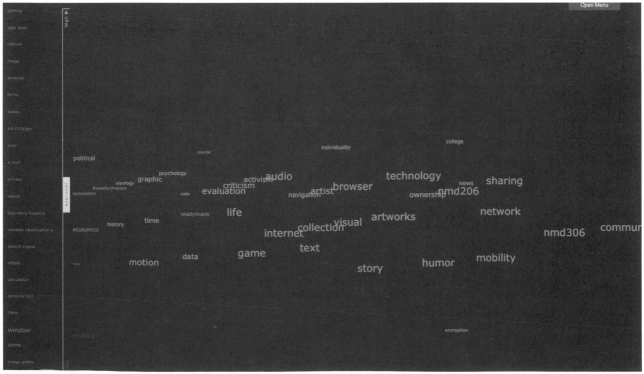

Recognition of Community by a Work

The converse of a community that can recognize the works of its members is an individual work that can recognize a community. Such acts of 'meta-recognition' can take two forms: creating an alternative interface for an established community, or improvising a self-aware community out of a group of people connected professionally or socially. *Conversation Map* is an example of a work that recognizes an established community; *Last Real Net Art Museum*, on the other hand, recognizes an improvised community of people connected to the artwork 'My Boyfriend Came Back from the War'.

Of course, online communities of sufficient size don't need an outsider to 'recognize' them, for they already have their own constituencies and can easily be Googled by potential members. Nevertheless, a creative interface can 're-cognize' even a well-known community by painting a revelatory picture of it. At first glance it may seem that the work of such 're-cognizers' is free of the ethical responsibilities that weigh on the designers of the communities' own interfaces, who have to cultivate loyal followers and represent their contributions fairly. However, maps designed by such hijackers can sometimes end up serving as bona-fide alternative interfaces for the community itself, influencing its self image and valuation. When *StarryNight* launched, for example, its code represented all the texts in the Rhizome textbase equally, as a random assortment of dim stars spread across the screen. As soon as a few visitors used the site to select specific texts, however, the stars corresponding to those texts began to shine more brightly – even if the texts were originally selected by clicking on random stars. The minute difference in luminosity was enough to lead more visitors to click on these stars again, and their brightness increased as a result. This positive-feedback loop, in which 'the rich get richer', is a problem of many online interfaces – even the universally popular search engine Google.[36] The builders of alternative interfaces, like the proverbial scientific observers of quantum-mechanical experiments,[37] can have a measurable impact on the communities they record.

Improvised networks, on the other hand, had no default interface – at least until Friendster. This online site for helping members locate friends of their friends is based on the 'small world' theory of human society. While research on the remarkable connectivity of human networks began in the 1950s, the Internet has both multiplied these connections and provided new tools for visualizing them.

GOSSIP AND GARDEN PLOTS
Judith Donath and Rebecca Xiong, *Visual Who,*
Loom, PeopleGarden, **and** *WebFan*

Judith Donath's Sociable Media Group at MIT has
pioneered several conversation visualizations in
the manner of *Conversation Map*. *Visual Who* maps
people's affinities to mailing lists, while *Loom*
traces the eruption and decay of activity over time
on Usenet's public discussion boards. The *Loom*
project has explored a number of visualizations,
each revealing a different dynamic of electronic
conversation. In one variation, the vertical axis
represents individual contributors, so a row with
many dots indicates an active participant. The
horizontal axis represents time, so a cluster of
activity crowded into a single column represents
a period of intense email exchange.

Departing from scientific-looking node diagrams
and graphs, Rebecca Xiong turns to organic or

feminine metaphors to portray Web-based group
discussions. In *PeopleGarden*, each contributor is
a flower whose petals are messages, with colors
representing their sequence. *WebFan* resembles
Martin Wattenberg's *Idealine* in that branching
segments reveal the evolution of a community effort,
but here the chronological scale is shorter and
updated in real time, reflecting the immediacy of
the medium – email – tracked by *WebFan*.

Studies for *Loom*.

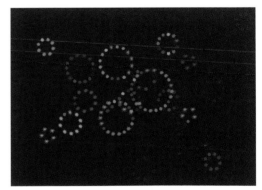

DRUMBEATS IN A GLOBAL VILLAGE
Mark Hansen and Ben Rubins, *Listening Post*

In their 1959 book *The Global Village*,[38] Marshall McLuhan and Bruce R. Powers claim that the world of global electronic communications harks back to an age when the human perception of space was more acoustic than visual. At the time the book was written, the acoustic electronic space it described was pure metaphor. *Listening Post* turns this metaphor into fact by translating the conversation occurring in real-time Internet chat-rooms and messageboards into rhythmical humming, beeping, and synthetic chanting. To complement the acoustic representation of this virtual chatter, visitors to the installation also find themselves surrounded by a grid of two hundred electronic screens, which display the same text fragments in sync with their reverberating aural counterparts.

Of course, the drumbeats McLuhan and Powers describe in *The Global Village* emanate from indigenous communities, whose rhythm of life has kept them alive and sane for the last ten thousand years. By contrast, the tips traded by stock brokers in the chat rooms surveilled by *Listening Post* have a shelf life of a few hours and are unlikely to foster long-term trust – raising the question of whether the increased reach of online communities comes at the cost of their sustainability.

Below and Opposite
Listening Post.

Recognition of Disconnected Communities

The explosive growth of virtual communities has reinvigorated the debate over what constitutes a community. Proponents of a strong definition argue that connection and communication are essential prerequisites, rendering meaningless popular expressions such as 'retiree community' or 'prison community'. In a provocative gesture that counters this presumption, some interlopers deliberately set out to reveal 'disconnected communities', networks of strangers linked by some common interest who nevertheless aren't aware of each other's existence. The interfaces they design typically map connections among shared themes rather than connections among people, for it's quite possible that there are no two people in these networks who even know each other.

EAVESDROPPING ON A GLOBAL CONVERSATION

Cameron Marlow, *Blogdex*

Originally little more than tour guides for the Web, the electronic journals known as blogs have evolved well beyond annotated bookmarks to include **RSS** feeds, **syndication**, and **trackback** — all of which multiply the connections among blogs and the news items they often comment on.

Below: *Blogdex.*

Blogdex is a research project of the **MIT Media Laboratory** tracking the diffusion of information through the weblog community. Ideas can have very similar properties to a disease, spreading through the population like wildfire. The goal of Blogdex is to explore what it is about information, people, and their relationships that allows for this contagious media.

Blogdex uses the links made by webloggers as a proxy to the things they are talking about. Webloggers typically contextualize their writing with hypertext links which act as markers for the subjects they are discussing. These markers are like tags placed on wild animals, allowing Blogdex to track a piece of conversation as it moves from weblog to weblog.

Blogdex crawls all of the weblogs in its database every time they are updated and collects the links that have been made since the last time it was updated. The system then looks across all weblogs and generates a list of fastest spreading ideas. This is the list shown on the **front page**. For each of these links, further detail is provided as to where the link was found, and at what time.

Since it went online, Blogdex has been joined by a number of other tools which provide similar services, Daypop, Technorati and Popdex to name a few. Taking from the design imperative made popular by Google, the guiding force in developing Blogdex has been to "Do one thing, and do it right". In the ecosystem of weblog aggregators, I hope that Blogdex will be the best tool for tracking emergent media.

Blogdex has been providing a service to weblogs for two years, and as a living research experiment it depends on people to help shape it as a tool. If you have any suggestions, please feel free to let us know; they will undoubtedly be useful.

INFORMATION
About Blogdex
Recent News
Search
Add your weblog
XML: **RSS 2.0**
Contact Blogdex

all content copyright © 2001, 2002, 2003 **MIT Media Laboratory**
Special **thanks** to **Wikipedia** for the blogdex.net domain name

While this web of connections depends on the efforts of individual bloggers to link to each other's sites, one of the earliest and most inventive of blog-related innovations, *Blogdex*, reveals emergent relationships among blogs that *aren't* deliberate. A project of MIT's Media Lab, *Blogdex* is a top-40 list of Web sites most commonly cited in blogs around the world. Because it is dynamically generated, this list changes daily; as the site itself explains,

> Webloggers typically contextualize their writing with hypertext links which act as markers for the subjects they are discussing. These markers are like tags placed on wild animals, allowing Blogdex to track a piece of conversation as it moves from weblog to weblog.

Of course, the list is subject to the caprice of the blogging community; on the Thursday before Thanksgiving 2003, for example, one company's claim to having introduced a 'Turkey & Gravy'-flavored beverage ranked higher than President George W. Bush's speech to the English Parliament. Nevertheless, *Blogdex* offers an unprecedented index of the interests of individuals worldwide, taking the collective temperature of an increasingly networked society.

STRANGE MUSICAL BEDFELLOWS
Jason Freeman, *N.A.G.*

Jason Freeman's *N.A.G.* (Network Auralization for Gnutella) automates the popular DJ practice of collaging short samples of popular music into an anarchic musical tissue. Freeman's application echoes the search-and-download interface of the peer-to-peer *Gnutella* network on which *N.A.G.* is built. However, rather than simply downloading the **MP3** files returned for a query on, say, 'Beatles', *N.A.G.* shuffles in real time between snippets of the MP3s as they appear in the list, resulting in a lyrical hodgepodge that might skip from 'Yesterday' to 'Look at all the lonely people' to 'All you need is love' in one ten-second burst. The work is an update on John Cage's 1951 'Imaginary Landscape No. 4', a work in which performers generated random musical juxtapositions by twiddling the dials on twelve radios. In a reversal of its predecessor, *N.A.G.* relies on people to supply the musical selections — the community of music swappers — and a machine to shuffle among them.

SEARCH-ENGINE POETRY
Maciej Wisniewski, *Turnstyle II*

The millions of people who happen to have passed through a given turnstyle in Grand Central Station in New York are not a community in any ordinary sense of the word. However, even though they don't know each other, the diverse members of this transient population nevertheless have shared a specific experience. A comparable claim can be made for many transient online demographics, such as the set of people who have browsed a particular book on Amazon.com or bid on a particular item on eBay. Of course, these demographics are usually invisible to all but the e-commerce firms that harvest such data for marketing their products.

With *Turnstyle II*, the Internet artist Maciej Wisniewski found a way to reveal one such 'disconnected community'. He wrote a search bot that trolled archived email lists and posted excerpts of conversations with certain keywords on a Web site that arrayed text fragments in poetic stanzas. The keywords he chose all related to love or loneliness; despite being stripped of their original context, the phrases in various languages juxtaposed by the bot amounted to a sort of lonely-hearts club on ticker tape. Arrayed in stanzas scrolling across the screen, Wisniewski's found poetry suggests how poor a substitute electronic connection is for emotional connection.

```
hi my name is ashley I live in oklahoma and just…

Sorry

Recover peace religion forgive

Amour, amitie ou aventure sur l' Internet

LE SICILEN OU L' AMOUR PEINTRE

I already told you where to find me pinhead…

Stampfen bis zur…
```

Top right: *N.A.G.*
Right: *Turnstyle II.*

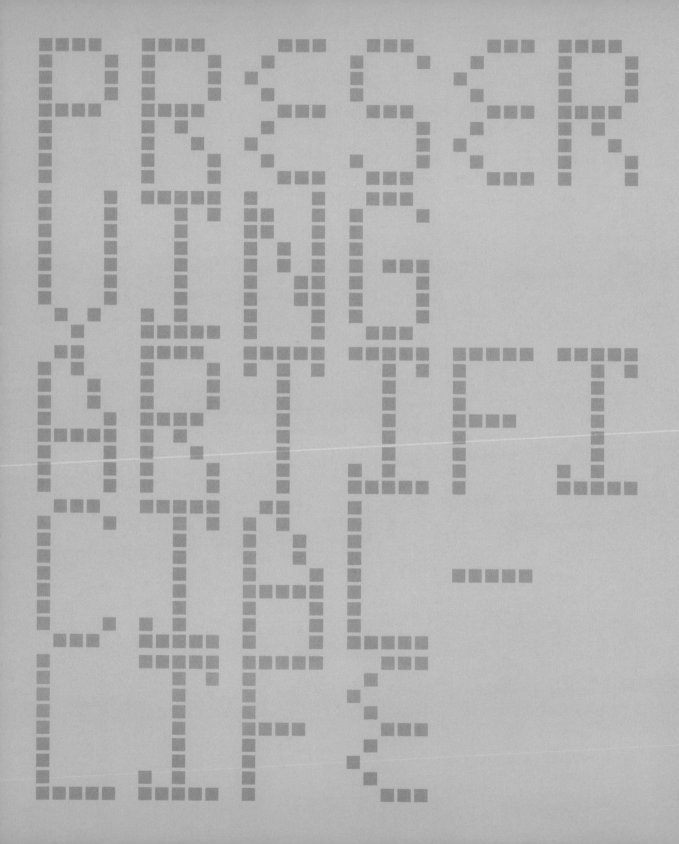

Culture on the cutting edge is not there for long, especially in this age of rapid technological progress and the seemingly equally rapid precession of aesthetic fashion. For traditional plastic art, this has exacerbated the difference between success and failure: sanctification in a hallowed hall of culture, or banishment to obscurity in an attic or garbage dump. A painting by Malevich that has served its tour of duty on the frontline of artistic research earns a final resting place on a wall at the museum of modern art in a major urban center. But what of the works in this book that are not by the avant-garde as defined by art historians but from the great ocean of the Internet and quasi-scientific research? The previous chapter surveyed new recognition networks which can attract attention to these radical works faster than traditional validation mechanisms; in theory, this discursive matrix may also sustain their memory for future generations. But memory is second-hand. New-media artists who want their works to be known more directly have to choose the final form their research will take with that in mind. And they have two diametrically opposed choices: to cast their work in traditional genres like ink or bronze, or to trust code to survive by means of its executability.

This chapter examines an emerging field in which the contrast between these two alternatives is greatest: so-called 'a-life', or artificial life, the creation with a computer of organisms that exhibit lifelike behavior. To complement this animate software, we'll examine parallel experiments with animate 'wetware': *E. coli*, rat brains, and other 'semi-living' entities confined to Petri dishes rather than hard drives. Many of these works have convincing art-like functions: they are executable as either digital or biological code (or both); they are revelatory of evolutionary mechanisms and even aesthetic taste; most of all, they are polymorphously perverse in their proliferation of new forms with no obvious utility.

In the domain of computer and biological scientists, a static visual record is rarely the expected end result of research. To satisfy the art world's predilection for colorful images to display in a gallery, however, a number of researchers investigating the expressive potential of artificial life have transmuted their algorithms into real-time images of **biomorphs** cavorting on video monitors or in wall projections. Others have even trained their synthetic organisms to print out pen-and-ink drawings, render Iris prints, and otherwise feed the art-gallery system inert formats it can recognize. But do these static end-products best preserve the volatility, and hence the immunological function, of live art? Or are they merely aesthetic vaccines – dead versions of once virulent originals that confer only partial and short-lived protection? If so, then it's not at all obvious how to preserve art whose medium is *E. coli* or rat brains. Nevertheless, the most potent biological immunity takes the form of somatic memory left by antibody responses to live pathogens. Likewise, the best art leaves a cultural memory – in this case, of encounters with technological assault by biological, digital, or ideological viruses – that perseveres and thus protects society. The degree of this perseverance is directly related to the extent to which the radical and dynamic nature of the original work is preserved over time and space. < >

A WILDLIFE SANCTUARY FOR COMPUTER VIRUSES

Tom Ray, *Tierra*

Tierra's gamekeeper, Tom Ray, is a zoologist at the University of Oklahoma and the Advanced Telecommunications Research laboratory in Tokyo. To create this 'wildlife sanctuary for computer viruses', he writes snippets of program code designed to copy themselves and then releases them onto his hard drive to reproduce. To this promiscuous mix, he adds two ingredients that make the network more Darwinian jungle than sedate server. First, he configures his operating system so that it will introduce occasional random mutations in the computer code of these viruses. Second, he lets loose a 'grim reaper' **subroutine** to weed out and erase any mutated algorithms which fail to function properly or cause errors. Once Ray lets the system go, it proceeds of its own accord, generating new viruses that are most fit to survive in the population.

Thanks to this magic combination of self-replication, mutation, and competition for disk space, Ray's little viruses evolve into new 'species' he never could have predicted. Their patterns of evolution are strikingly similar to those of biological organisms, despite the fact that they are just ones and zeros on a hard disk. Among the evolutionary milestones *Tierra* has produced are parasitic algorithms — snippets of program code embedded in other algorithms that are automatically reproduced when their hosts reproduce. As in natural ecosystems, such parasites can dominate a system until mutations give rise to a variation of the host's genome that is immune to the parasite, at which point immune hosts quickly dominate the population. Because it can be implemented over a computer network of interconnected hard drives, Ray's sanctuary has also produced nocturnal nomads: populations of algorithms that migrate, via a sort of guerrilla email, to the dark side of a global network in order to take advantage of computers that are available because their users are asleep. Although

Right: *Tierra* visualization shows how dominant organisms (red) can succumb to parasites (yellow), only to be succeeded by immune hosts (blue).

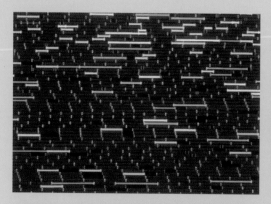

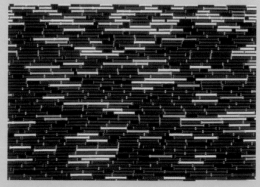

A 'SEMI-LIVING' ARTIST

Steve Potter and SymbioticA, *Meart*

Incorporating cutting-edge research in wetware and software, *Meart* is a radical experiment in synthetic life that ironically manages to eke out an artwork in conventional format. For the brains of this 'semi-living artistic entity', the neuroscientist Steve Potter cultured a network of a few thousand cells from the cortex of embryonic rats in his lab at the Georgia Institute of Technology in Atlanta. The habitat for this rodent Rembrandt is no ordinary Petri dish but a Multi-Electrode Array (MEA) outfitted with electrodes for communication between the cells and external electronics. The signals generated by these neurons — which, it must be said, are not necessarily focused on art-making — wend their way over the Internet to the SymbioticA lab at the University of Western Australia in Perth. Awaiting them is the brawn to go with the brain: a robotic drawing arm gripping three colored markers positioned above a white canvas.

As if this setup weren't a sufficient departure from the typical artistic process, the experimenters came up with an elaborate scheme for 'closing the loop' between brain and brawn, to make possible some degree of the feedback characteristic of truly animate systems. To begin the loop, visitors to SymbioticA are caught on a Webcam while they view the resulting drawing. Their eight-by-eight-pixel image, converted from this video capture into a datastream sent back to Potter's lab in Georgia, is fed into the sixty-four electrodes snaking into the Petri dish, which stimulates selected neural pathways of former rat brain. In a crude sense, the experimenters are tricking a rat in Georgia into 'seeing' a person in Perth.

In a further translation from cerebral to pictorial space, the electronics in Potter's lab record which regions of rat brain spark the most electrical activity from this input and then reroute these data back to Perth. There, the drawing arm marks the canvas in the same region where the rat brain was activated. The resulting composition may look like a work by Cy Twombly, but the concept is right out of

M. C. Escher: *Meart*'s arm is drawing its brain in the act of perceiving a face.

Researchers have mapped brain response to visual stimuli before, from Hubel and Weisel's experiments with cat brains in the 1950s to contemporary PET scans of humans observing images by Hanna and Antonio Damasio. Two factors make *Meart* more than a kooky variation on these experiments: first, its focus on creating an autonomous, 'semi-living' entity rather than studying ordinary life processes; and second, its deliberate provocation of the art world by creating a pen-and-ink drawing.

Of course, more biotech labs are outfitted with Petri dishes than robotic arms for penning artistic masterpieces. But SymbioticA is no ordinary research facility. It is the University of Western Australia's artistic laboratory dedicated to the research, learning, and critique of life sciences. *Meart* is but one of the loopy experiments in extreme science carried out by SymbioticA's researchers, which have included growing fish cells over microprocessors (*Fish & Chips*), living skin over worry dolls (*Tissue Sculpture*), and inch-long wing-shaped objects from living pig tissue (*Pig Wings*). Potter, the Georgia Tech neuroscientist, describes his goals in quasi-scientific terms: 'I hope that we can look at the drawings it makes and see some

Above: Meart.

their lifeblood pulses across modem lines rather than capillaries, Ray himself claims that his creatures are alive — in a way that even artificial-intelligence programs are not – due to the fact that they reproduce and evolve. In short, the algorithmic creatures in his virtual bestiary do almost everything that organic creatures do.

Except make drawings. As we'll see later in this chapter, experiments in artificial life are most likely to catch the art world's eye if they produce some aesthetic byproduct along the way: prints, plotter drawings, interactive installations. Researchers have even applied genetic algorithms directly to the task of making images as aesthetically pleasing as possible. And yet, like SymbioticA's artist-researchers, many of these picture-making experimenters justify their work by touting its relevance to or use of cutting-edge science. Ray, by contrast, emphasizes that his viruses are not beholden to some predefined fitness function such as the ability to run fast, display appealing colors, or grow into a recognizable shape; like natural ecosystems, *Tierra* follows its own nose when it comes to evolution. Has Ray crossed the line from art to biology by actually trying to achieve life rather than merely representing it? Or is his research not recognized as creative activity because he hasn't added an artificial 'fudge factor' to make his ecosystem look like art?

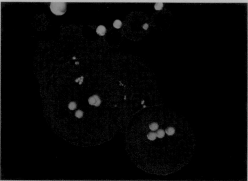

Above: Visualization of networked *Tierra*.

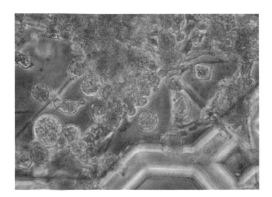

evidence of learning. Then we can scrutinize the cultured network under the microscope to help understand the learning process at the cellular level.'[1] However, as a clue that their value lies in perverse revelations rather than scientific advancement, SymbioticA's ventures seem to have been most welcome in new-media art contexts: *Fish & Chips* was exhibited at the Ars Electronica Festival in 2001, while *Pig Wings* appeared at the Biennale of Electronic Arts Perth. Yet as SymbioticA neuroscientist Stuart Bunt has suggested,[2] the atmosphere of SymbioticA's experiments changes subtly from workplace to spectacle in the migration from lab to art gallery. Once transported to a glassed-in exhibition chamber, Pyrex flasks and other run-of-the-mill staples of a research lab become exotic set pieces in an 'art installation', while the sustained attention that researchers give a deliberate scientific process is replaced by the passing glance of the typical gallery-goer. The focus shifts from research methods and data analysis to brightly colored scribbles taped on a wall and evocative close-ups of goldfish cells on video monitors — from scientific process to artistic product.

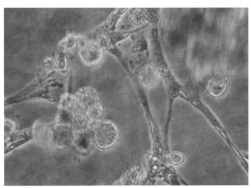

This loss in translation is familiar to anyone who has studied the history of process-oriented art in the twentieth century. Once it enters a museum's hallowed halls, any artwork that began life as performance, whether a Dada poetry slam from 1920 or a Fluxus piano-bashing from 1960, ends life as an installation in a white cube or as a poster in an antiseptic vitrine. The advent of digital media has provided new methods of translation but hasn't necessarily lessened its damaging effects, since the storage paradigm that desiccates performance art can also reduce dynamic media to static screenshots.[3]

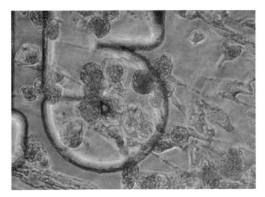

The Problem of Recognition

Tom Ray doesn't talk about his work as art, nor does he call himself an artist. The researchers of SymbioticA, on the other hand, explicitly refer to themselves as 'tissue engineering artists' or 'Wet Biology Art Practitioners'.[4] Nevertheless, it is not merely the intent that makes projects like *Tierra* less likely to be found in art contexts than projects like Meart. *Tierra* is less likely to be recognized as art by an art world accustomed to defining art by medium.[5]

Roman Verostko's biological metaphor, introduced earlier, can help clarify the difference between SymbioticA's approach and Ray's. Verostko describes the transition from rules to result as 'epigenetic' — that is, generating a phenotype (drawing) from a **genotype** (algorithm). For him, this is an analogy; although his atmospheric drawings are drawn by a software-driven plotter, the rules encoded in that software do not evolve in a literal sense.[6] The artists discussed in this chapter, however, turn Verostko's metaphor into digital reality by emulating the genetic processes of mutation and recombination to create vivid new forms of art and life.

Whether these new forms are cast in silicon or skin, the question of intelligibility is just as central for these works as it is for the software art discussed in the first chapter. For gussying up phenotypes in stylish dress only disguises their relation to their genotypes. When artists mystify their working process, it suggests they are trying to increase the value of their work by husbanding its artistic secrets instead of trusting to whatever inherent interest may be latent within it. This criticism can be lobbied at much of SymbioticA's work. Although *Meart* results in a familiar-enough ink drawing – one reviewer has likened it to 'the imaginative scribbling of a three-year-old'[7] – that image is made by a labyrinthine chain of techniques: Webcam > data array > **TCP/IP** > neuronal stimulation > electrical activity > TCP/IP > robotic actuators > pen-and-ink drawing. *Meart*'s phenotype may look familiar, but its genetic process is difficult to follow even for the technically inclined.

By contrast, *Tierra* produces no pretty pictures to hang on a wall and no familiar genres to document in an art magazine. This is primarily because it has no phenotype, unless you count Ray's diagrams representing the genomes in a given population as colored bricks in a wall or the proliferation of viruses across a computer network as spheres popping up in an abstract space. Importantly, *Tierra*'s straightforward visualizations involve no fudging – no chain of arbitrary translations from one discipline or medium to the next, no fitness function imposed by its creator to result in aesthetically pleasing or evocative imagery. *Tierra* does not even fit in the category of interactive art, since permitting viewers to twiddle the knobs after the evolution had already begun would undermine the very transparency that grants those same viewers an understanding of the relation between rule and result. As we'll see, it is ironically this truth to its own process that makes *Tierra* unlikely to persevere as an artistic artifact in the Modernist mold.

The Problem of Perseverance

Human history has seen two strategies for preserving culture. In the first, artists have emulated inanimate objects by chiseling stone and casting bronze – media that survive through durability. In the second, artists have emulated animate objects by composing songs and telling stories – media that survive through performance. The former media are static, built to last, secured in cold storage for safekeeping. The latter are dynamic, built to adapt, transferred from generation to generation like the genes of an evolving species.

From the clay tablets of 3000 BC up until the arrival of the Internet five millennia later, the number of dynamic media stayed roughly the same – dance, song, theater – while that of static media multiplied. Over time, many of the oral media of performed culture have been replaced by storage media of recorded culture: spoken stories have been written down in books, songs have been recorded onto vinyl, theater has been recast as film. Digital media have also generated their own panoply of storage techniques and devices, from diskettes to **DAT** tapes to DVDs. Yet in many forms of new-media art, and in artificial life in particular, the work's ephemeral, performative aspect is what is most interesting about it. Because most of them date from a century marked by an explosion in the number of storage media, brick-and-mortar museums – by default still the custodians of art in the early twenty-first century – are ill equipped to safeguard the temporal or contextual aspects of any artwork.

Some digital artists are content for museums to collect the by-products of their investigations even if they no longer preserve the executability that attracted those artists to digital media in the first place. For others, the ability to run a work is more important than the ability to save it. In describing a toolkit that preceded Adrian Ward's project *Auto-Illustrator*, Ward and collaborator Geoff Cox expressed this latter perspective: '*Autoshop* should only be appreciated as software, its output irrelevant. With this in mind, it is proposed that the next version of the software might 'patch' a bug so there is no 'Save As' feature at all.'[8]

In the hands of the creators profiled in this chapter, genetic processes promote the perseverance of many species of virtual or biological creatures. But only those genetic systems that are *themselves* designed to persevere dynamically hold out the hope of keeping their creatures alive rather than preserving them as inert output.

Modes of Perseverance

The labwork of investigators like Joe Davis or Oron Cats may never translate exactly into an experience that can be relived outside the lab. But *Tierra* might, for it depends not on Petri dishes and rat neurons but on computer hard drives and networks. *Tierra*'s denizens are native to cyberspace; they are already escapees from the lab. Their survival depends less on finding stable forms to stand the test of time than on maximizing their adaptability so they can change as their electronic environment changes.

Of course, the de facto custodians of culture – museum conservators – are poorly equipped for maximizing an artwork's adaptability, since they usually see their job as keeping it as static as possible. There is no way, however, that this paradigm will work for the rich panoply of artistic media born of the digital and Internet revolutions; storing a *Tierra* colony as a data file on Windows-formatted CD-ROM would only forestall its demise. For within five years the software to read the data would become obsolete, within ten the CD would have delaminated, within fifteen it might become impossible to find a CD-ROM drive, and within twenty Windows would be **dead media**.[9] For digital culture, storage equals death.

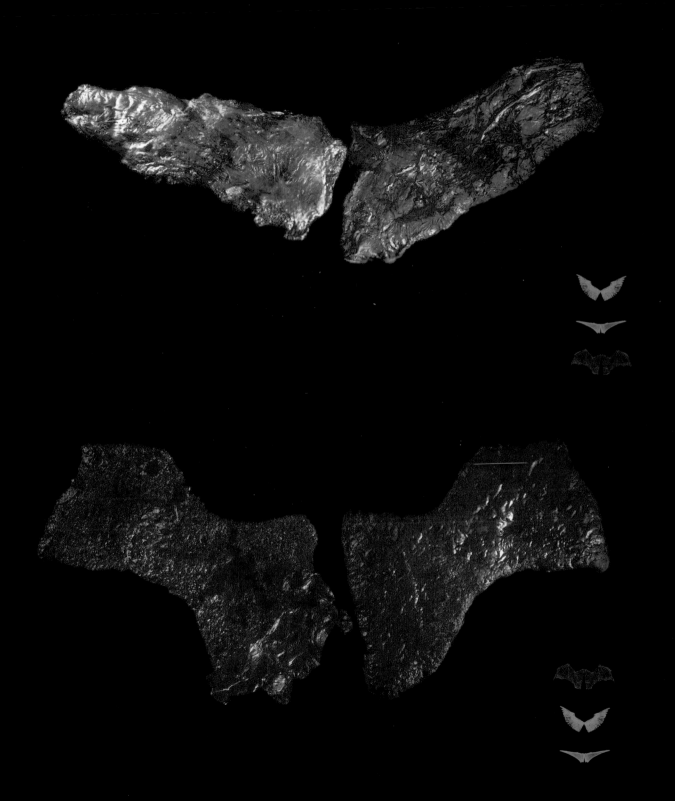

For media of the Internet age, the only alternative to storing fragments that point to a foregone experience is to accept the necessity of remaking that experience even if the experience changes in the process. If we are unwilling to accept a paradigm shift from fixed to **variable media**,[10] only those works with a static end product will survive. Some plotter drawings, Iris prints, and a handful of text explanations – what a meager memory the storage paradigm would leave of this fecund moment in art history. A SymbioticA drawing hung out of context on a museum wall would no longer be category-breaking but category-reinforcing – representing not artificial life but artificial death.

Artificial life isn't the only form of artistic research imperiled by static perseverance. The Introduction argued that art's power to tap into a culture's unconscious helps it confront future threats before they arrive on the doorstep or in an email inbox. Yet the art world's white pedestals and gilt frames exclude the most visionary art of all: artistic research. In order to accommodate the dynamic forms art takes in the Internet age, society's definition of art will have to expand to include research that is ongoing rather than discrete, dispersed rather than self-contained – a theme we will return to in the final chapter.

Perseverance of Static Works

Artificial life tends to get noticed as art when it cameos in a wall calendar or video clip. Genetic artists who produce such fixed products target them for museums, libraries, and other cultural-heritage systems premised on storage as the canonical preservation strategy, they take pains in their documentation to describe the works in terms curators and conservators will understand. While they gloss over the intricate technicalities of their genetic algorithms, many of these artists' Web sites go into great detail about the type of paper and printing procedures used to create their wall-based imagery, often describing them as 'archival', 'colorfast', and 'museum-quality'. These adjectives are not applied to the aesthetic quality of the images but to their durability as unchanging artifacts. Given that these same artists often extol genetic algorithms for their variability and serendipity, it is ironic how much attention they give to ensuring the end-product doesn't vary – a bit like breeding a butterfly for flight only to pin it to the wall.

ARTIFICIAL SELECTION
William Latham

Although clearly inspired by nature, artist William Latham describes genetic algorithms as a means to create something more savage, and perhaps more beautiful, than nature. In practice, his work began with a three-dimensional shape generated from the mathematical equivalent of genes: formulas like **polynomial**s or **sine wave**s which determine whether a form will be straight or twisted or wavy, and whether its color will be matte or speckled or gradated. Latham then applied a program he built with programmer Stephen Todd, called *Mutator*, to enable this formula to go forth and multiply — by mutation (changing a snippet of code in a particular formula), crossover (swapping code sequences between two formulae), or splicing (nesting one mathematical function in another). Of the handful of variations that resulted from this genetic

inbreeding, Latham would pick the spiral or squiggle he found most intriguing and let it sire a new generation. To keep things more interesting, there was no incest taboo to keep him from breeding, say, a shape with its genetic 'parent' or 'child', and no polygamy taboo to prevent a shape from breeding with more than one other shape. Latham would repeat this virtual orgy of artificial selection until he was happy with the image that resulted.

While Latham's forms could in principle have all kinds of strange relations, in practice this kinky sex required his consent, since *Mutator* didn't originally work on its own. Although he describes his computer as more than a utilitarian tool, Latham stayed firmly in control of the process.

Latham's coiled tendrils and twisted nautiloids have received varied reactions from art critics. Where some see 'fungal spores' or 'fossils from an alien civilization', others see brocade, jewelry, or the echoes of other decorative arts — implying that Latham's fine-art training at the Royal College of Art in London biased his work toward familiar forms

rather than his stated goal of uncovering ideas 'beyond the human imagination'.[11]

It's significant that Latham was originally known in genetic art circles for presenting his three-dimensional 'virtual sculptures' only as static images or non-interactive videos. If artificial-life artists are gods – to borrow writer Kevin Kelly's description of Latham's contemporary Karl Sims[12] – then Latham seemed to be an interventionist god, guiding evolution and editing its byproducts with no one to please but himself. More recently, however, he's targeted a broader audience with a *Mutator* screensaver that lets viewers breed their own shapes and even a computer game, *Evolva*, based on his 3D creatures. If creators of artificial life are akin to deities, Latham has decided to allow others to 'play god' – at least within the morphological and narrative paths he offers them.

'WHERE INFORMATION CAN GO, A VIRUS CAN GO WITH IT'[13]

Joseph Nechvatal

Another artist who trusts to static perseverance for his dynamically generated forms is Joseph Nechvatal, whose paintings are derived from the trails left by artificial organisms programmed to scavenge colors from a digital image. Given Nechvatal's high-tech process — employing **cellular automata**, viral mutations, and even a spray-painting robot — it is ironic that the final output is an acrylic painting on canvas. Furthermore, each virally modified Nechvatal canvas stands alone, in the style of an artistic masterpiece rather than the time-lapse photographs and diagrams that are so instructive for biological and artificial-life research. Once frozen on a single surface, the scientific allusions in his work take a back seat to artistic ones, whether the organic ornament of the graphic artist H. R. Giger or the ingratiating palette of the fabric artist Miriam Shapiro. Although he has recently experimented with interactive and animated formats, Nechtaval's primary ambition for a-life is to bring painting 'back from the dead'.[14]

FAMILY PORTRAITS OF PICTORIAL GENES

Philip Galanter

Perhaps because his background straddles art and computer science, Philip Galanter steps a little further outside the conventional forms of artistic expression to render his process more visible. He achieves this not through his choice of media — his prints, light-boxes, and video loops are familiar media to gallery visitors — but by his choice of presentation formats that demonstrate causal connections between multiple images rather than settling for a single 'optimum' output.

A grid of digital prints entitled *100 Random Chromosomes*, for example, displays the images that result from various recombinations of a predetermined number of pictorial 'genes'. Each gene controls the color, brush type, width, length, density, order, or shape of marks. The offspring of this diverse gene pool ranges from singular gestures dominating a relatively sedate ground,

to energetic calligraphic compositions where no gesture dominates, to 'pathological' monochrome canvases in which a brush mutates to become so wide that it covers the entire canvas in one stroke.

Some of the visual differences between Nechvatal's and Galanter's images most certainly arise from their different genetic algorithms. What is more striking than the stylistic differences, however, are their similarities — a fact that calls into question Latham's claim that artificial life can extend art 'beyond the human imagination'. Both approaches produce all-over compositions with decorative color palettes — a pictorial style with a clear precedent in the paintings and fabric works of the Pattern-and-Decoration artists from the 1970s. Whether the resemblance between Nechvatal's acrylics and Miriam Shapiro's quilts or Galanter's prints and Robert Kushner's oils derives from an accident of software or a deliberation of the artist's hand, these end-products of artificial life look surprisingly conventional from an aesthetic point of view, given how revolutionary their processes are from a scientific one.

Right: *100 Random Chromosomes*, with two details, opposite.

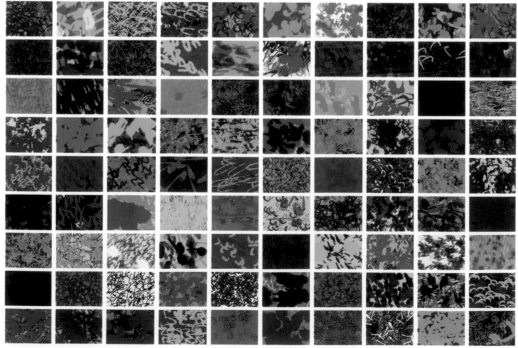

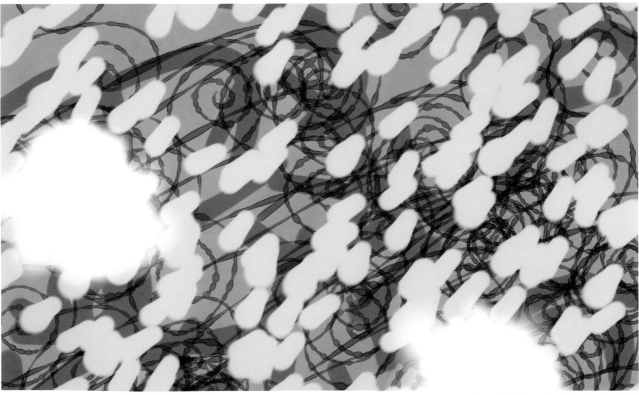

Perseverance of Dynamic Works

'People think about art as being nice "still lifes",'says William Latham, 'but my art is far more about the very processes which actually generate life.'[15] From an artificial-life perspective, his criticism is apt – 'still life' certainly is a contradiction in terms – but ironically, his critique is easily directed back at his own static products.

Of course, digital media don't need to stand still. Unlike pen plotters and Iris printers, interactive installations provide a mechanism for artificial life to remain dynamic rather than static. The recent shift by Latham, Nechvatal, and Galanter to interactive works seems to reflect the realization that, as Galanter puts it, generative art should move 'from nouns to verbs'.[16] But for viewers to grasp adaptive art requires it not merely to move, but to adapt. And in order for a system to be adaptive, it must respond to its environment – which in the case of an interactive installation means putting the viewer in the driver's seat.

BREEDING ART FOR THE GALLERY-GOER
Karl Sims, *Genetic Images* and *Galápagos*

Like Latham's *Mutator* or Galanter's genetic-algorithm software, called *GA*, the genetic program underlying Karl Sims's imagery breeds computer code by mutating the code of individual programs or swapping sequences between two of them. Unlike Latham, who generally remains in control, Sims is willing to put his viewer in charge of selecting the 'best' genes to be passed on to the next generation. Galanter has also packaged his software for other artists to use, but the lengthy time *GA* requires to render a visual phenotype from a chosen genotype prevents it from driving an interactive installation. Thanks to Sims's access to the powerful Connection Machine **parallel-processing supercomputer**,[17] he was able to illustrate the evolution of creatures in real time, enabling viewers to determine his imagery's genetic destiny.

Visitors to Sims's interactive installations at the Centre Pompidou in Paris or Ars Electronica in Linz, Austria, saw an arc of twelve to sixteen monitors arranged on pedestals. Each monitor initially displayed a different image generated from a combination of seeds in the form of mathematical equations. A sine function might produce a wavy image, while a random-number generator might produce an image of white noise; in *Genetic Images*, these seed functions were combined to make two-dimensional abstractions, while in *Galápagos* they combined to form three-dimensional biomorphs floating in a mathematical sea.

But it is not the imagery that makes Sims's installations different from their static counterparts. In both *Genetic Images* and *Galápagos*, viewers can express preferences for one image or another by stepping on a foot switch in front of each monitor; these choices designate the pictorial genes to parent the next generation of images. The mathematical equivalent of mutation and sex[18] among these genes begets another dozen images that in theory are closer to the viewers' tastes. Museum-goers can then select the best images among these 'children' and breed them to generate an ensemble of 'grandchild' images, continuing the process until they are satisfied with one or more of the resulting images.

Because they are guided by audience rather than artist, *Genetic Images* and *Galápagos* recall the tongue-in-cheek experiment in survey-based art-making *The Most Wanted Painting* by Witalij Komar and Alexsander Melamid. This duo of Soviet artists conducted a poll to ascertain viewers' tastes in art,

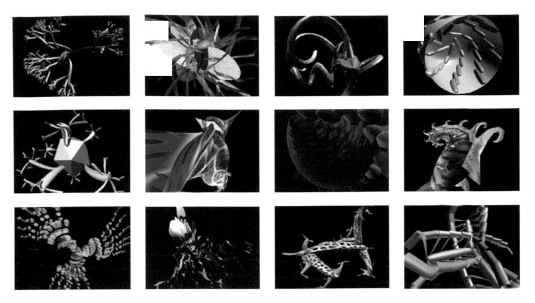

then hand-painted the traits reported most often in the poll — including wild animals, historical figures, and the color blue — into a single oil-on-canvas. However, while Komar and Melamid let viewers choose their preferred genotypes, Sims lets them choose among phenotypes. This is a more accurate approximation of the way nature works; just as the speed of a full-grown antelope guarantees survival in the Serengeti rather than the shape of its chromosomes, so viewers of Sims's genetic images are better off judging the final images than the mathematical algorithms that gave rise to them. (It may also explain why *The Most Wanted Painting* turned out to be an unsightly hodgepodge.) For Sims's interactive work, phenotypes function as a sort of visual paraphrase[19] for the genetic algorithms that underlie them. Non-mathematicians may not grasp how sine(x) bred with $\sqrt{1-x^2}$ yields sine($\sqrt{1-x^2}$), but they can guess that breeding squiggles and circles could yield squiggly circles.

Sims's interactive genetic art inspires the same hyperbole as Latham's static version, almost to the letter: Kevin Kelly pronounced in *Wired* that 'only evolution brings us things that are literally beyond our imaginations,' calling Sims's imagery 'the daydreams of machines'.[20] Later in his essay, however, Kelly seems to have changed his mind, crediting the inventiveness of Sims's imagery to

his artistic powers rather than those of his computer: 'The artist becomes a god, creating an Eden in which surprising things will grow.' Could one of the reasons Kelly resorted to contradictory metaphors be that Sims's viewer-centered images — like those of his artist-centered peers — turn out to be beholden to their own aesthetic? Like the islands of Galápagos themselves, Sims's *Galápagos* seems insular in its morphological range.

Why is such an open work constrained to a limited look? Could it be that any art made with sines and cosines will look like Sims's, because the off-the-shelf equations of mathematics span a limited aesthetic range? Or are his viewers to blame for electing according to bourgeois, average taste, as in *The Most Wanted Painting*?

The progression of Sims's imagery over the four years between *Genetic Images* and *Galápagos* suggests that although there is nothing inherently more natural about breeding three-dimensional objects than two-dimensional paintings, *Galápagos* deliberately grows tentacled 'blobjects' that 'look like' artificial life. Could it be that the aestheticized end-products of *Genetic Images* weren't sufficiently interesting for art viewers, so Sims biased his seed equations to produce end-products that would remind gallery-goers of science rather than art? Why did he adopt a forced graphic metaphor for

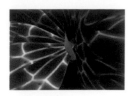

evolution to supplement his computer's literal emulation of an evolutionary process?

Kelly's claims to the contrary, the answer is that looking at a single product of Sims's image-making algorithms is no more enlightening than looking at a single static image of Latham's or Galanter's. To date, the static imagery of most artificial-life art has been more artificial than lifelike. For all their metaphors of pre-Cambrian or viral fecundity, the images are surprisingly antiseptic, bereft of painterly marks, errors, or other evidence of an organic or accumulative process. Although many of the formulae are calculated by iteration, computers render them as single images that pop onto the screen in one go or print on the plotter from one corner to another.[21] The scaleless images bear no reference to the size of the mark-making instrument or the position of a viewer, nor do they have any of the graininess that accompanies images of plankton or paramecia from a real sea. Noise in a signal can be evidence of a process, but there is no such evidence in these noiseless images.

So, Kelly and Latham are wrong: it is not evolution's look that is beyond human imagination but its process. Interactors with Sims's installations glimpse that process, but not curators or critics who catch one of his relatively banal images reproduced in art magazines.

Although he is the victim of the art world's focus on static imagery, Sims has speculated, 'Perhaps someday the value of simulated examples of evolution such as this will be comparable to the value that Darwin found in the mystical creatures of the Galápagos Islands.'[22] The hope that a future generation will see the value of such research should sound familiar, for we heard the same sentiment at the beginning of the book when Ken Musgrave claimed that society would someday see the value of Proceduralist art. But, like works of Performance and Conceptual art before them, no work of software art or artificial life will ever enter the art-historical canon as long as the latter's criteria are based on aesthetic aspects that survive by static perseverance.

Above: *Galápagos.*
Right: *The Most Wanted Painting.*

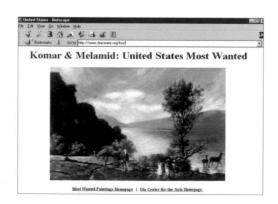

TRANSGENIC FLESH FOR AESTHETIC ENDS

Eduardo Kac, *Genesis*

A pioneer of wet artificial life, Eduardo Kac is best known for his plan to genetically engineer a glow-in-the-dark rabbit to be part of his family. While bioluminescent bunnies make headlines, they don't make installations as good as Kac's *Genesis*. *Genesis* begins with a Biblical quote that suitably sums up the hubris suggested by genetic engineering: 'Let man have dominion over the fish of the sea, and over the fowl of the air, and over every living thing that moves upon the earth.' Kac translated this sentence from English into a sequence of DNA nucleotides[23] and inserted this 'artist's gene' into a species of bacteria that glows green in the dark.[24]

The *Genesis* installation was clearly designed with a gallery-going public in mind. A spot-lit Petri dish sits on a pedestal in a darkened room; flanking this centerpiece is a magnified video of its bacterial contents dividing and interacting on one wall, with texts of the sentence from Genesis and its DNA equivalent spelled out on adjacent walls. Visitors need not get their hands dirty, because only remote viewers accessing the work through its Web site can interact with it. By triggering a burst of ultraviolet light, they both illuminate the portion of the bacterial colony contaminated with the 'artist's gene' and encourage mutation that may affect the future propagation of the bacteria.

While Kac's didactic presentation exposes the genotype behind the glow-in-the-dark bugs on display, his installation's dramatic lighting and pretentious title ironically reinforce the air of religiosity he hopes his work will undermine. When Kac etches his gene's translations and mutations into granite tablets, is he lampooning that religiosity or conceding to the art world's appetite for durable artifacts?

Below and following pages: *Genesis*.

Let man have dominion over the fish of the sea and over the fowl of the air and over every living thing that moves upon the earth

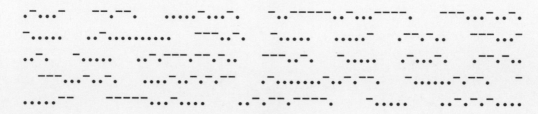

Morse to DNA conversion principle

DASH (-) = T   A = WORD SPACE

DOT (.) = C   G = LETTER SPACE

```
CTCCGCGTATTGCTGTCACCCCGCTGCCCTGCATCCGTTTGTTGCCGTCGCCGTTTGTCA
TTTGCCCTGCGCTCATGCCCCGCACCTCGCCGCCCGCCCCATTTCCTCATGCCCCGCACC
CGCGCTACTGTCGTCCATTTGCCCTGCGCTCATGCCCCGCACCTCGTTTGCTTGCTCCAT
TTGCCTCATGCCCCGCACTGCCGCTCACTGTCGTCCATTTGCCCTGCGCTCACGCCCTGC
GCTCGTCTTACTCCGCCGCCCTGCCGTCGTTCATGCCCCGCCGTCGTTCATGCCCCGCTG
TATTGTTTGCCCTGCGCCCACCTGCTTCGTTTGTCATGCCCCGCACGCTGCTCGTGCCCC
```

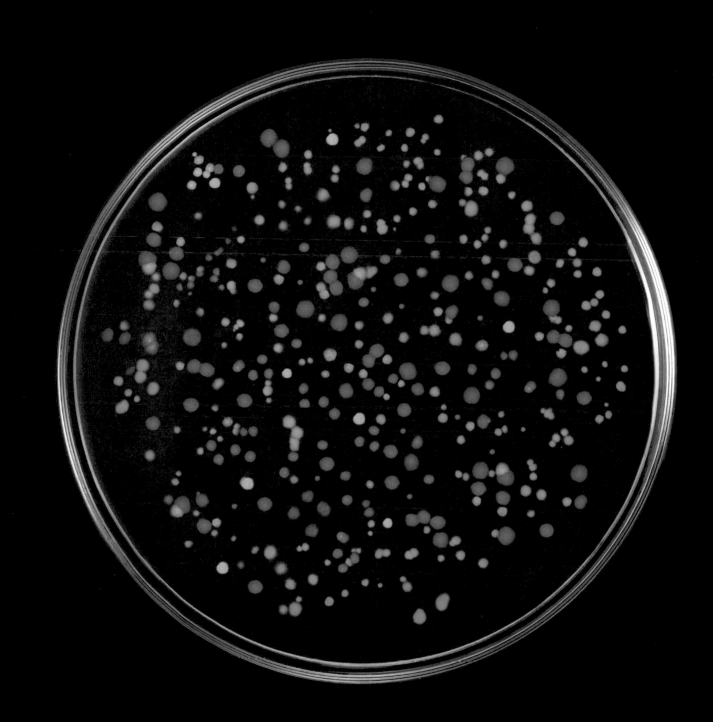

A CLONE LIKE NO OTHER
Natalie Jeremijenko, *OneTrees*

So far, the edge studies we've examined have put artists or viewers in the driver's seat of their species' evolution. Natalie Jeremijenko's *OneTrees* project illustrates a third alternative: letting the life forms determine the course of their own evolution. Her approach is the antithesis of Kac's: the dispersal of a simple natural phenomenon into the natural world instead of the gathering of a complex set of technologies into an art-world setting.

Jeremijenko collaborated with scientists to produce a hundred clones of a deciduous tree. Grown into saplings, her identical centuplets were exhibited together at the Yerba Buena Center for the Arts in San Francisco, but have since been planted across the Bay area at public sites where their divergent growth patterns will serve as a visible disproof of the prevailing myth — bolstered by the hype surrounding genetic engineering — that cloned individuals are identical.

LIFE IN TWO DIMENSIONS
Ed Burton, *Sodaplay*

Paintings, drawings, and even interactive installations aren't the best forms for revealing process, since their emphasis has traditionally been on pigment or pixels that can be perceived in the flesh — whether the flesh is physical or virtual. What's interesting about artificial life, however, is not necessarily the images produced as byproducts but the process intuited from those byproducts. Chapter 01 included artists less interested in retinal output than the structure of the software that generated that output. The situation is analogous for artificial-life art, and the strategy is comparable. By focusing on software that can be ported from machine to machine, even viewed over the Internet, some artificial-life researchers seem to be telling us to think about what's happening behind the screen rather than on it.

One of the most entertaining – and, for some users, emotionally engaging — of the Web sites devoted to experimenting with artificial creatures is *Sodaplay*, an online bestiary where Java-powered stick figures creep, crawl, and clatter their way across the screen. *Sodaplay*'s virtual arthropods aren't much to look at compared to Sims's stripy octopi, but their behavior in response to user intervention is most compelling. *Sodaplay*'s godlike users can control the underlying physics of the

Sodaplay world as well as the forms of its creatures — loosening or stiffening their muscles, adjusting the friction they encounter when clambering across floor or walls, even turning gravity up, down, or off.

What's surprising is how attached *Sodaplay* gods become to their **wireframe** children. The Web site is more of a virtual dog show than a zoo, since users can add their own creatures and contribute to online discussions. The site's 'Frequently Asked Questions' include headings for 'psychological' and 'emotional' queries:

> i think i've emotionally bonded with
> daintywalker. when i was too rough with it its
> leg twisted right round and it looked in such
> pain i had to close my browser. am i a cruel
> monster?
> we can assure you that sodaconstructor models
> don't feel pain, you can be as rough with them as
> you like. however some models are more fragile
> than others and don't survive extreme conditions
> very well
>
> *
>
> help me! i've been playing with sodaconstructor
> for hours. i don't work, i don't eat, i don't sleep.
> am i an addict?
> yes

Sodaplay suggests that the creation of life involves more than merely emulating a few natural processes: it can involve inspiring an empathetic bond between creator and creature — a premise explored by few other experiments in artificial life, scientific or artistic.[25]

Opposite: *OneTrees.*
Below: *Sodaplay.*

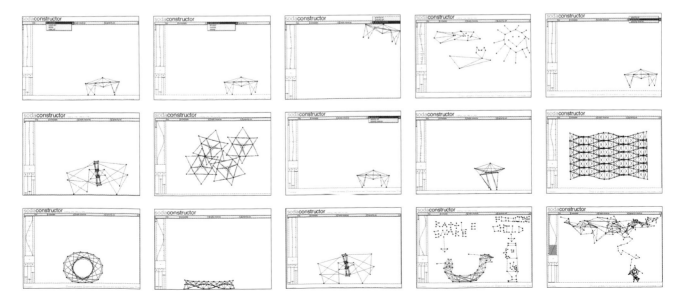

ALGORITHMIC SWIMMERS AND OTHER VIRTUAL ATHLETES
Karl Sims, *Evolved Virtual Creatures*

Despite the difference in look and computational power, *Sodaplay* is in some ways an homage to Karl Sims's work, a fact underlined by an interview Ed Burton conducts with Sims on the *Sodaplay* site. *Sodaplay* users can also launch a 'Sodarace' application that enables them to download creatures from the *Sodaplay* zoo and race them on a terrain of their own construction — a reference to Sims's *Evolved Virtual Creatures*, a work he made available online as a downloadable video.

To be sure, the video that documents Sims's experiments in evolving virtual creatures is not interactive, whereas much of what makes *Sodaplay* creatures engaging is how they respond in unpredictable ways as their owners twiddle the virtual knobs that govern their physics. Nevertheless, like the wind and sun that shape Natalie Jeremijenko's *OneTrees*, pressures from Sims's mathematical water and land gives rise to their own form of unpredictability.

In *Evolved Virtual Creatures*, Sims has abandoned the goal of emulating the look of nature in favor of emulating its behavior. The creatures are pieced together from the virtual equivalent of cardboard boxes rather than the elaborate biomorphic forms of *Galápagos*, a fact not lost on Ed Burton:

Ed: While the block creatures aren't as visually complex or colourful as some of your other work such as 'Genetic Images' … or 'Galapagos' … they nonetheless seem to have an elegance and beauty about them. Does aesthetics play a role in the process?

Karl: Aesthetics was not part of the selection criteria there, but I think the physical simulation and their resulting dynamic behaviour strongly affects how they are perceived. If something exhibits behaviour and obeys physics properly, unlike a lot of computer graphics, it can feel emotionally real even though the structure is simple.

Whereas William Latham's *Mutator* software requires him to choose the fittest images from each generation to interbreed to produce the next generation, Sims's software, like most genetic algorithms used in scientific research, only requires the artist to specify in advance a generic 'fitness function' describing the optimum characteristics of the final offspring. The fitness tests Sims applied to his boxy bestiary included swimming and walking speed, jumping height, and the ability to follow a light source. He compiled the results of this selective breeding into a video that depicts the most successful — or most perverse — species bred according to these benchmarks.

The result is an astounding wealth of evolutionary strategies for aquatic and terrestrial locomotion. Some creatures resemble wriggling water snakes or humans doing a sidestroke; the most revelatory, however, are uncanny behaviors

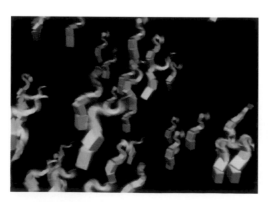
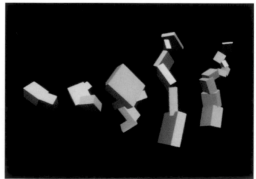

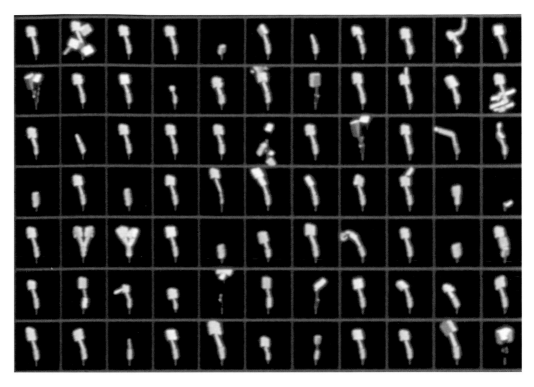

without biological precedent — limping, rolling, contorting combinations of articulated appendages that somehow hobble over virtual ground or swim through a virtual sea. These Special Olympians of the virtual world seem completely divorced from any naturalistic depiction, though of course they were evolved according to a naturalistic, Darwinian mechanism. Sims has also experimented with fitness functions that involve more than one organism — for example, by evolving organisms that fight over possession of a hockey puck. While such systems have been investigated in mathematical terms by game theorists,[26] Sims's animations suggest the true place of perceptual evidence in scientific research, for his athletic menagerie conveys at some gut level the raw power of genetic algorithms to breed new forms, making the case better than any genetically engineered Iris print could do that evolution is creative 'beyond human imagination'.

Sadly, the fact that Sims's creatures existed as a computer program rather than a print doesn't make their preservation any more secure. In his *Sodaplay* interview, Burton asks Sims whether he ever resurrects his software to revisit or evolve the blocky creatures. 'I have not,' replies Sims, 'because it only runs on old unsupported computers, but I do still enjoy watching the videos of them.'[27] Surely, Burton's realized that, barring a paradigm shift in the way digital culture is preserved, his own virtual wildlife will someday be extinct, captured only in static screenshots and video loops.

These pages: A selection of Sims' virtual swimmers, at comparatively unevolved (opposite, right) and advanced states (opposite, left).

Perseverance of Research

The final category of artificial life we'll examine is too performative or experiential to be summed up in a single format. Typically emerging from a scientist's lab rather than an artist's studio, this most dynamic of research generates no static objects, interactive installations, or even unique software releases.

Although it has been codified in software, Tom Ray's *Tierra* was originally produced for purposes of scientific research, and it maintains most of the dynamic perseverance expected of this paradigm. Unlike *Sodaplay* or *Evolved Virtual Creatures*, *Tierra* has no default visual rendering or interface. In fact, one of its distinguishing features is its independence from human intervention or experience. Even Sims's creature-centric genetic algorithms depend on a fitness function to select the strongest behaviors from each generation. Ray, in contrast, insists that *Tierra* has no fitness function. Its genetic diversity emerges solely from the basic conditions of life anywhere: competition for territory (disk space) and energy (**CPU cycle**s).

Tierra can operate in many electronic contexts – on a single hard drive, over a computer network, in an emulator that simulates one computer within another. One of the only habitats in which its scrappy little bugs have had trouble getting a foothold is the brick-and-mortar art world. In this section, we'll look at other artificial organisms highest on the endangered species list of media culture: scientific research bordering on art.

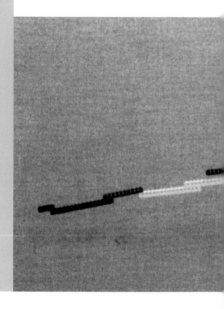

MAKING A-LIFE REAL
Hod Lipson and Jordan Pollack,
The *Golem* Project

One of the earliest visionaries of artificial life, the computer scientist John von Neumann, imagined a self-assembling machine that could reproduce by making copies of itself. Hod Lipson and Jordan Pollack have come closest to realizing von Neumann's proposal in their project *Golem* (*Genetically Organized Lifelike Electro Mechanics*), a lab in which custom software breeds designs for physical robots through evolutionary computation, then instructs a machine to fabricate the best designs with minimal human intervention through three-dimensional printing, a manufacturing technique used for rapid prototyping. The robots of each generation race in virtual or real space, and winning genes are fed back into the genetic algorithms to pass their mechanical adaptations on to the next generation.

As frightening as this concept may seem on paper, the actual contraptions bred and fabricated by this automated process are a long way from the Terminator — or even from R2D2. Although the notion of machines reproducing machines has long been a staple motif of science fiction, the products of the *Golem* Project are crude assemblages of thermoplastic, motors, and artificial neurons that wobble their way across parking lots. Indeed, one of the more surprising outcomes of this research is its deflation of the pervasive meme of technology run amok. To see such pathetically maladroit klutzes inspires pity rather than fear. The robots are as ponderous as their project's acronym.[28]

The *Golem* Project is a good example of a research project that attracts artists and critics but leaves them no static object or record with which to accord it the status of art. To infer from their official statement, jurors of the artificial-life festival Life 3.0[29] recognized the value of the *Golem* Project. However, while the other candidates under consideration lent themselves to presentation in a single screen or frame, the *Golem* Project required its viewers to assemble an understanding of it from documentary videos and text. In a gesture that both included and excluded it from the competition, the jury awarded the project a Special Mention for Innovation in Alife Research, thus segregating its scientific-research paradigm from the self-contained presentations of the other artistic entries.

A Lego bridge designed by evolutionary algorithms, created at Jordan Pollack's DEMO lab.

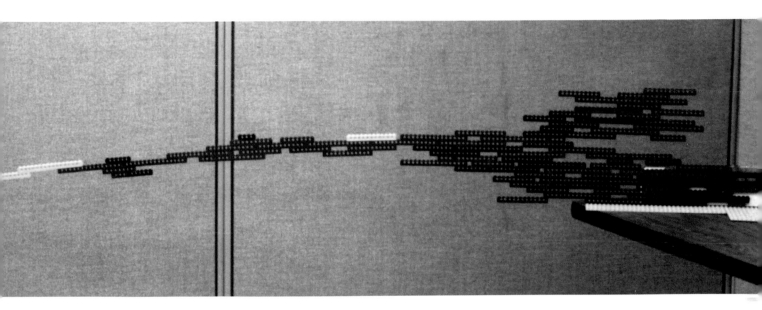

WHEN THREE EARS ARE BETTER THAN TWO
Stelarc and The Tissue Culture & Art Project, *Extra Ear 1/4 Scale*

One of the characteristics of scientific research that the art world's static paradigms have trouble accommodating is its performative character. The French philosopher Jean-François Lyotard has gone so far as to suggest that 'performativity' is the fundamental dynamic of science.[30] To be sure, there are performative traditions in art outside the conventional modes of music and drama, but the art world has often been reluctant to accept these expressions of the avant-garde except through the static documentation they've left behind.[31]

The Australian artist Stelarc cut his teeth on one of those avant-garde formats — extreme body art — though it might be more apt to say he cut his flesh.[32] In his most infamous early performances, Stelarc suspended himself in mid-air, hanging from the ceiling of a gallery by cables attached to hooks piercing his skin. In successive years, he has continued to explore the technological extension of his body, but now the hardware comes from a research lab rather than an abattoir: stomach sculptures, robotic arms, giant walking contraptions, each implanted in or molded to the artist's flesh. At this point, his work is most commonly classified under new media rather than performance.

Nevertheless, as Stelarc's technology has gradually crept beneath his skin, it has become more and more resistant to the static preservation expected even of interactive installations or software. How can a museum collect a work of Stelarc's if it's permanently attached to his body?

That question is raised quite literally in Stelarc's *Extra Ear 1/4 Scale,* a proposal to grow an ear fashioned from his own skin and cartilage and implant it on his forearm. Although the technology for reconstructing amputated human tissue has been around for decades, it's not the kind of thing you find in your average art-supply store. Stelarc spent six years trying to get reconstructive surgeons to help him realize his auditory prosthesis before he stumbled upon The Tissue Culture & Art Project, based at the SymbioticA lab – the same folks who introduced the world to rat-brain-powered plotter drawings.[33] Although the new ear cannot hear, in typical **cyborg** fashion Stelarc plans to implant a sound chip and proximity sensor so it can whisper to anyone who gets close enough. More in line with its

Right: Extra Ear 1/4 Scale.

original function, he also plans to add a modem and wearable computer so that he can broadcast the sounds picked up by the ear as **RealAudio** signals, using the Internet to amplify and extend his congenital sensorium.

FISHING FOR PARAMECIA
Joe Davis

Joe Davis coaxed researchers at MIT into helping him set up a deep-sea fishing rig for paramecia and commandeer million-watt radar to beam the sounds of vaginal contractions of Boston Ballet ballerinas into deep space — at least until the Air Force shut it down. In the Introduction, we asked what inspires top research scientists in one of America's most competitive academic environments to waste their time on zany schemes cooked up by their unofficial artist-in-residence. Perhaps they recognize in Davis's can-do naïveté something of the spark that attracted them to science in the first place — a spark that can be contagious even outside of the lab. Davis also inspired CalArts students to build a frog-leg-powered ornithopter that took wing at the Civilian Flight Test Facility in Mojave, California. As a *Scientific American* journalist observed about

Davis's Brobdingnagian fishing rod:

> It makes me wonder whether I could watch a protozoan take my hook, listen to it thrash, break a sweat as I fight it to a draw, and yet not come away with a new perspective on the ocean of microscopic life in which we are immersed, usually imperceptibly.[34]

The perspective Davis gives his high-brow lab mates is not that of a Newton or an Einstein standing on a peak high enough to expose nature's mysteries to his ken. It is the perspective of a child looking up at a mountain shrouded in mist, wondering how anyone could ever climb it. The stereotypic scientist — Mr Wizard — has all the answers. But real scientists save their attention for the questions; they stalk anomalies, hunt for holes in the theory; they're after the signal, yes, but there's no fun in uncovering it unless you dig through a veil of interesting noise first. And Davis has an ear for noise.

Lately, for example, he's been listening to protozoa. Naturally, this took some doing: although single-celled organisms spend a lot of their time

Above: Davis's audio microscope, *E. coli* specimens, and frog flier.

waving their cilia and whipping their tails, the frequencies and amplitudes of the resulting sounds are far beyond the range of any human-made microphone — except Davis's. Taking a cue from Alexander Graham Bell's experiments with sound-to-light conversion, Davis convinced MIT scientists to help him build an 'audio microscope'. This lens transduces the reflections of microscopic swimmers cast by a scanning laser into electric signals that Davis amplifies and plays on ordinary speakers. A typical engineer might have lost interest as soon as the problem was solved, but Davis wanted to hear the noise. After weeks of listening to his single-celled bestiary, Davis claims to be able to identify microscopic species by sound.

If the images produced by artificial-life researchers Philip Galanter and Karl Sims are clean and noiseless, Davis's work is messy, jury-rigged, full of noise in the signal. While his preoccupation with the unfinished and impossible endears him to those researchers who share his obsessions, the noise he revels in is almost impossible to translate out of its natural habitat in MIT's Building 68. Davis created a work of transgenic art a decade before Eduardo Kac's *Genesis* installation, yet while Kac's genetic creations have been exhibited widely and collected by major museums, Davis has at the time of this writing yet to exhibit his self-replicating creations in the US.[35] While he is a frequent lecturer at universities and conferences, he cannot sell his transgenic sculpture and relies on the unofficial largess of his colleagues for equipment, expertise, and even a place to lay his head.

Although science is often more accommodating of dynamic perseverance than art, to rely on science's liberal definition of research to preserve Davis's legacy isn't a sure bet either. Academic journals typically accept articles in which scientists explain how they cleaned up noise, not how they made more of it. And scientific textbooks and science museums, because they focus on teaching established principles rather than muddying the intellectual waters, present noise-free science — the opposite of the way in which scientists themselves experience their discipline every day in the lab.

Nevertheless, it's possible that Davis could have the last laugh when it comes to perseverance. This chapter has argued that life itself offers an especially adaptable model of preservation; if so, then Davis is one of the first beneficiaries of evolutionary longevity. In 1990, he convinced molecular biologists at Harvard Medical School and the University of California at Berkeley to help him encode an image as a sequence of twenty-eight DNA **nucleotide**s, with the hope that this message might someday be read by extraterrestrials. The forked image itself conjures up a Germanic rune, a vulva, or a peace sign without the circle — but to Davis, *Microvenus* represents a universal symbol for life. To distribute his message, Davis inserted this 'infogene' into the DNA of live *E. coli*, a microorganism he chose for its ability to survive the radiation and cold of outer space. Left in its beakers to replicate, these microscopic Monets multiplied into the billions, making Davis likely to be the most prolific artist of all time. 'I'm probably the most successful publisher in history,' he told *Scientific American*. 'There are more copies of my work than of Salvador Dali's, Escher's and all the rest of them put together.'[36]

Never mind that no American gallery has been willing to risk the public exhibition of genetically modified bacteria. Davis's work may well outlast pen-plotter drawings, Iris prints, even the very bricks of the museum itself.

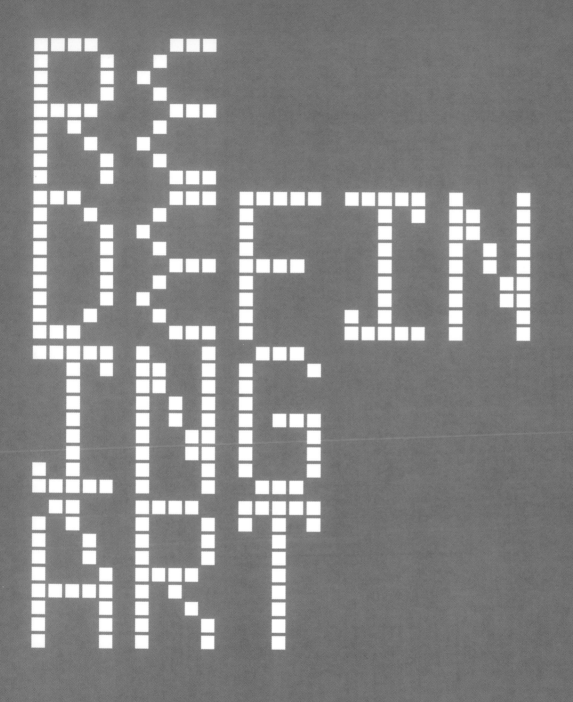

Art on Our Side

This book has surveyed six edges of art in the Internet age with the goal of uncovering a functional definition that can apply to these new cultural forms. The survey turned up six functions for a new kind of art: perversion — misusing programming, pixels, or paint to produce a multitude of forms; arrest — catching the eye or giving pause; revelation — seeing something in a new way; execution — propagating outside the studio or gallery to affect distant people or events; recognition — attracting public notice as worthy of attention; and perseverance — enduring beyond the moment to serve as cultural heritage.

Despite its viral powers, art of the Internet age is accountable to the society that births it — not only to prevent art from doing physical harm, but to permit it to liberate the imagination unimpeded by the laws and mores that govern political design. As an immune system for the social body, art at its best innoculates the collective unconscious against future threats by providing safe arenas in which it can face unfamiliar or disorienting situations. Art won't tell us what to do, because its job is to expose problems, not dictate solutions. (Van Gogh is reputed to have said, 'I am always doing what I cannot do yet, in order to learn how to do it.' 'Painting is what you don't know how to do,' agreed Abstract Expressionist Willem de Kooning.') Instead, art is provocative, in the etymological sense of 'speaking before' — representing something before or as it emerges in consciousness.

How can art anticipate the future? To prepare the social body for encounters with the new and unfamiliar, art recombines the stuff of culture, playing around with cultural codes until something interesting emerges. When the threat facing society derives from technological memes, then art tampers with those memes to play out their implications. Like a virus, art manipulates the codes of culture — but in the service of the 'social' immune system rather than against it. Art can be truculent, unnerving, and downright hostile — but under the right conditions it's on our side, engaging a deep curiosity about our world but in a way that we can survive. For this reason, art deserves the support necessary to create those 'right conditions'.

Toward a New Definition

But who will support these new forms of creativity erupting online? The sporadic and tentative nature of the art world's flirtation with online art makes it an open question whether the edge of art will expand to encompass these rival endeavors or retreat before them, reducing the scope of art to an esoteric trade in fetishized artifacts. Some argue that the art world is right to reject the rival forms of creativity birthed by new technologies, and hence to retreat to the traditional media and mechanisms of validation, from oil paint to auction houses. Others insist that the fires of artistic creativity are spent and that we should abandon the category of art altogether, a future Bruce Sterling envisions in his novel *Holy Fire* (1996). An unfortunate consequence of these reactions is the loss of occasions for deep listening or contemplation, as well as a loss in strategies for coping with change — practices that in an age of information overload are critical to social health and survival.

But what we are witnessing is not the dispersal or implosion of art but rather a seismic instability along the edge between art and non-art. If we are to embrace the proliferation of art-like creativity spawned in disciplines with no direct relationship to art history or the art market, then we must revise our understanding of what art can be, and we must work toward new definitions for this explosion of creativity. We must acknowledge that traditional sites of production and distribution like studios, galleries, and concert halls have lost exclusive claim to the nourishing or presenting of art. And we must adopt a view of art that is not solely defined by its context — its appearance in the tradition art world — but rather by the type and quality of experience it offers the viewer and its long-term effects on the social body.

Freeing Art from the Art World

Why has the art world not played a larger role in this Internet-enabled burst of creativity in the first place? Michael Kimmelman has written in the *New York Times* that there is no interesting art happening online. Students who want to make Web sites join Design instead of Art departments. And you can count on the fingers of one hand the number of museum curators who've heard of *Tierra*, DeCSS art, or ®™ark. What has kept the art world out of the loop?

There are many issues, but the most disturbing one is laziness. Not the physical kind — there are plenty of curators who jet back and forth from Kwangju to Kassel, studiously trolling for biennale *Wunderkinder* and art-school stars-in-training. No, what's holding the art world back is a philosophical laziness: a disinterest in or – worse — a refusal to rethink their definitions of the art they spend so much of their time trying to scare up.

This philosophical laziness is understandable — not so much because a modern definition of art has been hard to come by, but because it's become too easy. Marcel Duchamp let the art world off the hook by transforming a store-bought item with no obvious aesthetic import into art simply by plunking it on a pedestal next to bronze sculptures and oil paintings. To be sure, Duchamp may have meant to poke fun at the arbitrary line that divides art from non-art, but since his death those museumified bicycle wheels and bottle racks have slyly transformed from a critique of the art world's solipsism into a justification for it. If art is simply what fits under a gallery shingle or museum lintel, then curators and critics needn't trouble themselves with the question of whether something is art when they put it on display or write about it.

In theory, this contextual definition of art may sound open-minded and pluralistic, but in practice it has excluded a remarkable variety of creative activities whose distributed nature has kept them outside the art world's sacred circle. Most of them don't look like art. Many are not made by people who call themselves artists. And even if curators tried to squeeze them into a white cube, the act of uprooting these works from their own context — especially the Internet — would drain them of the links, literal and figurative, that made them interesting in the first place. If we want to find the sparks of emerging creativity, we have to be willing to step outside the art circles and practices that have made too many of us comfortable, launch our browsers or email clients, and engage in a kind of viewing and interaction destined to change our notions of what constitutes art – and, as a consequence, how we see life.

Freeing Art from the Market

For this redefinition to be rigorous, however, we must cast an unprejudiced eye not only on creativity outside the museum's white walls but also on creativity within them. For every scientist whose research fits a revised definition of art, there may be an oil painter whose work no longer qualifies.

Cultural works that serve a different function than art may be called 'applications'. Some applications — including décor, self-promotion, commerce, advertising, political design, and commodity speculation — are commonly confused with art, but their accountability to a predefined standard hampers their ability to be genuinely arresting or revelatory. A high percentage of fine-art paintings and prints are too ingratiating to serve as more than décor, whether their appeal is lowbrow (wildfowl landscapes) or highbrow (polite abstractions). The saleable objects produced by 'bad boy' artists as props for their publicity stunts, meanwhile, are instruments of self-promotion and little more. These works may grace the walls of collectors' homes, the pages of art magazines, and even the coveted catalogues of museum holdings. Context notwithstanding, however, they evidence few art-like functions.

Nor does every innovation outside the art world qualify as art. Airport sculpture and perfume bottles designed by artists typically serve Mammon more than Apollo; monuments and religious statues are often a form of advertising, and should be evaluated accordingly. Peer-to-peer file-sharing programs like Napster are revelatory and executable, but their success as political design has eclipsed their role as art. Even objects that began life as art may cease to be art if their social function changes. Van Gogh's *Dr Gachet* made headlines in May 1990 as the most expensive painting in history when it sold for $82.5 million at Christie's New York to the Japanese businessman Ryoei Saito. The work immediately disappeared from public view, and soon afterward Saito declared that he would literally take it to his grave.

Saito's case is unfortunately not unique. The buyers of 70 per cent of works sold at auction are not identified. Even when paintings are held by large institutions — as happened when banks seized Saito's assets in 1992 — these 'investments' frequently end up sequestered in a warehouse or vault. Many artworks disappear from the cultural record altogether; as reported by Japanese art critic Shin'ichi Segi, 'They exist in a kind of no man's land between their owners and the financial institutions that have seized them as collateral … we are losing so much still — and I don't mean just we Japanese … The trail is going cold, perhaps forever'.[2] Whether it is currently hanging above a bank president's chair in a boardroom or leaning alongside gold ingots in a vault, *Dr Gachet* is no longer the striking portrait that impressed contemporaries of its impoverished artist. It has become an investment, appraised at an extraordinary financial value that has cost the painting any future as art.

Degrees of Accountability

Application obscures art. If an artwork serves other functions, those functions must not eclipse the work's powers of arrest, revelation, or executability. It is up to the artist — and the artwork's custodians — to protect its fragile artistic value from being subsumed by decor, entertainment, or commerce.

Requiring that art not be beholden to another application rules out many oil paintings, bronze sculptures, and other objects that otherwise look like art. In their place, however, a functional definition admits experiences and artifacts that don't necessarily look like art. Moreover, to define art as an immunological agent allows us to broaden the range of its accountability beyond self-contained objects to embrace a spectrum of accountabilities, from artistry to research to genre.

Artistry

Artistry is the opposite of application, for artistry is that sudden and fleeting experience of awe not accountable to anything. Artistry need only be beheld, an arresting revelation experienced in the mind of a single viewer. Arresting moments are all around — on the beach at dusk, in rush-hour traffic, in a serendipitous dance improvisation or jazz riff, in a Botticelli painting at the Uffizi or in a child's doodle on a frost-covered window. If the art in an application is eclipsed by another function such as décor or commerce, the art in artistry is present but unmovable, intransigent, stuck in its original context and resistant to portability. For artistry, that context need not be an art object or setting — often it is not — but the experience in that context is always raw and real-time.

Frequently, trying to preserve artistry is like taking a snapshot of a sunset: the deficiency of the result only reinforces the futility of recapturing the original experience. In such cases, artistry lives on only in the memories of its witnesses, and once those memories have faded, it is gone altogether. On the other hand, some artistry leads to artifacts which can be recognized and which persevere. A pattern of dew on a spiderweb can inspire a haiku or photograph; the taste of a *madeleine* can motivate a five-hundred-page novel. The experience may not outlast the moment, but a recording or evocation of that experience may.

Following the diagram on the opposite page, we'll look at how the residue of artistry can give rise to two more lasting, and hence more accountable, forms of art: research and genre.

Research

Some art is more lasting than artistry (the glimpse of a sunset) but not as established as a genre (a painting by Cézanne). By analogy to science, we might call this investigative art 'research', since it is typically understood only by subcultures dedicated to its creation and study. Like artistry, research can be perverse and arresting. But in addition, research can also be revealed to others, and it often takes the form of executable culture to maximize its reach. Where research comes up against limits is in recognition and perseverance.

To recognize artistic research would mean to upgrade our eighteenth-century standards of authorship, originality, and framing to fit twenty-first-century reality. While artistry may lack these completely, artistic research embodies them, even if they take different forms in the Internet age than they did in the heyday of Modernism. Let's take them one at a time.

Authorship in research is inherently collaborative and community-based. In his account of the complex collaborations underlying scientific discoveries,[3] the historian of science Peter Galison notes that of all the authorship scenarios for the pursuit of modern

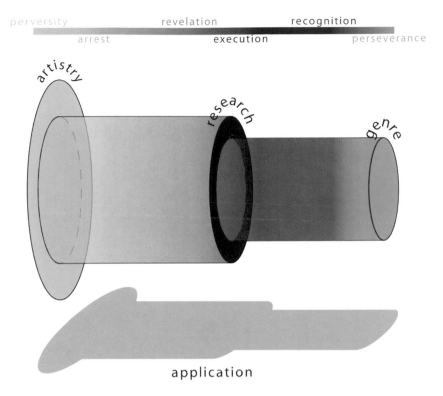

perversity   revelation   recognition

arrest   execution   perseverance

artistry

research

genre

application

The spectrum of artistic practices described in this chapter. Only a subset of artistry is able to circulate as research, and only a subset of research is able to persevere as genre.

physics — from graduate students co-publishing theoretical papers with their professors to international teams of experimenters coordinating experiments via the Internet — the only paradigm that is almost never true is that of a lone researcher at a workbench in an isolated lab. Yet, as we have seen, the myth of the solitary genius still pervades galleries, museums, and universities, where art is indexed by a single last name. Expanding its definition beyond the narrow interests of gallerists and other middlemen will require challenging the prevailing view of the artist as a solitary white male with an MFA and a studio in Manhattan. In a case such as the artists' list server 7-11, twenty or thirty names may be associated with a research project; in others, such as the artists' Web site 010010110101101.org, a hyperlink may be all that is necessary to refer to an artwork in the discourse that surrounds it.[4] Understanding research will require an understanding of its place in the community that birthed it; the contextual information in Olia Lialina's *Last Real Net Art Museum* is more illuminating than the exhaustive description of the work itself. An important conclusion of Chapter 05 was that individual recognition is the flip side of communal definition; what passes for art on Pandromeda.com would not pass for it on Rhizome.org, and vice versa.

Originality in artistic research may also have a more expansive definition than in other fields. While science has recognized more unusual forms of authorship than the art world, it has been less liberal in its definition of originality. Of course, no researcher should get a Nobel Prize for reconfirming Newton's theory that gravity makes apples fall. However, to see why science's limitations on originality may not apply to art, consider the Austrian biologist Wolfgang Maass, who uses computers to simulate connections between neurons in the brain. By emulating the stimulus-response network of the cerebral cortex, Maass hopes to devise a model accurate enough to reproduce empirical results from past experiments and predict the results of future ones. Although his goal is preordained, his working method is trial and error, tweaking his system parameters and throwing out any configurations that depart from known brain behaviors. Maass's allegiance to a predetermined 'fitness function' is not exclusive to biology; cosmologists at the Harvard-Smithsonian Center for Astrophysics in Cambridge study the evolution of the early universe by tweaking the cosmological equations encoded in a specially designed computer program, then watching as a flock of stars swarms across the screen, gradually coalescing into slowly spinning spirals. If this universe on a computer monitor doesn't look like the sky glimpsed through a real telescope, then the ingredients must be adjusted. The premise is that equations that result in spiral galaxies may be the same as those that govern our natural universe, while those that result in, say, helical galaxies obviously aren't.

But what if a cosmologist one day was intrigued by the helical universe and devoted a lifetime to exploring its unfamiliar intricacies? What if a biologist discovered some non-natural fitness function that made neurons dance and twist and sing? Surely, the best reaction they could expect from their fellow scientists would be puzzlement. And yet such 'useless' experiments, thanks to their extreme originality, may offer a window onto some future puzzle whose solution provides an essential stepping stone in the evolution of human awareness.

Unfortunately, only rarely does the jury for a scientific grant bestow awards on research that pretends neither to model the real world nor to engineer an improvement to it. Science cannot always reward curiosity for its own sake[5] — but perhaps art can. In that case, it would be more appropriate for the National Endowment for the Arts, rather than the National Science Foundation, to fund perverse research by the likes of Benoit Mandelbrot, Oron Catz, or Joe Davis — at least until a practical value for that research turned up.

Finally, research breaks the frame that has contained art for the past three hundred years. If the scientific community has been less tolerant of highly original work than the arts community, it has been somewhat more tolerant of research whose 'frame' is continuous rather than discrete. A researcher's contribution to science can't be reduced to a series of self-contained experiments or publications that can be viewed out of context; rather it may be defined by a lifelong devotion to testing and refining hypotheses in a cumulative fashion. In contrast, galleries and museums don't know how to sell artworks that are dispersed, collaborative, or ongoing.[6] Once museums got hold of him, Nam June Paik turned from avant-garde musician to video-installation artist, while Josef Beuys turned from performance artist to creator of scribbled blackboards and corners of fat in vitrines. When Basel's Plugin Gallery invited jodi to participate in their first gallery show, visitors could check out laptops, each of which featured a particular work; in the transition from online to offline, jodi's continuous Net-based research was divided up into discrete, recognizable projects. The unfortunate consequence of this insistence on framing is ultimately a misrepresentation of twentieth-century art history — a denial of the fluid and collaborative cultural matrix that gave rise to these artifacts. To recognize art that is pure research, on the other hand, is to admit the possibility of a practice that is continuously gradated, where it is impossible or misleading to draw a line to separate one artwork from another, whether the inquiry is jodi's, Dave Touretzky's, or Tom Ray's.

Respecting its lack of frame is important not just for the recognition of research but also for its perseverance. Unfortunately, a common strategy for preserving performances, Web sites, and other works in ephemeral media is to archive documentary photographs, audio, video, or props. But unframeable research loses a lot in the translation to documentation. Lynne Hull creates site-specific outdoor sanctuaries for birds whose migration patterns have been upset by deforestation and climatic change. To cut her work out of its original context and plunk it in a gallery would be to lose more than its context — it would be quite literally to sacrifice its primary audience, which is not even human. Birds feed from or take temporary residence in Hull's earthworks and sculptures. While an ornithologist could mine data on avian behavior from this work, it is ultimately the irreproducible results that make it interesting as site-specific art. Hull's photographs and maps should by no means be confused with her research.

Lynn Hull's environmental interventions.

Another example of research that failed to persevere due to the art market's substitution of documentation for otherwise irreproducible work can be found in Lynn Hershman's *Roberta Breitman* project. Roberta was a pseudonymous, alternative personality Hershman constructed while living in San Francisco in the 1970s. Roberta had jobs, a boyfriend, and credit cards; she was an early example of a constructed avatar *avant la lettre*. Sadly, when captured on videotape or in paint-embellished photos, these radical performances lose their edge, devolving into anemic documentation of a very real and live activity. If the art world were as accommodating of research as it is of artifacts, Hershman might not have felt the compulsion to drain the life out of the *Roberta Breitman* performances in the interests of making them look like art.[7] The same can be said for the 'domesticated' graffiti artists who showed in East Village galleries in the 1980s, whose framed tags and doodles quickly lost their verve in the transition from subway or street to white cube.

If the gallery system is especially inept at nourishing research, fortunately the Internet is especially adept at doing so. An example is the *Art Crimes* Web site, a gallery of graffiti art begun by Susan Farrell in 1994 that has grown to include three thousand photographs of graffiti *in situ* from two hundred cities across six continents. In many cases, the photographers know nothing about the artist's biography, motives, or even name (save what can be gleaned from the tag line). Nevertheless, the site petitions volunteers to help with the effort to preserve this marginal art form: 'Because it is so hard to get books published and to keep photos and blackbooks [graffiti sketchpads] from being seized and destroyed, the Internet may be the best way to publish and preserve this information. Please get involved in the effort … to help preserve and document the constantly disappearing paintings.'

Why did the Internet succeed in keeping graffiti in the cultural consciousness when the gallery system failed? The answer hinges on the difference between framing and connecting. Research on the Internet isn't isolated on a wall but interwoven into a matrix of text, images, and hyperlinks. When a curator ports graffiti from the streets into an East Village gallery, it becomes *framed*; when Farrell ports graffiti onto the *Art Crimes* Web site, it becomes *connected*. Research thrives on connections, whether definitions of jargon, references to historical context, or biographical notes more complex than a single last name. More than a

mere gallery of images, the *Art Crimes* Web site includes news, links, sketches, and cultural notes: 'We also want to spread the truth that this kind of graffiti, called "writing", is being done by artists who call themselves "writers", not by gangs.'

Ultimately, the static perseverance of research documentation, such as audio and visual recordings, can help support efforts at *dynamic* preservation. True, viewing a screenshot of *Web Stalker* is nothing like seeing it in action taking apart a Web site of your choosing; reading an online article about Joe Davis is nothing like walking into his lab. Nevertheless, screenshots and texts about these artists may be essential to re-creating their work in a dynamic way in the future.[8] At a minimum, research must be articulated in words or documented in image and sound in order to persist — whether by static or dynamic perseverance.[9] This enables research, unlike artistry, to be accountable, if only to a community of specialists.

Genre

While art of the Internet age may never achieve the complete autonomy to which Modernism aspired, nevertheless there are forms of art that are more self-contained, or context-independent, than artistic research. We will call these forms 'genre'.[10] If research is accountable only to local specialists, genre is accountable to the art-viewing public. This requires more stringent degrees of recognition and perseverance.

Genre is easier to recognize as a self-contained 'work' than artistic research. For this reason, almost everything found in an art-history text or art museum, from a Minoan potshard to a film by Matthew Barney, has become genre.

Where one draws the line between research and genre is often a matter of perspective. The average attendant of an Ars Electronica conference will know that ®™ark fits in the hacktivist genre, but the average patron of the Museum of Modern Art in New York may not even acknowledge ®™ark as art. In order for research to become genre, exposure to that medium or movement must expand outside the subculture that birthed it. This destiny will only befall a subset of artistic research.

Genre art is highly accountable, but that doesn't mean it is always accessible in the sense of appealing to a wide range of tastes. It may be well framed, but its experience can still be jarring, disorienting, or otherwise disturbing. Indeed, because it is audience-centered, it is all the more important that it not pander to its audience.

Genre typically implies a stable author or author function associated with the work. One of the 'hooks' that can help lay viewers remember, evaluate, and appreciate art is the ability to track an artist's career from style to style and medium to medium. Originality, on the other hand, is not as important for genre as for research. The public is less informed about originality than art experts, and requiring viewers to look up every reference to an artist's contemporaries would defeat the genre's goal of encapsulating art to make it appreciable by a wider audience. Generally speaking, only works that were valuable originally as research retain a strong sense of originality once they have been accepted as genre.

By contrast, many well-known artists create works that are not original yet are of value as visual artifacts to the lay observer. Seen individually, the *Cold Mountain* drawings by the American painter Brice Marden are noted for their graphic intensity and evocation of Chinese calligraphy. But Marden made hundreds of these pen-and-ink

Train art began in New York City in the 1970s. Trains are a moving target and are often well guarded. They are hard to paint and difficult to photograph. Either one can get you arrested or even killed.

Read what happened to Slick when he tried to save his friend in a tunnel. Paint fumes in tunnels can explode with a spark. Don't let it happen to you! Bence, AM7 MSG was crushed to death by a train October 18, 1997. Sk8 CBS RIP. OEPZ-ONE RIP.

Sadly, these guys knew what they were doing, had lots of experience, and they were still killed by trains. Please stay away from tracks because trains can silently sneak up on you. They can also jump suddenly, when cars bang into them, so always use the ladders to cross trains and hold on tight.

Americas

Passenger Trains

Chicago
Milwaukee
New York 1 2 3 4
Washington DC

Freights

Albuquerque 1 2
Canada 1 2 3 4 5 6
Brazil 1 2 3
East Coast (US) 1 2 3
Los Angeles
Miami 2
Midwest
New York
North America 1 2 3 4 5 6 7 8 9 10 11 12 13 14 15 16 17 18 19 20 21 22 23 24 25 26
Ohio
Oregon 1 2 3 4 5
Philadelphia
Pittsburg 1 2
Rochester 1 2 3 4
U.S. (various) 1 2 3 4 5 6 7 8 9 10 11 12 13 14 15 16 17 18
Vermont
West Coast 1 2 3 4 5 6 7
Wisconsin
Seattle

Freight Monikers 1 2 3 4 5 6

Other North and South American Train Sites

Ancient Ones
Addicted 2 Freights
Aerosol Aesthetics
Anonymous Art
B-More Careful
Bayones
Bellingham Bomb
Bombing Science
Bottle in the Ocean
Blade
Buenos Aires Graff
Connections
CTA trains and more
Deathinthedirt-Felts
Dr. Revolt
DareCIA
Fear Graffiti
FrSorade
Freightlife
Fucking Freights
Fuk 1 Burke
Getlesht
Government Cheese
Graffiti Organizado
Graffiti Tracks DC
Harmful Art
Ill Effect
Illegal Escarpments
Keep it Rail
Letters and Text
New York City Graffiti @ 149 St.
Nitty Gritty Graf Page
Not Without Opposition
NYC Trains
Pasconer
Obscyville
Railwhores
Sacramento Graffiti
Silent Weries
Steel Vandals
Subway Outlaws
St. Louis Freghts
TC Freights
Underground Art
Uncle Feasers
Visual Cancer
Visual Orgasm: The Canadian Climax
Wallnuts
Yes2Krylon

Europe

Passenger Trains

Amsterdam, Holland 1
Czech Republic 1
Denmark 1
France 1 2 3 4 5
Paris 1 2 3 4 5
Germany 1 2 3 4
Munich, Germany 1
Greece
Holland 1
Hungary 1 2
Italy 1 2 3 4 5 6 7 8 9 10
Italy and France 1
Rome, Italy 1 2 3 4
London, England 1
Portugal 1 2 3 4 5
Prague, Czech Republic 1 2
Serbia 1 2
Slovakia 1 2 3 4 5 6 7
Spain 1 2 3
Sweden 1 2
Zurich, Switzerland 1
Mixed passenger trains 1 2 3 4 5 6 7

Freights

Finland

Other European Train Sites

AK-47
Aerianweeb Spain
AR graffiti Switzerland
Artiste de
Autograff
BDMSK
BGS
Bigonzo
BrnoVision
Buffstuff
Cantalizm
Colored Steel
Cromatics
Damage
ddzgraff.com
DJK Bratislava
Direct Effect
Dirtues Rome
DOUBLE-H, Hamburg Graffiti
Dutch Damage
Dutch Deals
effeno invisible on line Sicily
Endstation
FnneGAS Italy
Fixart.de
Free Art Group Russia
Flashbereich.de
Full Effect
Graff of DK
Grafflighten Germany
Graffiti Hamburg 80
Graffiti Mainz
Graffiti AG
Hard 2 Burn

drawings, with little variation or progression over the course of the series. By the time these more-or-less interchangeable drawings numbered in the double digits, he had ceased doing original research, even as he continued to produce new examples of the genre.

In general, genre tends to persevere better than research. Many forms of research do not survive the transition to genre because of a confusion between experience and documentation. To be sure, documentation often looks more like art; a photo-collage documenting a street performance by Vito Acconci looks more like art than watching Acconci follow someone down an alley. Yet making something accessible to the public doesn't mean making it *look* like art; it means encapsulating it in a form that can be experienced outside its original context without diminishing its impact.

Research that impersonates genre loses its edge. And the standards for evaluating genre are different from those for evaluating research. Research draws original and non-intuitive connections, often among disparate fields, while the focus of genre is more internal than external. If research rewards expansive or associative thinking, genre rewards a close reading. Successful research is interesting; successful genre is good.

Of course, it's easier to decide what's good for older genres like portrait painting than it is for emerging genres like executable art — not because newer genres are immature or because older ones are sclerotic, but because expectations for older genres are well established and can be easily subverted or expanded. Diego Velázquez's portrait *Las Meninas* (1656) is one of the most subversive artworks of all time, partly because the painter was able to twist perspective to call into question the privileged position of his spectator, the king of Spain. But perspective had already been around for 250 years, offering Velázquez a well-established genre to hack for political ends. ®™ark created its GWBush.com subterfuge when the Domain Name System was only seventeen years old, which explains why ®™ark is not yet genre outside of a narrow subculture that understands its practice. It's harder still to predict the expectations to come from the very latest technical innovations; so when Christophe Bruno bases his *Google Adwords Happening* on a form of advertising barely a year old, we must evaluate his project according to the standards of research rather than genre.

The Four Stages of Accountability

The spectrum of art practice ranges from individual moments of awe to culturally sanctioned cases of recognition. *Artistry* occurs during those fleeting moments of individual perception, and thus cannot be accountable to any larger social group. *Research*, an intuitive and original investigation at the boundary of intelligibility, is accountable to a limited community with specialized knowledge. *Genre*, creative work within an established set of expectations, is accountable to the art-viewing public that has internalized those expectations. *Application* is art-like activity so fully accountable to another end that it's hard to experience as art. The creative spectrum moves from individual glimpse to community recognition, from inarticulate bewilderment to practiced appreciation.

Each of these stages of accountability stresses different artistic functions. As art becomes more social, it loses some of its originality but gains reach. So, artistry is often perverse or arresting but is too fleeting to show more than limited revelation and execution. Research must be articulated and shared; it can be recognized by specific subcultures and can persevere through documentation or discourse. Genre is more easily recognized and preserved than artistry or research, even if it is sometimes less arresting than artistry or less revelatory than research.

Learning to discern the six functions of art dispersed across a spectrum of art-like practices may give us the intellectual suppleness to appreciate and engage with the explosion of creative practice in the age of the Internet. But this model, like any categorization scheme, can be misapplied.

For example, an artwork can be weakened by expecting it to straddle large sections of the spectrum. Often a work will have one effect with one audience but the opposite with another. For tech-savvy critics who never thought of misusing JavaScript for artistic ends, jodi's HTML hijinks may be liberating, but to a public already intimidated by technology, they merely reinforce a sense of disempowerment. This fact needn't weaken the appreciation of jodi.org as long as the work is judged or understood as research rather than genre — at least until the public gets up to speed with the cognoscenti.

A reverse problem occurs when work that functions primarily as genre or application masquerades as research. Critics wax philosophical about the way Peter Halley's brightly colored compositions mirror prison architecture, silicon-chip design, and suburban tract-home planning; it's possible that some collectors of his work even slog through the two-hundred-page book of his collected essays so they can spout the same deconstructionist vocabulary when describing the work to their friends. You can bet, however, that their friends just see a pleasing geometric abstraction hanging above the couch, complete with the Day-Glo colors and stucco texture found in motel-room 'art'. Likewise, the artist collective Big Room creates TV commercials with subliminal references to politics. But how subversive are such references if the average consumer reads them simply as marketing? Like Halley's decorative paintings, Big Room's commercial spots whisper subversive footnotes to critics in the know, but these arcane references are drowned out by the glitzy appeal these ads present to the general public. It's hard not to fault these artists for packaging their work as genre with one hand while verbally defending it as research with the other.

Oliviero Toscani's advertisements for Benetton, by contrast, combine punchy phrases with stark visuals to go beyond art-world in-jokes and affect a huge swath of public viewers. His imagery — school kids of different skin colors holding hands, a blood-stained Yugoslavian army uniform — is overt rather than covert. Perhaps because they cannot be confused with research, his advertisements manage to slip from application into genre art — an extraordinary accomplishment for magazines and bus posters so strongly branded with a corporate identity.

Who Gets the Grant?

Like the antibodies' immunological crazy quilt, the perverse activities of artists claim little justification by comparison to applications with obvious social value. Yet these creative practices, analogous to basic research in science, deserve attention and support — and calling them art supplies a rationale for it.

For example, if art were distinguished from décor, the American '1 per cent for art' program that mandates architects reserve a fraction of their total budget for art could go for something more revelatory than a big red steel sculpture next to a building's entrance. Imagine, for the sake of argument, that the rule applied to every social structure of sufficient scale, rather than just to buildings. What if high-tech companies, media corporations, even particle accelerators[11] were required to set aside money for artists-in-residence? The notion is not as farfetched as it might seem; Xerox and AT&T each maintained artist residencies for a time. The artist and art writer Paul Brown was artist-in-residence at the Centre for Computational Neuroscience and Robotics at the University of Sussex, Oron Catts was a Research Fellow at Harvard Medical School, and Karl Sims was artist-in-residence at Thinking Machines Corporation. These are not the day jobs artists held in the 1940s and '50s, when Robert Ryman was a guard at New York's MoMA and Dan Flavin worked in the Guggenheim Museum's mailroom. Ryman and Flavin were surrounded by art but not making it; Brown, Catts, and Sims were selected for the value and relevance of their own research rather than for their knack for sorting envelopes or deterring vandals.

While supporting art-like activity in technological settings could broaden the reach of art beyond the narrow confines of galleries and museums, society will still need communities of local experts — if not a coterie of insiders, then at least recognition networks. Left to their own devices, the physicists running a particle accelerator might easily pick the most conservative works — illusionist paintings of scientists with microscopes, or decorative posters of fractal images — for their 1 per cent. To take full advantage of the opportunities of distributing art to these untapped nodes of culture will still require experts. The difference is that experts will no longer acquire their credentials by frequenting the right museum openings and gallery parties — or chairing Physics departments for that matter. Such people will scan culture at large, armed not with a rolodex or an NSF grant but with an open mind and a strong sense of definition. The Internet obviously offers the ideal school for these artistic equivalents of *médecins sans frontières*, and certainly provides an ideal breeding ground for the emergence of expertise from the very communities engaging in creative work.

Must all art enthusiasts hold to the definition proposed in this book? No. As diverse antibodies make the body more adaptable, so society will be more adaptable if it recognizes and nurtures more kinds of art — and more ways of discerning, appreciating, and supporting it. Holding to one particular definition is less important than relinquishing received assumptions in order to press the question 'Is this art?'. Only by abandoning the comfortable foregone conclusion offered by Duchamp's misinterpreters can we reinvigorate our understanding beyond the hothouse flowers of the mainstream art world.

This book has taken you on a long and varied journey. From the Web site of a wacky MIT researcher, you've followed links to such diverse destinations as software art, autobotography, gaming, political design, community art, and artificial life. Having opened and closed each of these browser windows one by one, you're finally back at the Web site where you began, with Joe Davis describing his proposals to build frog-powered aircraft or to go fishing for paramecia. The question is: Does Davis's work look any different now? And if you had a grant to give to an artist, would you give it to someone like him?

REFERENCES

INTRODUCTION

1 www.viewingspace.com/
   genetics_culture/pages_genetics_culture/gc_
   w03/ davis_joe.htm, accessed 28 June 2004.
   Technically this is a third-party Web page
   rather than Davis's home page.

2 One of the few art-related venues to exhibit
   his work is Austria's Ars Electronica
   (www.aec.at/festival2000/timetable/
   personen.asp?tid=1260).

3 Shulgin continued, 'Forget those silly fetishes
   — artifacts that are imposed [on] you by
   suppressive system[s] you were obliged to
   refer your creative activity to.' See Rachel
   Greene, *Internet Art* (London, 2004), p. 38.
   Another early contributor to creative email
   lists, Frederick Madre, said in an interview
   with
   net critic Josephine Bosma that he did not
   want his work 'to be labelled as [art] because
   it does not add anything to say so. There
   is no need to call it art'. Laudanum.net/cgi-
   bin/media.cgi?action=display&id=985961178,
   accessed 28 June 2004.

4 Tim Griffin, 'Apropos: Every Age Has Its Artist',
   paper presented at the conference 'Stubborn
   Practices in the Age of Bio and Information
   Technologies' in conjunction with the
   exhibition 'Tenacity: Cultural Practices in
   the Age of Bio and Information Technologies'
   (Swiss Institute New York, 24 March—13 May
   2000; Shedhalle Zurich, 30 June—6 August
   2000).

5 Michael Lewis, *The New New Thing* (New York,
   2000), pp. 91, 119.

6 Griffin, *op. cit.*

7 The closest the Internet has come to a dot-art
   suffix is the acceptance of .museum by the
   International Committee for Assigned Names
   and Numbers. This suffix has met with
   indifference or scorn among the online art
   community. See Jon Ippolito, 'An Open Letter
   on Dot-Museum', three.org/ippolito, accessed
   28 June 2004.

8 Cultural historian Leo Marx argues that this
   'will' is illusory, though he doesn't go so far as
   to claim art helps counteract this illusion.
   See 'Technology: The Emergence of a
   Hazardous Concept', *Social Research* 64/3 (Fall
   1997),
   pp. 989—1017.

9 Oliviero Toscani, conversation with Jon
   Ippolito, 5 September 2001, translated by
   the authors.

10 Manuel de Landa, *War in the Age of Intelligent
   Machines* (New York, 1991).

11 Studies linking autism and mercury-based
   vaccines such as HIB and Hepatitis B are only
   one instance of this. See www.safeminds.org,
   accessed 5 June 2004.

12 Marx, *op. cit.*

13 Marshall McLuhan, *Understanding Media:
   The Extensions of Man* (New York, 1964), p. 71,
   quoted in Leonard Shlain, *Art and Physics:
   Parallel Visions in Space, Time, and Light*
   (New York, 1991), p. 19.

14 As if to reinforce the antibody metaphor,
   artists such as John Simon — whose work we'll
   examine later— incorporate random processes
   in their work.

15 news.com.com/2102-1001_3-
   983197.html?tag=ni_print, accessed 28
   June 2004.

CODE AS MUSE

1 Cornelia Solfrank, presentation at CAT
   symposium, Aula do Risco, Lisbon, July 2000.
   Sol LeWitt's statement, 'The idea becomes a
   machine that makes the art,' from 'Paragraphs
   on Conceptual Art', *Art—Language 1*, no. 1 (May
   1969), pp. 11–13; reprinted in *Sol LeWitt:
   A Retrospective* (exh. cat.) (New Haven, 2000),
   p. 369.

2 Ken Musgrave, 'Formal Logic and Self
   Expression', www.wizardnet.com/musgrave/
   FLnSE_text.html, accessed 28 June 2004.

3 Some of Simon's recent laser-cut sculptures
   resemble fractals, but these hand-drawn
   shapes in fact reflect a return to more
   traditional art- object production in his
   later work.

4 In this equation, c is a constant number such as
   5, and z is a variable. To iterate this equation,
   Mandelbrot plugged in a seed number for z on
   the right-hand side — say 1 — and calculated
   the result (12 + 5 = 6). Then plugging this new
   result for z into the right-hand side again,
   getting a new result (62 + 5 = 41), he continued
   a third time (412 + 5 = 1686), a fourth, and so
   on. For most initial choices of z, the result
   seemed to get bigger indefinitely, but for
   others the results seemed to converge to a
   finite, fixed target.

5 Musgrave, *op. cit.*, section 2.2. Of course,
   artists sometimes deliberately choose
   unnatural constraints that enhance their
   aesthetic output. The artist with the greatest
   impact on 20th-century painting, Cézanne,
   defined his practice as describing nature via
   'sphere, cone, and cube' — a scientifically
   questionable constraint but one that led to
   Cubism and other important movements.

6 Musgrave, *op. cit.*, in a section on 'Global
   Parametric Control' (2.4.2). In the same essay,
   Musgrave writes: 'Proceduralism, the practice
   of encoding behaviors in formally defined,
   deterministic functions, is at the very heart of
   this process. Strict adherence to this practice
   is whence the intellectual significance we
   claim for the process emanates' (section 6.1.2).

7 *Ibid.*, section 3.5.

8 *Ibid.*, section 2.7. Emphasis in original.

9 *Ibid.*, section 5.4.

10 *Ibid.*, section 6.2.

11 The relationship between Conceptual practices
   of the 1960s and software art of the 1990s and
   2000s is often misunderstood. See Jon
   Ippolito, 'Where Did All the Uncertainty Go?',
   Flash Art International, 29/189 (July—August
   1996), pp. 83, 85—7.

12 New York University computer scientist and
   artist Philip Galanter's characterization of the
   group's common agenda from the eu-gene list,
   quoted by Florian Cramer in an interview with
   Cornelia Solfrank at userpage.fu-berlin.de/
   ~cantsin/homepage/#softwareart, accessed
   28 June 2004. See also Adrian Ward's nearly
   identical definition at www.generative.net/
   wiki/index.cgi?Generative_Art_Definition,
   accessed 28 June 2004.

13 Matthew Fuller, 'It Looks Like You're Writing
   a Letter', www.heise.de/tp/english/inhalt/
   co/7073/1.html, accessed 28 June 2004.

14 Amy Alexander *et al.*, 'QuickView on Software
   Art', art.runme.org/1046615440-32394-
   0/runme_interview.htm, accessed 28 June
   2004.

15 Florian Cramer, 'Concepts. Notations.
   Software. Art', userpage.fu-
   berlin.de/~cantsin/ homepage/#softwareart,
   accessed 28 June 2004.

16 Paik's hot-wired TV had in fact been
   anticipated as early as 1950 by Ben F.
   Laposky's *Oscillon*, which used an oscilloscope
   to display geometric curves on a television
   monitor. But while Laposky generated his
   signals artificially, Paik chose to screw up
   everyday broadcasts, thus emphasizing the
   misuse of a predominant form of technological
   expression over the *ex nihilo* creation of a new
   one. For more on Laposky's device, see Cynthia
   Goodman, *Digital Visions*, exh. cat. (Everson
   Museum of Art, Syracuse; New York, 1987), pp.

12, 19.

17 For more on what is and isn't artistic misuse, see Jon Ippolito, 'The Art of Misuse', in *Telematic Connections: The Virtual Embrace*, CD and Web site co-published by Independent Curators International and Walker Art Center, Minneapolis, 2001, at telematic.walkerart.org/overview/ overview_ippolito.html, accessed 28 June 2004.

18 This conclusion seems to be reinforced by this definition of artistic software from www.macros-center.ru/read_me/abouten.htm: Following works can be referred to as artistic software:

1. Instructions (read_me) on adjusting standard (commonly used) software, as well as patches and any kind of impact on software, whose results are not planned by producers and application of which leads to creation of an artistic product.

2. Deconstruction of existing software products, including computer games.

3. Written from scratch program with purpose differing from usual rational software purposes, i.e. refusal of the idea of a program as a purely pragmatic tool.

19 For more on the relation between Conceptual and technological art, see Ippolito, *op. cit.*, pp. 83–7.

20 The output of Simon's later programs, especially in his digital sculptures, is rococo compared to *Every Icon* and *Combinations*.

21 As the title of a paper by computer scientist Eric Weiss attests: 'In the Art of Programming, Knuth Is First; There Is No Second'.

22 Donald Knuth, 'Computer Programming as an Art', in *Literate Programming* (Stanford, 1992), referred to in artenumerica.com/inspiration/knuth.en.html, accessed 28 June 2004.

23 Cramer, in Alexander *et al.*, 'QuickView', accessed 28 June 2004.

24 Cramer, in 'Concepts. Notations. Software. Art'.

25 See The Jargon File, www.catb.org/~esr/jargon/, accessed 28 June 2004.

26 runme.org/feature/read/+duffsdevice/+9/, accessed 29 June 2004.

27 www.lysator.liu.se/c/duffs-device.html, accessed 28 June 2004.

28 runme.org/project/+forkbombsh/, accessed 28 June 2004.

29 For more on *Limosine*, see Alain Depicas, Jon Ippolito, and Caitlin Jones, eds., *Permanence Through Change: The Variable Media Approach*, (Montreal and New York, 2003), pp. 100–07.

30 Reena Jana, 'Real Artists Paint by Numbers', Wired.com, 8 June 2001, wired.com/news/print/ 0,1294,44377,00.html, accessed 28 June 2004.

31 Perhaps the earliest translation of photographic imagery into ASCII took place at Bell Labs, where researchers Leon Harmon and Kenneth Knowlton computer-processed a nude photo of dancer Deborah Hay in 1966 (Cynthia Goodman, *Digital Visions: Computers and Art* [New York, 1987] p. 34). Since then, nudity has been a common theme among ASCII 'artists' — including an entire rendering of the classic porn flick *Deep Throat* by the ASCII Art Ensemble.

32 Amy Alexander, 'Notes on Google Groups Art' at runme.org/feature/read/+googleart/+42/, accessed 28 June 2004.

33 Goodman, *Digital Visions*, or see www.dam.org/nake/, accessed 28 June 2004. Music by electronic composer James Tenney played in the background; as noted earlier, the interplay between computer scientists and composers has a long and interesting history beyond the scope of this book.

34 A. M. Noll, telephone conversation with Jon Ippolito, 26 April 2005.

35 Douglas Hofstadter, *Metamagical Themas* (New York, 1996), p. 207.

36 Harold Cohen, 'Colouring Without Seeing: a Problem in Machine Creativity', crca.ucsd.edu/~hcohen/cohenpdf/colouringwithoutseeing.pdf, accessed 11 August 2005. Cohen distinguishes his project from Noll's by emphasizing his disinterest in superficial imitations of existing models in favour of exploring a new model for producing art. Harold Cohen in private email to Jon Ippolito, 11 August 2005.

37 In 'Art Ex Machina' (1970), Noll wrote, 'In the computer, man has created not just an inanimate tool, but an intellectual and active creator partner that, when fully exploited, could be used to produce wholly new art forms and possibly new aesthetic experiences.' The essay is cited in Mihai Nadin, 'Art, Artists, and Computer', at www.code.uni-wuppertal.de/uk/all_pdf_files/art.pdf, accessed 28 June 2004. Nadin extends the metaphor: 'We adapted a technological product … and have done our best to force the "monster" into "drawing," "singing" and "dancing".'

38 Harold Cohen in private emails to Jon Ippolito, 7 and 9 August 2005.

39 Cohen's claim, 'I'd be happier if AARON's work in the future were LESS like human work, not MORE like human work,' suggests this situation may change in the future. www.pbs.org/safarchive/3_ask/archive/qna/3284_cohen.html, accessed 11 August 2005.

40 Roman Verostko, 'Epigenetic Painting: Software As Genotype – A New Dimension of Art', www.dam.org/essays/ verostko01.html, accessed 11 August 2005.

41 www.ericjhellergallery.com/index.pl?page=aboutart and www.harvardmagazine.com/on-line/0101122.html, both accessed 28 June 2004.

42 www.harvardmagazine.com/on-line/0101122.html, accessed 28 June 2004.

43 Color is more useful than other graphic signs because it can demarcate a two-dimensional area yet correspond to a continuously and predictably varying parameter. At a presentation of his work at the Guggenheim Museum, New York in 1990, Mandelbrot acknowledged that color had a special utility for scientists independent of its aesthetic value, and that he chose the palette for his fractal images (which demarcate the speed at which the iterated formulas move toward infinity) based less on subjective preference than on maximizing the amount of insight conveyed by the image. In this prognostication, Mandelbrot echoed the virtues espoused by other scientifically inclined designers, including computer artist Manfred Mohr and graphic-design guru Edward Tufte.

44 From www.ericjhellergallery.com/index.pl?page=aboutart, accessed 28 June 2004.

45 'Heller has been influenced by Sol LeWitt, whose meticulous and often geometric creations he admires.' From www.ericjhellergallery.com/ index.pl?page=aboutartist, accessed 28 June 2004.

46 As we'll see later, allowing the audience to modify the *genotype* can be a much more illuminating approach.

47 Despite his proclivity toward process, Wattenberg is not above offering prints of his diagrams for sale as well. Clearly his notion of aesthetic experience still involves a static object as one teleology.

48 runme.org/feature/read/+monteyoung1/+30/, accessed 29 June 2004.

49 See James Buckhouse's exhibition *Refresh* at www.artmuseum.net/, accessed 28 June 2004. In his critique of the show, Tilman Baumgaertal claims that 'some of the commercial screensavers of the past have approached this topic in a more radical way' (www.eyestorm.com/feature/ED2n_article.asp?

article_id=188&caller=1, accessed 28 June 2004).

50 See the statement of the read_me 1.2 jury, mirrored at netartcommons.walkerart.org/ article.pl? sid=02/05/21/0510256& mode=thread, accessed 28 June 2004.

51 Software artist Adrian Ward's misuse of his first computer exemplifies the approach of a software artist at www.generative.net/papers/ autoshop/ index.html, accessed 28 June 2004.

52 For more on Maeda's creative output, see Jon Ippolito, 'John Maeda: Post Digital (Billboard)', *Artex*, no. 73 (May—July 2001).

53 See Jon Ippolito, 'Deconstruction or Distraction?, *Artbyte*, 2/1 (April—May 1999), pp. 22—3.

DEEP PLAY

1 D. W. Winnicott, 'Playing: Its Theoretical Status in the Clinical Situation,' *International Journal of Psychoanaysis*, 49 (1968), pp. 591—9.

2 Clifford Geertz, 'Deep Play: Notes on the Balinese Cockfight,' in *The Interpretation of Cultures* (New York, 1973); also webhome.idirect.com/~boweevil/ BaliCockGeertz.html

3 Henry Jenkins, 'Games, The New Lively Art', web.mit.edu/21fms/www/faculty/henry3/Game sNewLively.html#_edn7

4 www.c-level.cc/projects.html

5 waco.c-level.cc/media/timeoutny.pdf

6 Dyske Suematsu, 'Understanding the Medium of Video Game', www.rhizome.org/thread.rhiz? thread=10828&text=20967

7 waco.c-level.cc/media/timeoutny.pdf

8 waco.c-level.cc/

9 Benjamin K. B. Johnson, 'The Play's the Thing', www.gamegirladvance.com/zine/200307play/ the_plays_the_thing.html

10 *Dope Wars* for Palm OS, by Matthew Lee (2000), was originally based on a game called *Drug Wars* for MS-DOS, by John E. Dell (1984). See www.methodshop.com/palm/articles/MustHave PalmGames.stm

11 Galloway's hack arrests hardware as well as software, for to keep his skater in 'the groove' he binds the buttons on his game console with rubber bands. Galloway's tricked-out console recalls the piano John Cage 'prepared' by inserting screws and other obstructions between the strings.

12 The *Vincennes*' degree of automation prompted some Naval officers to deride it as a 'Robocruiser'. See www.countries.com/

messageboard/messages/1621.html; www.geocities.com/CapitolHill/5260/ vince.html, both accessed June 30, 2004.

13 Scene witnessed by the authors in a playground, Orono, Maine, 2003.

14 www.fullspectrumwarrior.com/ gm_game.php

15 www.specialforce.net/ english/indexeng.htm

16 www.underash.net/

17 www.eddostern.com/sheik_attack.html

18 Matthew Southern, 'The Cultural Study of Games: More Than Just Games', www.igda.org/ articles/msouthern_culture.php

19 See Matthew Mirapaul, 'A War Game (Sort of), But You Can't Control the Action', *New York Times*, 26 November 2001.

20 One might compare the effects of wargaming on kids in *Enders Game* with Klaus Theweleit's analysis of emotional and psychic numbness produced by Hitler Youth programs in *Male Fantasies*, vols 1 and 2 (Minneapolis, 1987—9).

21 From Amy Harmon, 'More Than Just a Game, but How Close to Reality?', *New York Times*, 2 April 2003; see also www.peostri.army.mil/ PAO/ pressrelease/moreThan.jsp

22 www.furtherfield.org/rcatlow/ rethinking_wargames/docs/overview.htm

23 agoraxchange.net/index.php?page=218

24 See www.cjfearnley.com/fuller-faq- 3.html#ss3.3, accessed 30 June 2004.

25 Mary Flanagan, 'Hyperbodies, Hyperknowledge: Women in Games, Women in Cyberpunk, and Strategies of Resistance,' in Mary Flanagan and Austin Booth, eds., *RELOAD: Rethinking Women + Cyberculture* (Cambridge, MA, 2002).

26 zanzarah.de/storyuk.php

27 www.gamespot.com/pc/adventure/ longestjourney/reader_review.html?id=337079

28 www.gamespot.com/pc/adventure/ longestjourney/reader_review.html?id=509395

29 lx.sysx.org/biotek/index.html

30 lx.sissyfight.com/

AUTOBOTOGRAPHY

1 To the extent that the body's immune system can identify its own antibodies and their relationship to the larger natural world, and also can confront cancer cells — versions of self that are not under the body's own control — it too can reveal aspects of the self that are often hidden.

2 Georges Gusdorf, 'Conditions & Limits of Autobiography', in James Olney, *Autobiography* (Princeton, 1980), p. 28.

3 *Ibid.*, p .29.

4 *Ibid.*

5 TIA (Total Information Awareness, an act amended in 2003 to Terrorist Information Awareness), gives US government law enforcement the Orwellian ability to collect, centrally store, and access private information about ordinary citizens. ECHELON is an international version of similar spy technology deployed by the US, Britain, Canada, Australia, and New Zealand. See encyclopedia.thefreedictionary.com/Total%20I nformation%20Awareness and www.echelonwatch.org/.

6 'The Gadget Lover: Narcissus as Narcosi', in Marshall McLuhan and Lewis H. Lapham, *Understanding Media: The Extensions of Man* (Cambridge, MA, 1994).

7 Donna Haraway, 'A Cyborg Manifesto: Science, Technology, and Socialist-Feminism in the Late Twentieth Century', in *Simians, Cyborgs and Women: The Reinvention of Nature* (New York, 1991), pp. 149—81; online at www.stanford.edu/dept/HPS/Haraway/ CyborgManifesto.html

8 www.jennicam.org/

9 'If something is boring after two minutes, try it for four. If still boring, then eight. Then sixteen. Then thirty-two. Eventually one discovers that it is not boring at all.' See Cage quotes online at www.english.upenn.edu/~afilreis/88/ cage- quotes.html

10 'Smart Clothing: The Wearable Computer and WearCam', wearcam.org/ personaltechnologies/

11 *Ibid.*

12 Curiously, this citizen-enabled defense is the only strategy that worked in the 9/11 hijackings, according to an article by Elaine Scarry. Citizens with cell phones on flight 93 were able to ascertain the threat, decide on a plan of defense, and put that plan into action. See 'Citizenship in Emergency', www.bostonreview.net/BR27.5/ scarry.html.

13 A colleague who has met Steve Mann on a number of occasions notes that this technology has its costs: Mann usually 'jacks into' his computer to identify this colleague rather than relying on human facial recognition, and also declined a visit to an art museum complaining of his inability to see except at the close range of his glasses. If accurate, this is an eerie and McLuhanesque 'amputation' that accompanies the extension of Mann's faculties. Does connection with non-local communities compromise our connection to local ones?

14 A later chapter algorithmic forms of life.

15 From the last entry on William Gibson's blog, explaining his decision to give up the practice. See www.williamgibsonbooks.com/blog/blog.asp

16 Max Langdon, in *Reload* blog, October 2003; see cordova.asap.um.maine.edu/~blaisj/cgi-bin/reload/

17 Donna Haraway, *op. cit.*, p. 151.

18 *Ibid.*, pp.180–81.

19 N. Katherine Hayles, *How We Became Posthuman, Virtual Bodies in Cybernetics, Literature, and Informatics* (Chicago, 1999).

20 See Mary Flanagan's essay on *Iphage]*, www.maryflanagan.com/ phage%20flanagan.doc

21 www.rhizome.org/object.rhiz?1856, accessed 30 June 2004.

22 Consider 'askpang''s 3 October 2003 post on the *Future Now* blog (blogger.iftf.org/Future/000160.html):
   Recognizing that players acquire rights with our online characters has implications for all kinds of online data. For example, if I have certain property rights over things I create in a game world, might I also have rights over the data I create in my Amazon profile? Saying that players and their online characters have rights that players alone do not also begins to expand our legal notions of ourselves.

23 Rosa Allucquere Stone, 'Will the Real Body Please Stand Up?', www.rochester.edu/College/FS/Publications/StoneBody.html.

24 Julian Dibbel, 'A Rape in Cyberspace', www.levity.com/julian/bungle.html

25 www.artwarez.org/femext/content/femextEN.html

26 Not all avatars challenge the status quo. While Solfrank's virtual artists destabilize museum practice, Kurzweil's female rock-star persona satisfies a mainstream fantasy of fame and erotic power.

DESIGNING POLITICS

1 Keynote speech at the H2K '"Hackers on Planet Earth"' convention, salon.com/tech/feature/2000/07/20/hacktivism/index.html, accessed 10 July 2003.

2 www.reamweaver.com, accessed 10 July 2003.

3 Ball echoed the elision between hacktivist art and design when he wrote, in a private email to Jon Ippolito on 14 December 2004, '... we certainly think of our graphs as art (a la Tufte]'. Yet Ball's invocation of graphic design guru Edward Tufte confirms that his goal is clarity rather than confusion.

4 www.rtmark.com/more/articles/whitneymirapaul.html, accessed 10 July 2003.

5 See for example www.activism.net/cypherpunk/crypto-anarchy.html, accessed 10 July 2003.

6 For an argument about how protocol has become the new form of social control, see Alexander Galloway, *Protocol: How Control Exists After Decentralization* (Cambridge, MA, 2004).

7 '"Attacks Called Great Art"', www.nytimes.com/2001/09/19/arts/music/19KARL.html?searchpv -nytToday, accessed 28 June 2004.

8 The Internet has provided a testing ground for many nongeographic nations, including Sinta, Refugee Republic, and Jennifer Government.

9 James F. Moore, 'The Second Superpower Rears its Beautiful Head', Berkman Center for Internet & Society, Harvard Law School, March 2003. cyber.law.harvard.edu/people/jmoore/secondsuperpower.html.

10 Mark Napier, presentation at the Ars Electronica Festival, 2002.

11 www.msnbc.com/news/601205.asp?0si, accessed 10 July 2003.

12 There is nothing mysterious or overly technical about downloading someone else's Web files, provided they are not fed from a hidden database on that person's server. In fact, the simple act of browsing a Web page automatically loads all of the text, code, and images for that page into a folder on the end user's hard drive called the 'cache'. Cosic and the artists of 0100101110101101.org simply moved the files that are usually captured in this way onto their own servers and opened them to public view.

13 Reinhold Grether, 'How the Etoy Campaign Was Won', *Telepolis* (26 February 2000); www.telepolis.de/english/inhalt/te/5843j/1.html, accessed 10 July 2003.

14 Private email from etoy.ZAI to Jon Ippolito, 13 January 2002.

15 .art frontiers: Partnerships in Art and New Technologies Industry, conference organized by The Kitchen and Ground Zero, Menlo Park, 2–3 November 2000.

REWEAVING COMMUNITY

1 Telephone conversation with the authors, 17 July 2003.

2 Olia Lialina's suspicions about this migration seemed to be confirmed in 2003 when the New York Digital Salon decided to show only four of the twenty online works they had selected — and moreover to present screenshots of the projects rather than providing live links to the works. The cost of trading online recognition for institutional recognition often becomes the replacement of a dynamic artwork with a static document — a trade-off examined in detail in a later chapter. See art.teleportacia.org, accessed 1 August 2003.

3 See Jon Ippolito, 'Death by Wall Label', in Christiane Paul, ed., *Curating New Media* (Los Angeles, forthcoming).

4 Joseph Kosuth argues against morphological definitions of art in his 1969 essay 'Art After Philosophy', in Gabriele Guercio, ed., *Art after Philosophy and after: Collected Writings, 1966—90* (Cambridge, MA, 1993).

5 Rather than artists abandoning the art world for more creative spaces, Sack believes that people who stumble into these spaces are transformed into artists by the questions they prompt. Personal conversation with the authors, 17 July 2003.

6 Private conversation with Jon Ippolito, Linz, September 2001.

7 For more on the importance of research as a cultural activity, see Stephen Wilson, 'Research as a Cultural Activity', at userwww.sfsu.edu/ ~swilson/papers/researcheditorial.html, accessed 28 June 2004.

8 See especially Jonah Peretti's work on 'contagious media' at www.contagiousmedia.org/, accessed 28 June 2004.

9 Peter Galison, *Image and Logic: A Material Culture of Microphysics* (Chicago, 1997), p. 46.

10 Research may port better than genre. 'When art is understood as an experiment rather than the making of a masterpiece, the gallery system loses its competitive edge over faster distribution systems' (Craig J. Saper, *Networked Art* [Minneapolis, 2001], p. 26).

11 A rare analog precedent for this is Carol Churchill's *Cloud Nine*, a play in which the actors swap roles during the intermission between the first and second acts, and the techniques of Augusto Boal's 'Theater of the Oppressed'.

12 Like most online communities, the Plaintext Players rely primarily on textual communication, which they justify by claiming that online performance 'takes advantage of the fact that what is perceived as the lowest of low tech in the computer world (text) is paradoxically an enormously high-bandwidth medium for ideas, for personal adventure, for imaginal experience generally' (yin.arts.uci.edu/~players/faq.html, accessed 28 June 2004).

13 Clay Shirky, 'Community, Audiences, and Scale',

www.shirky.com/writings/community_
lscale.html, accessed 28 June 2004.

14 See Dieter Daniels's presentation in 'Who
Controls New Media: Open Art in Closed
Systems', Guggenheim Museum, New York,
21 March 2002. Webcast archived at
cyber.law.harvard.edu/whocontrols/who_contr
ols.html, accessed 28 June 2004.

15 See, for example, Jeffrey Benner, 'When Gamer
Humor Attacks', wired.com/news/print/
0,1294,42009,00.html, accessed 28 June 2004.

16 www.2walls.com/RANTING/
ranting_oddtodd.asp, accessed 28 June 2004.

17 'All new language to describe the new medium
of interface … will depend on the interfaces
designed to represent communities of people
rather than private workspaces' (Steven
Johnson, 'Interface Culture', quoted in Saper,
op. cit. p. 149).

18 Indeed, one of Rhizome's signature line
contributors, Eryk Salvaggio, began life as
a graffiti artist.

19 rhizome.org/rsg/pastslogans.txt, accessed
28 June 2004.

20 The metaphor of a night sky has a history
in digital art, from the interactive
map *Electric Sky* (1995—6, archived at
cyberatlas.guggenheim.org) to Wattenberg's
Starry Nights (1999) and *Copernica* (2001).
More at www.hq.nasa.gov/copernica/cadb/
essay.html, accessed 28 June 2004.

21 See, for example, cultural critic Mark
Dery's critique of e-poetry on *nettime*,
www.nettime.org/Lists-Archives/nettime-l-
0105/msg00118.html, posted 21 May 2001.
Interestingly, no such revolution occurred in
'postal' mail art, probably because the means
of propagating artistic expression via the post
office is so much more time-, labor-, and cost-
intensive than via email.

22 See www.muthesius.de/~virtual/ texts/
000001.html, accessed 28 June 2004.

23 www-apparitions.ucsd.edu/~bookchin/
finalProject.html, accessed 28 June 2004.
Bunting received an A for his assignment.

24 Conversation between Alex Galloway and Jon
Ippolito, 18 July 2003.

25 See Keiko Suzuki's interview with Josephine
Bosma at www.nettime.org/Lists-Archives/
nettime-l-9711/msg00038.html, accessed
28 2004.

26 The Neoists pioneered the practice of multiple
participants sharing a single pseudonym.
See Saper, *op. cit.*

27 Alexei Shulgin, in private email to Jon
Ippolito, 20 August 2005.

28 Daniels, in 'Who Controls New Media'.

29 radioqualia.va.com.au/, accessed 28 June 2004.

30 See Kenneth Goldberg, ed., *The Robot in the
Garden: Telerobotics and Telepistemology in
the Age of the Internet* (Cambridge, MA, 2000).

31 Although often referred to solely as 'Linux',
GNU/Linux is built on the copylefted GNU suite,
and hence beholden to its 'free software'
distribution model. See **open code** in the
glossary.

32 This critique recalls the call for legibility – of
the underlying processes, if not of the actual
source code – developed in an earlier chapter.

33 The site's creators drew on such metaphors as
pebbles on a beach and synapses in the brain.
Margot Lovejoy, private email to Joline Blais,
18 August 2005.

34 Several Fluxus artists imagined democratic
forms of art-making and distribution,
including Hans Haacke's *Visitor Profile* and
Nam June Paik's top-ten chart for art. Saper
has argued that 'the alternative art scenes
during the 1960s all had a peculiar and intense
fascination with networks' codes rather than
any individual breaking through all codes with
some supposedly outrageous performance'
(Saper, *op. cit.*, p. 115).

35 Rob Malda, private email to Jon Ippolito,
16 August 2005.

36 Google's page-rank algorithm ranks the
importance of a Web page by how many other
pages link to it.

37 Technically, interface designers *perturb*
the communities they record, while quantum-
mechanical investigators inadvertently *create*
the phenomena they record.

38 Marshall McLuhan and Bruce R. Powers, *The
Global Village: Transformations in World Life
and Media in the 21st Century* (Oxford, 1989),
pp. 36—8, 101, 107.

PRESERVING ARTIFICIAL LIFE

1 Georgia Institute of Technology, 'Researchers
Use Lab Cultures to Create Robotic "Semi-
Living Artist"', 8 July 2003, mirrored at
www.wireheading.com/ article/hybrots.html,
accessed 28 June 2004.

2 Stuart Bunt, presentation at Ars Electronica
Festival, Linz, 3 September 2001.

3 See Jon Ippolito, 'The Museum of the Future:
A Contradiction in Terms?' in *Artbyte*, 1/2
(June—July 1998), pp. 18—9; reprinted in
Spectra, 25/4 (Summer 1998), pp. 22—3;
mirrored at three.org/ippolito/, accessed
28 June 2004.

4 From the Tissue Culture and Art Web site,
www.tca.uwa.edu.au/atGlance/galnceMainFram
es.html, accessed 28 June 2004.

5 Fortunately, the art world's medium myopia
has been somewhat rectified lately by advances
in digital art forms such as the software art
examined in an earlier chapter. One of the
central contrasts of that chapter, however, is
between programmers who focus on process
versus those who focus on product, and this
book has argued that an overly aestheticized
product often diminishes the viewer's
understanding of the work as a whole.

6 Roman Verostko, 'Epigenetic Painting:
Software as Genotype, a New Dimension of
Art', at www.dam.org/essays/verostko01.htm,
accessed 16 November 2004.

7 Georgia Institute of Technology, 'Researchers
Use Lab Cultures To Create Robotic "Semi-
Living Artist"', www.gatech.edu/news-room/
release.php?id=160, accessed 18 August 2005.

8 Adrian Ward and Geoff Cox, 'How I Drew
One of My Pictures: or, The Authorship of
Generative Art', www.generative.net/papers/
authorship/index.html, accessed 8 August
2003.

9 For more on dead media, see Bruce Sterling,
'Digital Decay', in *Permanence Through
Change: The Variable Media Approach*
(Montreal and New York, 2003), online at
variablemedia.net, accessed 29 June 2004.

10 For more on the variable-media approach, see
variablemedia.net, accessed 29 June 2004.

11 Pablo Baler, 'The Doors of Expression: The
Work of Art in the Age of Quantum Processing
Power', *Sculpture*, 21/4 (May 2002), online
at www.sculpture.org/ documents/scmag02/
may02/doors /doors.htm, accessed 29 June
2004.

12 Kevin Kelly, 'Genetic Images', www.wired.com/
wired/2.09/ features/sims.html, 26 August
1998, cited in Adrian Ward and Geoff Cox, 'How
I Drew One of My Pictures: or, The Authorship
of Generative Art', www.generative.net/
papers/authorship/ index.html, accessed
8 August, 2003.

13 This quote of Nechtvatal's appears in his Web
site and related publications.

14 As of this writing, Nechvatal has begun work
on a game-like immersive collaboration based
on his virus software (www.music2eye.com/
vca/abstractvca.html, accessed 18 August
2005). He confirms, however, that painting
remains his passion in a 2005 essay, 'Fast and
Beautiful: The A-Life Undeadening of Painting
via the Digital', www.cyberartsweb.org/cpace/
art/nechvatal/1.html, accessed 18 August 2005.

15 Jim McClellan, 'William Latham: CSPACE', at www.cuttlefish.net/nemeton/axis-mutatis/latham.html, accessed 16 November 2004.

16 Galanter's rhetoric and vision – which include splashing nano-machines from buckets – recalls sculptor Richard Serra's lists of verbs and splashed lead 'castings' from the 1960s. See Philip Galanter, 'Generative Art Is As Old As Art', www.artificial.dk/articles/galanter.htm.

17 In the 1990s Karl Sims was an artist-in-residence at Thinking Machines Corporations. Although artist appointments in scientific labs or high-tech industries are rare, they offer a critical antidote to the art world's insularity — a point to which we will return later.

18 For the technical details of how these behaviors translate into programming, see Sim's 'Artificial Evolution for Computer Graphics', *Computer Graphics*, 25/4 (July 1991), pp. 319—28, online at www.genarts.com/karl/ papers/siggraph91.html, accessed 29 June 2004.

19 This concept was introduced in an earlier chapter in connection with John Simon's work *Combinations*.

20 Kelly, *op. cit.*

21 Such a process is almost unknown in the plastic arts, though painter Neil Welliver is reputed to begin his landscapes in one corner and finish them in the opposite one.

22 Karl Sims's artist's statement at www.genarts.com/galapagos, accessed 16 November 2004.

23 DNA is made of combinations of four nucleotides, adenosine, cytosine, guanine, and thymine. Kac first translated the Biblical passage into the intermediary cypher of Morse code, which he claimed symbolized the dawn of the information age, then converted dots into thymine, dashes into cytosine, word spaces into adenosine, and letter spaces into guanine: 'Let man...' -> '._..._ __.__. ' -> 'CTCCGCGTATT...'

24 Technically, Kac inserted the gene into *two* species, each of which already existed as genetic modifications created by the scientific community to respond differently to ultraviolet light, one by glowing yellow and the other cyan. It is typical of his work that he incorporates surplus complication into his installations.

25 For more on the 'synthetic ethics' of artificial life, see Jon Ippolito, 'Should You Feel Guilty Turning off the Computer?', *Artbyte*, 1/6 (February—March 1999), pp. 16—7.

26 For a useful discussion of Robert Axelrod's iterated Prisoner Dilemma tournaments, see Gary Flake, *The Computational Beauty of Nature: Computer Explorations of Fractals, Chaos, Complex Systems, and Adaptation* (Cambridge, MA, 2000).

27 sodarace.net/sims/, accessed 29 June 2004.

28 The acronym was inspired by the Jewish folktale of the golem, a creature brought to life from inanimate materials.

29 www.telefonica.es/fat/vida3/concurso/elipson.html, accessed 29 June 2004.

30 Jean-François Lyotard, *The Postmodern Condition: A Report on Knowledge* (Manchester, 1984).

31 One of the few shows of performance art to gain the art world's attention recently, Paul Schimmel's exhibition 'Out of Actions — Aktionismus, Body Art & Performance, 1949–1979' (MAK, Vienna/MOCA, Los Angeles), substituted large-scale photographs for 1970s-era performances — prompting one critic to close his review with the note, 'You had to be there.' See articles.findarticles.com/p/ articles/mi_m0268/is_4_40/ai_80856183, accessed 29 June 2004.

32 This tradition has a variety of geographic strains, including the American artist Chris Burden's body piercings, the animal sacrifices of the Viennese Aktion group, and the ritual scarification of Aboriginal peoples.

33 At the time of writing, TC&A are not pursuing a graft of the ear onto Stelarc's flesh, both for technical reasons and because their interest lies more in partially living organisms than augmented humans. Oron Catts in private email to Joline Blais, 20 July 2005.

34 For more on Davis's biography and work, see W. Wayt Gibbs, 'Art as a Form of Life', *Scientific American*, online at www.viewingspace.com/genetics_culture/pages_genetics_culture/gc_w03/davis_j_webarchive/davis_profile_sciam/jd.htm, accessed 29 June 2004.

35 It was not until fourteen years after its creation that *Microvenus* saw public light, along with didactic explanations of Davis's process, in a positive-pressure containment facility at the 2000 Ars Electronica Festival in Linz, Austria.

36 Gibbs, *op. cit.*

THE REDEFINITION OF ART

1 *Painters Painting* (Mystic Fire [video], 1972).

2 Stephanie Strom, 'Art Treasures Bought by Japanese in Better Times Now Quietly Resold Abroad', *New York Times*, 19 August 1999, mirrored at www.tamu.edu/mocl/picasso/archives/1999/opparch99-261.html, accessed 29 June 2004.

3 See, for example, Peter Galison, *Image and Logic: A Material Culture of Microphysics* (Chicago, 1997), p. 431.

4 Florian Cramer has exposed the vulnerabilities of such generic hyperlinks as shorthand for authorship. See www.0100101110101101.org/texts/ rhizome_perm-en.html, accessed 29 June 2004.

5 To be sure, science sometimes comes to appreciate perversions after the fact — if they satisfy criteria such as reproducibility of results, objectivity of measurement, and quantifiability. Gauss was embarrassed to publish his discovery of non-Euclidean geometries even though they later became the foundation of general relativity.

6 Director Richard Schechner claims Happenings resembled scientific lab experiments rather than finished artworks. See Craig J. Saper, *Networked Art* (Minneapolis, 2001), p. 114.

7 As noted in an earlier chapter, Joseph Kosuth argues against morphological definitions of art — 'It's art because it looks like other paintings or sculptures I have seen' — in his 1969 essay 'Art after Philosophy', in Gabriele Guercio, ed., *Art after Philosophy and after: Collected Writings, 1966—90* (Cambridge, MA, 1993). That said, the definition Kosuth offers in place of this misapprehension is more solipsistic than the definition offered in this book.

8 For example, in his discussions on variable media, Mark Napier acknowledges that contemporary 'recordings' of his work *net.flag* will help future preservation specialists rewrite the work from scratch. See variablemedia.net/e/preserving/html/var_pre_session_three.html, accessed 29 June 2004.

9 Although he doesn't use terms like *artistry* and *research*, Saper describes a comparable distinction in *Networked Art*, p. 151.

10 The term *genre* in this context is broader and more neutral than the pejorative tone it takes on in the art-historical phrase 'genre painting'.

11 The notion of being an artist-in-residence at a particle accelerator came up in a class taught by Janet Cohen, Keith Frank, and Jon Ippolito at the Yale School of Art, New Haven, in 1998.

actuator A mechanical component that extends or retracts in response to electronic signals.

ad banner An advertisement in the form of a clickable horizontal image positioned at the top of a Web site.

advergame A simple electronic game used to advertise or market a product or service.

AI Artificial Intelligence, a computer program designed to mimic human mental processes such as thought or judgment.

algorithm A mathematical formula, especially one calculated as part of a computer program. For example, computers can build complex fractal shapes algorithmically by repeatedly solving formulae such as $z = z^2 + c$.

anti-aliased image An image, especially one optimized for the Web, whose edges are algorithmically smoothed rather than pixilated.

antibody A protein on the surface of a human immune cell designed to detect a foreign agent such as a virus or bacterium.

applet A small computer program, such as an animation or user interface, written in Java and designed to run on the Web.

arrest The act of giving pause; a break in the flow that produces an opportunity for reflection or change.

artificial life Programs on a computer designed to evolve in a manner analogous to organisms in a natural environment

ASCII American Standard Code for Information Interchange, the default character set – A–Z, 0–9, @, #, and so on – that all Internet applications can read.

asynchronous Occurring sporadically, punctuated by intervals of inactivity; used to distinguish email and other processes from synchronized communication such as telephone conversations.

author function A term used by Michel Foucault to suggest the social construct of a work's creator defined by textual references, public biography, and the like, as opposed to his/her biological identity.

avatar A virtual representation of a user on a network, typically in textual or graphic form. Avatars are often assumed identities with only an oblique relationship to their real-world counterparts.

biomorph A shape resembling a living being, typically suggesting a soft, rounded, or animate presence.

bitmap A digital image whose array of colored pixels has not been, or cannot be, reduced to pictorial formulas. For example, scanned photographs are bitmaps, while forms composed of geometric shapes can be described via formulas.

blog A single- or multi-user online journal automated by software that facilitates daily entries, hyperlinks, and dynamic cross-references to other blogs. From 'Weblog'.

bot A small computer program designed to handle a specific task on the Internet, such as automating replies to email or imitating human conversation in a chat room.

browser An application, such as Firefox or Internet Explorer, that recognizes, interprets, and views Web documents (usually coded in HTML) on the World Wide Web.

bug The cause of a computer error, usually due to a mistake in the code such as a typo.

C A powerful programming language capable of building standalone applications such as video players.

canalized genes Genetic code evolved for stability, so that minor variations still produce the same organism. For example, slight mutations in a giraffe's DNA may still generate a long-necked animal.

cascading style sheet (CSS) An efficient design protocol that allows programmers to define precisely the look of a Web site, including its colors and layout.

cellular automata Primitive but lifelike processes emerging from a class of computer programs that determine the future states of adjacent cells in a grid according to a set of predefined rules.

chat room An online environment in which participants converse via successive lines of text typed into their computers.

click-and-drag An interface feature that allows users to move an item on the screen by clicking on it and then dragging their mouse.

codework A term coined by Alan Sondheim to describe artistic approaches to software, especially the allusion to computer syntax in online poetry.

compiler A software utility that renders source code readable by computers instead of humans. For example, Java source code is compiled into an applet, but HTML code is interpreted directly by the browser without being compiled.

convergence In mathematics, a process that tends toward a specific number over time, as opposed to processes that diverge to infinity. For example, the sequence 1, 1/2, 1/4, 1/8, ... converges to zero.

copyleft A form of copyright that requires any re-use to be as freely accessible as the original. For example, programmers who base a product on copylefted source code cannot hide the new source code from other users.

CP/M operating system A textual computer interface developed in the 1970s, a precursor to graphical interfaces such as Windows and Macintosh.

CPU cycle The rate at which a computer's Central Processing Unit processes data; the 'clock' of a computer.

cyberpunk A genre used to describe writers from the 1980s such as William Gibson and Pat Cadigan, who depict dystopias mediated by information technologies in which underground figures resist the control of a technological élite. From 'cybernetic' + 'punk'.

cyborg A human-machine hybrid. From 'cybernetic' + 'organism'.

DAT Digital Audio Tape, a high-quality format for recording sound.

dead media A term coined by writer Bruce Sterling to include the vast number of historical media that have become obsolete, from homing pigeons to Web protocols.

DHTML Dynamic Hypertext Markup Language, a version of HTML that enables advanced control over a Web site's elements, layout, and overall style. For example, DHTML can enable users to show and hide portions of a Web page at will.

distributed production The grass-roots creation of useful or cultural artifacts, whether software, encyclopaedias, or artworks, especially using the Internet.

do loop A programming statement that instructs the computer to repeat a set of commands multiple times.

document.write A programming method that writes text or other content to a computer screen.

domain The name registered for a Web

address, such as cnn.com or whitehouse.gov.

do-while A type of do loop that instructs the computer to repeat a set of commands only while a certain condition is true.

ECHELON An Anglo-American spy network allegedly employed to search for hints of terrorist plots and other illegal activity. ECHELON's critics contend that its pervasive access to email and other electronic transmissions creates the opportunity for flagrant abuses of privacy.

'else if' clause Part of a computer program that is only executed when a previously stated condition is unmet.

emoticon An emotional expression conveyed through text characters, such as :) to mean 'happy', used as shorthand in text based networks such as chat rooms or instant messaging.

engine Generic term for software to perform a perfunctory task, as in 'game engine' or 'search engine'.

executability The ability to trigger an existing system to automate a task that changes the state of that system. From computer parlance for the act of running a program, as when a user launches a word-processor or spreadsheet.

finger An Internet protocol that supplies information about a user's login status, email address, and full name.

first-person shooter (FPS) A genre of electronic game depicting an environment filled with adversaries from the perspective of a weapon-wielding protagonist. *See* 'third-person shooter'.

flame war An exchange of accusatory or vilifying messages among participants in an online conversation.

Flash An animation technology developed by Macromedia Inc. for use on the Web. Unlike other visual formats, Flash files can employ scripting to enable sophisticated interface design.

forkbomb A program that overloads the system and crashes the computer, for example by endlessly repeating a useless command.

fractal One of a class of geometric shapes discovered by the mathematician Benoit Mandelbrot whose structure is similar across different scales. A fractal coastline would look equally rugged on a map on the scale of miles or of inches.

game engine Software that renders a navigable, interactive environment from a set of 3D data and behaviors.

genotype The representation of an organism as the sum of its genes, i.e. its DNA.

GIF Graphic Interchange Format, a proprietary bitmap format that was a de facto Web standard for still images and primitive animations in the early 1990s.

glocal A condition in which local cultures and politics are responsive to global issues and empowered by global networks.

Google The dominant application for searching the Web as of 2005.

gradient A scale running from one value to another, such as from low to high or from red to blue.

Graphical User Interface (GUI) A visual system for interacting with a computer, such as a metaphorical 'desktop' on which the user can 'drag and drop' 'files' into 'folders'.

grayscale An image rendered in black, white, and gray tones.

hacker A skilled computer user adept at overcoming limits, especially in establishing access to remote computers. Within the computer community, the term is ethically neutral or positive; in mass-media contexts, it suggests a nefarious purpose.

home page The official or default Web page for an individual or organization.

HTML Hypertext Markup Language, the code used to generate hypertext documents on the Web through the use of tags and attributes. 'Hyper' implies that users can jump quickly to other files on the Internet by clicking on linked text or images. Viewing an HTML document requires a Web browser.

hypernovel An interactive, book-length story.

hypertext Any text navigated by links between pages, whether online or standalone.

'if then' statement Part of a computer program that is only executed when a specific condition is met.

interface A means of interacting with a computer, either via hardware such as a mouse or via software such as a screen menu.

Java A powerful, Web-friendly programming language developed by Sun Microsystems that gives programmers substantial control over their application's appearance and function.

JOIN statement A programming command that relates sets of data by combining records from different parts of a database.

karma In the online community *Slashdot*, a user's credibility as calculated from the net rating their posts have received from other slashdotters.

LAN party An informal event in which participants set up and play networked games in a physical space such as a home or dormitory. From 'LAN' ('Local Area Network').

LCD Liquid Crystal Display, a thin screen used predominantly for displaying computer output.

lymphocyte A white blood cell capable of detecting and responding to a foreign agent such as a virus.

machinima The repurposing of a game engine to produce an animated movie. From 'machine' + 'cinema'.

macrophage A type of immune cell that eats anything that is not healthy tissue, including viruses or infected body cells.

maxima High points in a field of data, such as the highest test scores in a class of students.

meme A term coined by the biologist Richard Dawkins to suggest an idea that propagates through culture the way genes propagate through a biological population.

messageboard An online site, such as a Web forum or Usenet group, in which users can post commentary or questions so that others can respond.

meta-tag A part of a Web page that describes the general characteristics of that page, such as its subject or creation date.

microprocessor A silicon chip, such as the Intel Pentium, that serves as the central controller of a computer.

MIDI Musical Instrument Digital Interface, a protocol for transmitting data between electronic instruments such as synthesizers and drum machines.

mod An altered version of an electronic game. From 'modification'.

MOO Multi-user Domain, Object-Oriented, a text-based online environment in which participants can avail themselves of virtual objects with pre-programmed behaviors. For example, a participant in MOO might access text hidden inside a 'book' object by typing the command 'open book'.

Moveable Type A prominent software package for blogging.

MP3 A highly compressed audio format suitable for exchanging music files over the Internet.

From 'Moving Picture Experts Group [MPEG] 1, Layer 3'.

nucleotide One of the four types of base pairs that serve as the rungs of the DNA molecule's double helix.

open code A technique for writing software in which the original author makes source code freely available for modification or improvement. Some examples of open code may be incorporated into closed-code projects, while others require that any re-use be open as well (a requirement known as copyleft). The general category of open code is often referred to as 'open source,' while the copylefted variety is known as 'free software'.
open source *See* open code.

packet The unit of information by which the Internet transmits email, Web pages, and other messages; each packet may travel an independent route to reach the destination.
parallel-processing supercomputer A high-performance computer that employs many microprocessors working simultaneously to solve problems that can be divided into parallel tasks.
parameters Variables that control the state of a system. For example, the parameter of time determines the position of a pendulum.
Pascal A programming language developed in the 1970s, popular for its logical structure and ability to run on the earliest personal computers.
patch A snippet of code that corrects a bug or alters a feature in a previous version of a computer application.
pathogen A disease-causing organism introduced into the body, especially a virus or bacterium.
peer-to-peer application A computer program that enables communication among a number of personal computers rather than between a personal computer and a Web server.
peripherals Hardware devices external to a computer's main casing, such as a mouse or keyboard.
Perl A programming language adept at extracting information from text files, now used predominantly on Web servers to perform tasks such as routing email or retrieving information from databases.
perseverance The ability to endure, whether in biological or cultural memory.
perversion The ability to misuse codes, whether genetic, technological, or social, to produce new

forms of biological or cultural expression.
phenotype An organism as represented by the sum of its physical characteristics, i.e., the expression of its genes. For example, an antelope's phenotype includes its antlers and legs, while its DNA is included in its genotype.
pico A simple programming language and text editor.
pine A simple email application; pine implementations for the Unix server require users to type commands at a command prompt.
pirate radio Radio broadcasts, especially organized by local communities or political activists, that usurp frequencies from 'official' networks.
pixel One of the minuscule colored dots that make up an image on a computer screen.
plotter An apparatus for translating computer data such as a table of numbers or a screen image into a drawing on paper.
polynomial A class of algebraic expressions containing powers of a single variable.
procedural In computer parlance, a method of programming in which all the code is run as one long sequence.
Proceduralist aesthetic A philosophy of software art that privileges the production of rich output from concise and consistent code. For example, the Mandelbrot Set generates complex visual patterns from a mere six characters.

QuickTime Apple Computer's application for creating and playing streamable, downloadable, and interactive audio or video.

RealAudio RealNetwork's format for streamed, or downloaded, audio.
recognition The process by which an entire system becomes aware of, and responds to, a new phenomenon in its midst.
recombination In genetic or computer code, the process of altering the order of individual sequences to produce a new outcome, as when a child receives a recombination of its parents' genes.
recursion A process in which a formula or procedure is repeatedly fed back upon itself. For example, a treelike shape can be generated by repeatedly forking a line segment.
revelation The process by which an individual becomes aware of a new phenomenon and signals its presence to others.
role-playing game (RPG) An adventure game in which live participants take on characters from a hypothetical narrative. RPGs were originally

played in actual rooms but increasingly form an important genre of electronic games.
RSS Really Simple Syndication, a protocol for summarizing the current stories on another Web site, especially for news sites and blogs.

screenshot A static picture recorded from a live computer screen; most of the pictures in this book are screenshots.
sine wave A smoothly varying, periodic mathematical function.
spam Unsolicited email advertisements, especially when mass-emailed from unscrupulous marketers.
spread spectrum A technique for overlapping radio broadcasts across a range of frequencies, thus enabling more transmissions and higher fidelity.
string In computer parlance, a sequence of characters such as 'pelham123'.
stylesheet *See* 'Cascading Style Sheet'.
subroutine A module of a computer program that can be called and run repeatedly from different points in the program.
suite An ensemble of software applications. For example, Adobe Corporation's Creative Suite includes tools for editing digital photographs, creating vector graphics, and publishing on the Web.
switch In computer code, a statement that tells the program to branch to different options depending on a condition such as a user's name or the number of times the program has been run.
syndication The practice, common among bloggers and online news organizations, of using RSS to furnish a condensed version of the original Web site — typically headlines and links — for others to re-present on their own sites.
synthesbian Computer-generated actors such as Max Headroom or Ananova.
system resources The combined memory available to a computer.

tag On a Web page, code for a particular function or formatting, such as <title> or <bold>.
TCP/IP The fundamental protocols that govern communication over the Internet. IP determines how an individual computer encodes and decodes packets of information, while TCP determines how those packets are sent, routed, and received among computers on the Internet.
third-person shooter A genre of electronic game depicting an environment filled with adversaries from a perspective directly above

and/or behind a weapon-wielding protagonist. *See* 'first-person shooter'.

Total Information Awareness A US Defense Department program begun in 2002, meant to gather information about people worldwide through their Internet activities, purchases, and records of all kinds. The project has been largely abandoned in response to claims that it violated fundamental privacies.

traceroute algorithm A procedure for determining which routes a piece of information (such as an email message) took to travel from one node to another on a network (such as the Internet).

trackback A feature of some blog software that automatically records when any of the blogger's entries have been linked to by another blogger.

transgenic Created from the genetic code of more than one life form, as in Eduardo Kac's rabbit enhanced with glow-in-the-dark jellyfish DNA.

translator In computer parlance, an application that converts one form of data (such as a word-processing document) into another (such as a Web page).

trust metric A measure of how much someone in a community is respected by other members of the community; the term originated in the social sciences but has recently been applied to self-policing online communities.

UNIX A highly influential multi-task and multi-user computer operating system originally developed at AT&T's Bell Labs. Variants of Unix have provided prominent examples of open-code software.

URL (Uniform Resource Locator) A Web address, such as www.variablemedia.net/ index.html.

Usenet The Internet's default discussion groups, where participants can post news or questions on everything from TV sitcoms to vaccine controversies.

variable media A paradigm proposing that the best way to preserve artworks in ephemeral formats is to encourage artists to describe them in a medium-independent way, potentially including the option to translate them into new media once their current medium becomes obsolete.

Visual Basic A event-driven, interface-based programming language devised by Microsoft Corporation for building applications for its operating system.

VRML Virtual Reality Modeling Language, used to create navigable 3D environments on the Internet. A VRML browser or plug-in must be downloaded to a Web browser to view VRML files.

Webcam A video camera whose feed, such as the view of a city skyline, can be viewed online in real time.

Weblog *See* 'blog'.

wiki A collaboratively produced Web site, built with software that permits any user to edit the site's contents over the Web.

wireframe A transparent geometric approximation of a three-dimensional object, represented by a skeletal framework of joined polygons.

worm In computer parlance, a variant of computer virus that can replicate itself without being embedded in another program. Worms are typically transmitted via email unbeknownst to the sender and receiver.

XP (Experience Points) In the Web site Everything2.com, a trust metric analogous to Slashdot's karma. In operating systems, a version of Microsoft Windows introduced in 2001.

Projects strongly associated with a single artist or collective name are indexed by creator; all others are alphabetized by the work's title. Except where noted, Web addresses begin with http:// and were valid at the time of writing; when the original link had expired, a link describing the project may be substituted. All works are copyright the creators unless otherwise indicated.

To my father, who would have disagreed with almost all of this book. —J.I.
To my children and your children, to whom we entrust our future. — J.B.

This book would not have seen the light of day without Lucas Dietrich's unflagging enthusiasm, Victoria Forrest's lucid design sense, and Andrea Belloli's keen eye and light touch. The authors are also grateful to the researchers who helped track down the images for this book: Starr McCaleb, Kristen Murphy, Suhjung Hur, and Josep Arimany-Piella.

Illustration credits are found in the index, pages 254–55.
Page 2: Golan Levin, *Floccus* from the *AVES* suite (p. 49).

First published in the United Kingdom in 2006 by Thames & Hudson Ltd,
181A High Holborn, London WC1V 7QX

www.thamesandhudson.com

British Library Cataloguing-in-Publication Data
A catalogue record for this book is available from the British Library

ISBN-13: 978-0-500-23822-6
ISBN-10: 0-500-23822-7

Designed by Victoria Forrest at SMITH, London
Printed and bound in China by Hong Kong Graphics & Printing Ltd